PAYMENTS FOR ENVIRONMENTAL SERVICES AND GOVERNANCE OF NATURAL RESOURCES FOR RURAL COMMUNITIES: BEYOND THE MARKET-BASED MODEL - AN INSTITUTIONAL APPROACH

CASE STUDIES FROM NICARAGUA

PROEFSCHRIFT VOORGELEGD TOT HET BEHALEN VAN DE GRAAD VAN
DOCTOR IN ONTWIKKELINGSSTUDIES AAN DE UNIVERSITEIT ANTWERPEN

SUBMITTED IN FULFILLMENT OF THE REQUIREMENTS FOR THE DEGREE OF
DOCTOR IN DEVELOPMENT STUDIES AT THE UNIVERSITY OF ANTWERP

GERT THEMBA VAN HECKEN

SUPERVISOR:
PROF. DR. JOHAN BASTIAENSEN

EXAMINATION COMMITTEE :
PROF. DR. ESTEVE CORBERA
PROF. DR. GUIDO ERREYGERS
PROF. DR. KRISTIN KOMIVES
PROF. DR. HELLE MUNK RAVNBORG
PROF. DR. AVIEL VERBRUGGEN

Gert Van Hecken
Doctoral dissertation

ISBN: 978-90-5728-324-6
Depot number: D/2011/12.293/7

This research was funded by a Ph.D. grant of the Flemish Interuniversity Council (VLIR-UOS).

To my wonderful son Jonathan. I love you so much.

TABLE OF CONTENTS

CHAPTER 4:

A CRITICAL ASSESSMENT OF DEMAND SIDE CHARACTERISTICS IN LOCALLY-FINANCED PES — INSIGHTS FROM A WATERSHED STUDY IN MATIGUÁS, NICARAGUA

LIST OF TABLES

LIST OF FIGURES

LIST OF ABBREVIATIONS

AMAT	*Empresa Aguadora de Matagalpa* (Water Utility Matagalpa - Nicaragua)
BPP	Beneficiary Pays Principle
C$	Nicaraguan Cordoba
C&C	Command-and-Control
CATIE	*Centro Agronómico Tropical de Investigación y Enseñanza* (Tropical Agricultural Research and Higher Education Centre – Costa Rica)
CDM	Clean Development Mechanism
CG	*Campesino Ganadero* (Cattle peasant)
COMUFOR	*Comisión Municipal Forestal* (Municipal Forestry Commission - Nicaragua)
CPC	*Consejo del Poder Ciudadano* (Citizen Power Council - Nicaragua)
CPT	*Campesino Pobre con Tierra* (Poor peasant with land)
CV	Contingent Valuation
ES	Ecosystem/Environmental Service
ESI	Environmental Service Index
FAO	Food and Agriculture Organisation
FG	*Finquero Ganadero* (Cattle farmer)
FSLN	*Frente Sandinista de Liberación Nacional* (Sandinista National Liberation Front – Nicaragua)
GEF	Global Environment Facility
GPC	*Gabinete del Poder Ciudadano* (Citizen Power Cabinet – Nicaragua)
Ha	Hectare(s)
ICDP	Integrated Conservation and Development Project
IEE	Institutional Ecological Economics
INAFOR	*Instituto Nacional Forestal* (National Forestry Institute – Nicaragua)
IOB	*Instituut voor Ontwikkelingsbeleid en –Beheer* (Institute of Development Policy and Management – University of Antwerp)
IPES	International Payments for Environmental/Ecosystem Services
IUCN	International Union for the Conservation of Nature
MA	Millennium Ecosystem Assessment
MAGFOR	*Ministerio Agropecuario y Forestal* (Ministry of Agriculture, Ranching and Forestry – Nicaragua)
MARENA	*Ministerio del Ambiente y los Recursos Naturales* (Ministry of the Environment and Natural Resources – Nicaragua)
MES	Markets for Environmental/Ecosystem Services
MINSA	*Ministerio de Salud* (Ministry of Health – Nicaragua)
NGO	Non-Governmental Organisation
PES	Payments for Environmental/Ecosystem Services

PGP	Provider Gets Principle
PLC	*Partido Liberal Constitucionalista* (Constitutional Liberal Party – Nicaragua)
PPP	Polluter Pays Principle
PSA	*Pagos por Servicios Ambientales* – Payments for Environmental/ Ecosystem Services
REDD	Reduced Emissions from Deforestation and Forest Degradation
RISEMP	Regional Integrated Silvopastoral Ecosystem Management Project
TA	Technical Assistance
UCA	*Universidad Centroamericana* (Central American University - Nicaragua)
UNFCCC	United Nations Framework Convention on Climate Change
US$	US American Dollar
VLIR	*Vlaamse Interuniversitaire Raad* (Flemish Interuniversity Council – Belgium)
WTP	Willingness to Pay
WWF	World Wildlife Fund

ACKNOWLEDGEMENTS

More than six years ago, in August 2004, I remember arriving in Nicaragua for the first time, in the company of two friends from my university, Ruben Vanleene and Koen Jaspers. Our professor Johan Bastiaensen offered us the opportunity to conduct, with a grant from the Flemish Interuniversity Council (VLIR), field research for our Master thesis in Matiguás, a rural town in central Nicaragua. I still vividly remember the culture shock I experienced during these first hours in Nicaragua, driving around in the chaotic centre of the capital Managua. Even today, I still dream of that first taxi trip: I again see us packed in that old cab, our luggage hanging out of the trunk, inventively tied together with a pair of shoe strings. I still can hear us sharing our first impressions: 'look, that man there is selling a toucan at the traffic light', or 'why is there a horse walking loose on the highway?' - 'why are there so many little kids selling bags of water, shouldn't they be at school?' And I still feel our confusion and embarrassment when this man without arms and legs begged for a coin after he ordered his son to clean the taxi windscreen. And all these kids on the street, walking barefoot on one of Managua's many garbage dumps, collecting empty beer cans...

Looking back to that first day in Nicaragua, I now realise how profoundly it changed my life. That day I met my Nicaraguan host family. Esmeralda and Fermín, my Nicaraguan 'mother' and 'father', and Luis Carlos and Filemón, my new 'brothers', welcomed me in their small apartment close to the Central American University, and told me that from now on they would treat me as their son and brother. And ever since that day, they have been treating me like that, though now they have a good reason for doing so: a few hours after this warm welcome, a beautiful young woman entered the apartment, introducing herself as my Nicaraguan 'sister' Virginia. Well, you may have guessed by now that it was this very same 'sister' who a few years later turned my host family into my real family, and that this 'sister' became one of the main motives for the many Nicaraguan chapters in my life.

For me, this little personal story illustrates how the doctoral project that I present in the next chapters is in fact part of a much broader 'life project'. It is an integral part of my life, and - as life - it has been shaped by a network of people. Every single one of them - each in their own way - has contributed to the document that lies in your hands. Although the following list is by no means exhaustive, I hope that those of you whom I may have omitted by accident, will forgive me for my poor memory.

I also hope that you will agree with me that, before anybody else, I address my heartfelt thanks in the first place to my supervisor Johan Bastiaensen. Johan has without any doubt been the main catalytic force behind this doctoral project. He is the most passionate 'Nicaragua-phile' I ever met, and he has the exceptional gift of being able to convey his contagious enthusiasm to other people. His expertise in microfinance and institutional economics, his many years of field experience in Central America, and especially his willingness to apply and expand his academic expertise to environmental themes continue to inspire me in many ways, and made him the best supervisor I could ever have hoped for. Johan constantly kept encouraging me to believe in this project, and whenever my motivation went through a dip, he was there with a pep-talk session, reminding me that a Ph.D. is not about 'changing the world', but simply about proving that one is able to conduct one's own research. I must admit that if it hadn't been for his enthusiasm and dedication, I might have given up this project a long time ago. Johan, during the last five-six years we have come to know each other better, and our professional relationship has steadily evolved into friendship. From the bottom of my heart: thank you for your continuous support during all these years and for steering the project to its conclusion.

My thanks also go to the many other colleagues and friends at the research institutes that I have been cooperating with during my project. In Belgium, my gratitude goes to all colleagues at the Institute of Development Policy and Management (IOB, University of Antwerp). More particularly, I would like to thank the members of our research group 'Poverty and Wellbeing as a Local Institutional Process', Tom De Herdt, Griet Steel, Kristof Titeca, Inge Wagemakers, and Nanneke Winters. It has been an intellectual challenge and a real pleasure being a colleague of every one of you! Special thanks also go to An Ansoms, Sara Dewachter, Martin Prowse, Ana Rivas, and Jos Vaessen, who provided me with useful and encouraging comments. Greet Annaert, Hans De Backer, Hugo De Craen, Katrien De Smet, Joelle Dhondt, Nicole Dierckx, Patricia Franck, Katleen Van Pellicom, An Vermeesch and all other support staff also deserve my gratitude for the assistance they provided along the way. In Nicaragua, my gratitude extends to the staff of the Research and Development Institute Nitlapán (Central American University), and in particular to Miguel Alemán, Omar Dávila, Adela Delgado, Selmira Flores, Arturo Grigsby, Yuri Marín, Silvia Martínez, Francisco Paíz, Tania Paz, Elías Ramírez, Roberto Rivas, Alfredo Ruíz and Alfredo Woo for sharing with me their theoretical and practical understanding of rural development in Nicaragua, and for their valuable support during the field work and data processing. I also want to thank Dries Cleiren and Jaqueline Zeledón, as well as the enthusiastic students who were part of the local survey team in Matiguás. I am also greatly indebted to a number of colleagues and friends from research institutes around the world, such as Bram Büscher, Frédéric Huybrechs, Kathleen McAfee, William Vásquez, Mette Vinqvist and Marc Wuyts.

This study greatly benefitted from the many comments and suggestions on previous drafts. All persons who helped reviewing a chapter (or the article on which it is based) are mentioned at the beginning of that chapter. The members of my doctoral jury also provided me with very useful comments and suggestions: I am indebted to Esteve Corbera, Guido Erreygers, Kristin Komives, Helle Munk Ravnborg and Aviel Verbruggen, who presided over the jury. Special thanks also to Stephen Windross and my father Guido Van Hecken for reviewing some of the chapters on language and structure.

As is the case with most research projects, also this one would not have been possible without the financial support that I received along the years. I sincerely thank the Flemish Interuniversity Council (VLIR-UOS) for providing me with a four-year Ph.D. Grant. I also would like to thank Dina Franceschi and William Vásquez for co-funding part of the fieldwork through a Faculty Research Grant of Fairfield University. My gratitude also extends to Johan Bastiaensen and the Institute of Development Policy and Management for funding the last three months that I needed for finishing this dissertation.

During the many field trips to Nicaragua and the two years that my wife and I lived in Managua, we made a lot of new friends who supported us in many ways. My sincere gratitude goes to all of them. In Managua, I am highly indebted to our dear friends Juan José Barrios and Francesca Viserto, who supported us in all possible ways and who were always there for us! Mil gracias! I also would like to thank Juan Carlos Polvorosa for the inspiring discussions and logistical support. Other people who made life in Nicaragua a beautiful experience are Marianne and José Antonio, Claudia and David, Grace, Isabel, Doña Doris and Doña Fefa, Noel, Karine and my beautiful godchild Román, Onno and Tjitske, Juan Carlos and Humberto, our temporary house companion Mario, mis hermanos Filemón, Luis Carlos, Rigoberto, Tamara and Franklin, and many other friends whom I may have forgotten to mention. In Matiguás, I owe special thanks to Josué Montoya and 'el chele' Jorge Blandón for explaining and showing me many aspects of life on the 'campo' and for their continuous concern for my wellbeing. I would also like to thank all farmers, peasants, and other research 'subjects' (although I prefer the word 'partners') in Matiguás and Río Blanco. Their openness and willingness to share their experiences with me motivated me and made it possible to write this thesis. Gracias!

There is no doubt that the encouragement, support, discussions, comments and suggestions of all these people have deepened my insights and understanding and have greatly improved the quality of the work before you. I do, however, bear sole responsibility for any omissions, factual errors and misinterpretations that it may contain.

A sincere thank you also goes to all friends and family in Belgium and around the world: naming all of you would take me too long, but you all contributed to making me who I am, and therefore in some direct or indirect way you also contributed to the present work. Thank you for keeping contact with me when I didn't, and thank you for reminding me that there is more to life than only work. I owe a deep gratitude to my dear friend Dries Cleiren, who not only supported me in all possible ways, but who also came over to Nicaragua and helped me with the survey work in Matiguás. Dries, you truly are an amazing person. Thanks for always being there!

Very special thanks also to my parents Nora and Guido. They really are the best (grand)parents that any person can possibly hope for. They taught me so many things, and they gave and continue to give me all the love and care that any person could ever wish for. They have created so many unique opportunities for me and continuously motivated me to seize every one of them. They gave me all the strength and energy that I needed in difficult times, and they are always there for me, no matter what! Thanks for all your support! The same goes for my dear brother Joost and his girlfriend Karin (my little sister). The last few years we were separated so many times, all of us living and working in different places. I miss you all, but our mutual love transcends all dimensions of time and space.

Last, but certainly not least, my deepest love and recognition go to my lovely wife Virginia and our beautiful son Jonathan. Virginia, you truly are one of the persons that I most admire in this world. I admire your optimism, dedication, patience, honesty and perseverance. Already more than six years ago in Nicaragua you taught me that anything can be achieved, as long as one truly believes in it. And the next moment you were standing there at the airport in Brussels, not afraid of leaving behind your job, studies, family and social life. I know it has not always been easy to live with a Ph.D. student, especially after the birth of our wonderful son Jonathan. Nevertheless, you did everything possible to create an enabling environment for me to finish this project. I am so grateful for your unconditional support and patience. Te amo, mi vida! Jonathan, you are still too young to understand these words, but some day you hopefully will. You can't imagine how happy you make your parents; you really are the joy of our life. You truly are the most precious gift that I ever received, and therefore I would like to dedicate this work to you. I love you so much!

Estelí, Nicaragua, March 2011

ABSTRACT

The concept of Payments for Ecosystem or Environmental Services (PES) has attracted growing attention in both academic and policy circles. The main premise of this approach is appealing: land users, who tend to be poorly, if at all, motivated to protect nature on their land, may be encouraged to do so through direct payments from ecosystem service buyers. The theoretical underpinnings of PES emanate from a Coasean externality framework, which holds that - under certain circumstances - private negotiations through the market can lead to socially optimal situations. The presumed superiority of PES over other conservation mechanisms is, however, not unequivocal. From an institutional ecological economics and political economy perspective and through a variety of theoretical and empirical chapters this Ph.D. discusses the potential and limitations of the so-called Coasean or market-based PES approach. The central argument throughout this Ph.D. is that one of the reasons for the poor performance of the dominant market-based PES approach is that it tends to overlook a broad range of important social, cultural, and economic dynamics that relate to effective environmental governance.

Chapter 1 provides the theoretical background on PES and gives an extensive review of the literature. It frames the development of the PES concept within the broader literature on market-based conservation instruments and discusses the environmental economics perspective to market-based PES. It contrasts the latter with two alternative views that have recently entered the PES literature. Through the elaboration of a simplified typology of PES perspectives, it indicates the main subjects of discussion dominating current PES debates. Chapter 2 provides a theoretical discussion on some of the main assumptions underlying market-based PES. More specifically, it qualifies the positive externality/ecosystem services framework underpinning PES and shows how this framework risks obfuscating some of the real political choices underlying environmental governance, which contains the risk of perpetuating and deepening regressive financing of global public goods by poor local communities.

Chapters 3 and 4 comprise the empirical research of the thesis, which is based on two Nicaraguan case studies. From a supply-side perspective, chapter 3 reassesses the Nicaraguan component of the international GEF silvopastoral project, which piloted the use of PES in several Central and Latin American countries. Based on extensive field research, this chapter assesses farmers' motivation for adopting environmentally-sound land use practices. It suggests that a mixture of economic and non-economic factors, connected to a broader pathway of change in milk production, motivated farmers to adopt the envisaged silvopastoral practices and that the actual role of PES is mistakenly understood as a simple matter of financial incentives. Chapter 4, in turn, empirically investigates the under-researched demand-side aspects of PES by assessing local willingness to pay for water and watershed services in an upstream-downstream setting. It combines both quantitative and qualitative research approaches and shows how local perceptions of agricultural externalities and entitlements affect the feasibility of local PES schemes.

The Ph.D. concludes that a narrow market-based or Coasean approach to PES may not adequately explain the typically complex socio-political and cultural dynamics operating in the field. In line with recent contributions to the PES literature, it argues that PES approaches should be understood as a part of a broader process of local institutional transformation rather than as a market-based alternative for allegedly ineffective government and/or community governance. A more flexible approach recognising the complex (intended and unintended) outcomes of institutional interplay and processes of institutional 'bricolage' may therefore be a more appropriate framework for further investigation of PES mechanisms. This means that PES research should not only focus on market structures, but should more explicitly recognise the variety of complementary governance structures that may play a role in environmental governance.

INTRODUCTION

1. SETTING THE SCENE

> 'As the demand for food, fibre and fuel has increased, so has the demand for clean air and water, unspoilt landscapes and other environmental services provided by forests. Where forests are converted to other land uses, the services they supply are diminished. Maintaining such services poses challenges, especially where trade-offs between the production of goods and the provision of services must be addressed ... With non-state actors playing an increasing role in resource management, a need for incentives for the provision of environmental services has become evident.' (FAO, 2009: 72).

The citation above from the latest FAO report on 'The state of the world's forests' illustrates how current conservation strategies are increasingly drawing on economic metaphors in order to communicate the severity of the environmental situation to society. It seems pretty obvious: human beings have a demand for clean air and water, but at the same time they are destroying the resource bases that are responsible for supplying these environmental services. This metaphor of ecosystem stocks as the producers of environmental or ecosystem services has proven to be a very powerful one. In fact, the metaphor is so powerful that it has started developing a life of its own, making it increasingly difficult to disentangle the ecological and economic arguments underlying current conservation strategies. Moreover, it has exceeded its original aim of evoking public interest in environmental problems, and is now widely used as the underlying framework for experiments with so-called 'innovative' market-based instruments that aim to offer financial incentives for the provision of environmental services. These instruments are founded on the belief that environmental degradation is mainly caused by a general failure of conventional markets to account for the many public goods or positive externalities that ecosystems provide to society. From this perspective, the new concept of 'Payments for Ecosystem (or Environmental) Services' (PES) has attracted growing attention among a wide audience of scholars as well as conservation and development practitioners[1].

The core idea of PES is that private landowners, who tend to be poorly, if at all, motivated to protect nature on their land, can be encouraged to do so through direct

[1] The literature on PES refers to both payments for 'ecosystem' services and payments for 'environmental' services. Although some authors make a clear distinction between 'environmental' and 'ecosystem' services — the former emphasising the enhancement of 'nature' services, while the latter also encompass amenities provided by the 'built' or 'actively-managed' environment (Bulte et al., 2008; Muradian et al., 2010) — we will in this work use both terms interchangeably. For an overview of other terminologies of the same PES concept, see Wunder, 2005. Although there exist some ideological differences in the use of various other related terms, such as *compensations, markets*, or *rewards* instead of *payments* (Ravnborg et al., 2007), the differences in practice are rather semantic, but could have significant implications for the local framing and acceptance of or resistance to the concept (Wunder and Vargas, 2005).

economic incentives from ecosystem service (ES) beneficiaries in return for adopting environmentally-sound land use practices that secure ecosystem conservation and/or restoration (Engel et al., 2008; Pagiola et al., 2002; Wunder, 2005). PES schemes can thus be considered as novel institutional arrangements attempting to compensate those who produce public goods or positive externalities (Landell-Mills and Porras, 2002). The approach has mainly emerged from a general dissatisfaction with traditional governmental regulatory approaches or more community-based integrated conservation and development projects (ICDPs) and educational approaches, which are often deemed to be ineffective in halting further degradation (Baland and Platteau, 1996; Ferraro, 2001; Pagiola et al., 2002, Wunder, 2005). Rather than ineffective sanctioning of 'bad behaviour', the PES approach explicitly recognises difficult environmental and developmental trade-offs and seeks to reconcile conflicting interests through payments (Wunder, 2005). PES theory thus generally builds on a market-governance model, as it aims to change individual decision making by means of price incentives[2]. Moreover, it is held that institutionally-simple and direct incentives through the market will not only lead to expanded opportunities for private conservation funding, but will also lead to the most efficient allocation of scarce conservation funds (Ferraro and Simpson, 2002, Pagiola and Platais, 2007; Pattanayak et al., 2010). Indeed, scarcity of public funds makes some authors argue that the ES demand side of the market should be further developed in the future (Wunder et al., 2008), thereby allowing society 'to give the invisible hand of free market economics a green thumb' (Wilson, 1992: 283). This paradigm shift is increasingly reflected in global debates on climate change, such as 'Reducing Emissions from Deforestation and Forest Degradation' (REDD) (Harvey et al., 2010), and has led to growing research and implementation of PES mechanisms in the field.

The huge popularity of the concept and the mushrooming of new initiatives all over the globe illustrate that the scientific and political community has been gradually embracing and adopting PES as the new conservation paradigm, especially for halting further agricultural land expansion in the developing world, where most of the world's remaining biodiversity is located. Several multilateral organisations,

[2] In this thesis we will use the terms 'market-based' and 'market-governance' models to indicate a governance model that mainly builds upon the belief that compliance and individual or collective action should be accomplished through the use of decentralised and individual price incentives. More specifically, the use of the terminology is based upon Uphoff (1993), who distinguishes between three main governance models (bureaucratic or command-and-control models, market-based models, and community-based or voluntary action models), which each use different instruments and underlying philosophies to stimulate compliance and collective action. As noted by Uphoff (1993): in the market-based model 'decisions are left to individuals to calculate private advantage without reference to broader interests of the public good' (ibid: 610). It is important to note that market-based models do not necessarily require the presence of a functioning market. Nevertheless, mainstream PES advocates often refer to the market as the ideal scenario in wich PES would flourish (e.g. Wunder et al., 2008), and they generally use the market (and the related efficiency criterion) as the model legitimising PES (Vatn, 2010).

such as the World Bank and the Global Environment Facility (GEF), and global conservation NGOs, such as the International Union for Conservation of Nature (IUCN) and the World Wildlife Fund (WWF) have been driving forces behind the current global discourse of substituting unattractive and state-regulated conservation projects for market-based PES programmes (Ervine, 2010; McAfee, 1999). The presumed superiority of PES over other conservation mechanisms is, however, not unequivocal, to say the least. Scientific evidence is still limited and often points to the fact that ongoing PES initiatives have had limited additional positive environmental and development effects (Kosoy et al., 2007; Muñoz-Piña et al., 2008; Pattanayak et al., 2010; Robalino et al., 2008). Moreover, in many cases the promised efficiency gains of PES have been proven hard to demonstrate (Muradian et al., 2010). The rather uncritical promotion of the concept makes one suspect that its popularity is mainly based on ideological grounds, rather than on sound empirical evidence. Redford and Adams (2009), for example, note how the seductive idea of PES is 'being adopted with great speed, and often without much critical discussion, across the spectrum of conservation policy debate and developing a life of its own independent of its promulgators' (ibid: 785). Landell-Mills and Porras (2002: ix) and Muradian et al. (2010), in turn, note that a large part of the existing PES literature is written by market instrument proponents who often take the creation of markets as desirable in itself, without any further critical discussion.

As we will argue in chapter 1, the bulk of PES research has indeed been guided by a rather narrow and somewhat normative research agenda, mainly defined by environmental economists, who largely focus on the potential efficiency gains that can be obtained by harnessing market forces and offering individual price incentives. This perspective mainly refers to the Coase theorem (Coase, 1960) which — according to the interpretation of environmental economists — holds that 'socially suboptimal situations (e.g., too little provision of environmental services) can be resolved through voluntary market-like transactions, provided that transaction costs are low and property rights are clearly defined and enforced' (Pattanayak et al., 2010: 256). This dominant perspective to PES has resulted in a vast body of fairly technical publications on (economic) models related to 'efficiency-enhancing' institutional design of market-based or so-called 'Coasean' PES schemes, with limited meticulous reflection on the broader local institutional embeddedness of these arrangements and their appropriateness as policy instruments. This approach and the associated research agenda has, however, been increasingly criticised during the last few years. Some authors are either largely rejecting PES as improper and neoliberal commoditisation processes that attempt to cash ecosystem services through the development of new markets (e.g. McAfee and Shapiro, 2010; McCauley, 2006), while others rather call for conceptual modifications of the market-based PES approach, mainly by adopting a broader and more hybrid institutional governance perspective to PES (e.g. Corbera et al., 2009; Muradian et al., 2010; Vatn, 2010). While the former position has somewhat foreclosed a more constructive debate on the potential of PES, the latter opens a whole new and multidisciplinary research agenda, one that explicitly broadens the narrow focus on efficiency to other important criteria such as equity and sustainability, and one that is more sensitive to the many institutional contexts in which PES schemes are implemented. It is from the latter perspective that we will investigate the potential and limitations of market-based PES in a broader environmental governance approach.

2. RESEARCH QUESTIONS AND CENTRAL ARGUMENT

Because of the novelty of its agenda, the empirical research on PES from this broader institutional perspective is still very limited and rather inconclusive. Indeed, it was not until three years ago that empirical research articles with a more explicit focus on equity-, legitimity- and sustainability-related aspects of PES schemes started to appear in leading scientific journals (Kosoy et al., 2007, 2008; Corbera et al., 2007a, 2007b). These studies emphasised how PES schemes are in practice largely mediated by land entitlements and local political dynamics, and warned against the possible exclusion of poor minorities from the potential benefits that these schemes might deliver. They also showed that PES schemes are not only about markets and financial incentives, but are largely influenced by the local institutional context and other 'intangibles', such as cultural perspectives and the levels of trust and understanding between the actors involved. Moreover, the studies showed that non-financial incentives, such as agricultural extension support or social 'pressure' can be even more important motivations to participate in land stewardship schemes, and suggested that monetary compensations through PES may not necessarily improve economic efficiency and sustainability of conservation actions, but may even contain the risk of 'crowding out' non-profit-based motivations for environmental governance. These many new insights culminated into a reconceptualisation of PES (Muradian et al., 2010; Vatn, 2010), and simultaneously also indicated the many analytical and empirical gaps that still need to be addressed (Corbera et al., 2009).

The aim of this doctoral thesis is to discuss the potential and limitations of the Coasean or market-based approach from an institutional perspective. It thus aims to contribute to an expanded research agenda and provide additional empirical and analytical insights that have been largely neglected by the market-based approach to PES. Moreover, we are mainly interested in the many institutional factors and interactions that may play a role in effective environmental governance in the context of PES. The central question that guides the research in this work can thus be formulated as follows:

> *What are (some of) the theoretical and practical limitations of the mainstream Coasean or market-based PES approach?*

The main sub-questions that underlie the present work are the following:

> *Are payments the only motivation for the adoption of environmentally-sound land use practices? What other motivational factors might play a role? And how do PES schemes affect these other factors?*

What fairness implications might different types of PES schemes have on local communities?

Which contextual factors might interact with PES schemes? How do these interactions influence the acceptance or rejection of local PES schemes? To what degree are PES mechanisms and their associated discourses compatible or in conflict with local views on environmental governance?

The broad theoretical review of the different perspectives to PES in chapter 1 will make it easier to contextualise these questions and to understand their relevance to the broader PES debate.

The central argument we will elaborate throughout the thesis is that the mainstream market-based PES approach tends to overlook a broad range of important social, cultural, and economic dynamics that relate to effective environmental governance. We argue that PES mechanisms may have a role to play, but that their potential role should be analysed from a broader institutional governance perspective. This means that it should not only focus on market structures, but should more explicitly recognise the variety of complementary governance structures that may play a role in environmental governance. It should also acknowledge that efficiency is only one among many other socio-ecological criteria that need to be taken into account when evaluating PES schemes and their outcomes. Finally, this paradigm shift should also take into account that deliberately 'crafted' institutions will inevitably interact with socially embedded rules and practices, and that therefore research should be much more sensitive to the (local) institutional context in which PES schemes are to be implemented.

At the same time, it is also useful to clearly delineate the scope of our investigation. This study has no ambition to offer 'clear-cut' institutional design principles for 'better-functioning' PES schemes in all circumstances (in fact, this would be inconsistent with the central argument of the thesis, which emphasises context dependency), nor does it aim at offering a 'fully-fledged' governance alternative to PES. Such aspirations would be far too ambitious for a single doctoral thesis. Our research rather aims to 1) demonstrate some of the limitations of market-based frameworks for PES; and 2) offer new insights into some of the contextual factors that may have an important role to play at the moment of implementing PES in the field. In this way, we hope that the theoretical and empirical material in this work may help to demonstrate the relevance of the new research agenda, and will contribute to building a stock of knowledge for a more appropriate contextualisation and a more effective and fair implementation of 'second-generation' PES schemes as part of an integrated rural development strategy.

Finally, it is also important to emphasise that the present study does not pretend to offer an all-encompassing comprehensive analysis of all possible conceptual and practical limitations that the market-based PES approach may entail. This too would be far too ambitious. Instead, the study points to some (among possibly many other) essential elements that have so far not — or perhaps only superficially — been discussed elsewhere. Each chapter is indeed based on a separately-published article or paper (and therefore also stands on its own) that sheds some light on a specific aspect of the market-based PES approach. Chapter 2, for example, discusses some of the negative consequences ensuing from an over-reliance on the externality framework, underlying market-based PES approaches. It does not, however, pretend to discuss all theoretical weaknesses underlying market-based PES; it does not include, for example, other important theoretical discussions on the conceptualisation of opportunity costs, or on the theories behind the quantification of ecosystem services, which obviously also deserve more attention in future research[3].

[3] For a general discussion on the problems associated with the quantification of ES and the use of the concept of opportunity costs in PES schemes, please refer to Van Hecken and Bastiaensen, 2009, §5.1.

3. THEORETICAL FRAMEWORK

In chapters 2, 3 and 4 we will investigate the research questions mentioned in the previous section from different perspectives, taking explicitly into account the wide variety of political, cultural, behavioural, ecological, economic and social factors that may play a role in environmental governance. The many dimensions that need to be considered call for a multidisciplinary research approach, building on insights and concepts from economic sciences, as well as social, political and environmental sciences. As mentioned before, each of these chapters is based on a separately-published article or paper, and therefore develops its own theoretical framework relevant for the specific topic under investigation. Although we do not think that our analysis fits into one single 'all-encompassing' theoretical framework, many of the arguments that we will expound in this work are inspired by insights and concepts borrowed from a school of thought that has recently been coined 'institutional ecological economics' (IEE) (Paavola, 2007; Paavola and Adger, 2005; Slavíková et al., 2010; Vatn, 2005a, 2005b, 2009). Authors pertaining to this approach explicitly aim at developing a multidisciplinary framework that allows understanding and examining the design of environmental policies and governance institutions by capitalising on the many insights from institutional economics (Paavola and Adger, 2005: 353). Rather than restricting the analysis to institutional design principles for the governance of (mainly local) common pool resources (e.g. Baland and Platteau, 1996; Ostrom, 1990; Ostrom et al., 1994, Young, 2002a), the IEE approach expands the field of analysis to all types of resources and property regimes across different governance scales (Paavola, 2007; Paavola and Adger, 2005).

From a general perspective, IEE can thus be considered the synthesis between ecological and institutional economics (Paavola and Adger, 2005). The concept of 'institutions' should then be understood in the sense of the 'rules of the game' in a society, consisting of both the formal and informal human-devised constraints that govern — but not necessarily determine — individual behaviour and structure social interactions (see e.g. North, 1990). Instead of taking institutions as an exogenous variable, ecological institutional economists explicitly acknowledge that institutions play a central role in articulating values and in forming preferences, and thus regulate the way in which humans interact with their environment (Dietz et al., 2003; Vatn, 2005a). As such, they focus on the role of institutions in explaining human behaviour and collective action in the context of environmental governance (Paavola and Adger, 2005). In this context 'environmental governance' means 'the establishment, reaffirmation or change of institutions to resolve conflicts over environmental resources' (Paavola, 2007: 94), where 'conflict' refers to a conflict of interest, and not necessarily to an open conflict, between involved parties (ibid: 94). As a consequence, processes of institutional interplay or the intended and unintended environmental outcome of interactions between different (formal and informal) institutions also deserve due attention in institutional analysis (Young, 2002a, 2002b). Furthermore, the IEE approach prioritises ecological sustainability and social justice over market efficiency (Paavola, 2007; Paavola and Adger, 2005; Slavíková et al., 2010) and builds on concepts such as value and motivational pluralism, which refer to the multiple and often incommensurable values that inform agents' preferences in a choice situation (Paavola and Adger, 2005). Considerations of pluralism and fairness also imply that more attention should be given to 'participatory' or 'communicative' processes and procedures in environmental decision making, instead of limiting policy analysis to individual cost-benefit analyses (Paavola, 2007, Paavola and Adger, 2005; Vatn, 2005a, 2009). Moreover, the IEE approach explicitly highlights how trust, engagement, culture, beliefs and other forms of 'social capital' can influence the effectiveness of governance solutions (Paavola and Adger, 2005).

We do, however, want to emphasise again that the IEE approach is not the only theoretical framework we draw upon. The empirical chapters also use insights developed by Cleaver (1998, 2002, 2005), who has indicated some limitations of institutional approaches. Cleaver emphasises that these still largely have as their starting point the belief in institutional design principles for devising successful and sustainable arrangements for environmental governance (see e.g. Baland and Platteau, 1996; Dietz et al., 2003; Ostrom, 1990; Ostrom et al., 2002). Cleaver is very sceptical about the extent to which social and environmental change can be brought about by simply 'getting the institutions right' and she 'questions the idea that appropriate mechanisms can be designed to ensure optimum resource use, beneficial collective action and hence to build social capital' (Cleaver, 2002: 11). Through the concept of 'institutional bricolage', she shows 'how mechanisms for resource management and collective action are borrowed or constructed from existing institutions, styles of thinking and sanctioned social relationships' (ibid: 16). The implementation of deliberately 'crafted' institutions will thus always be subjected to a process of evolution mediated by the social and cultural practices of everyday life (ibid). As will become clear in the empirical chapters of this thesis, and in line with Cleaver's work, we will argue that PES interventions should be 'based on a socially informed analysis of the content and effects of institutional arrangements, rather than on their form alone' (Cleaver, 2002: 12), and should mainly focus on ways to complement or reinforce the positive aspects of socially embedded arrangements (ibid: 28).

4. METHODOLOGICAL REFLECTIONS AND RESEARCH SITE

As mentioned by Petheram and Campbell (2010), to date most research on PES has primarily depended on quantitative research methodologies, with only few examples of qualitative approaches 'aimed at in-depth understanding of perceptions of PES' (ibid: 1140). For our assessment of PES and in our explicit focus on the broader institutional context and motivations behind specific behaviour, we employed a mix of several research approaches. The two empirical chapters both rely on a combination of qualitative and quantitative data generation methods, which will be discussed in more detail in the methodology section of each of these chapters. We believe that the adoption of different methods can provide us with important and complementary insights into the relevant research theme, as it allows for the 'triangulation' of different types of data obtained in distinct ways (Denzin, 1978). Thus it is important to keep in mind that quantitative results should be interpreted with care, because 'numbers do not speak for themselves ... [and are therefore] not an absolute that exists outside of the meaning that people give it' (Rubin and Rubin, 2005: 29). The use of qualitative methods can also give us better insights into 'the intricate details of phenomena that are difficult to convey with quantitative methods' (Strauss and Corbin, 1990: 19).

The combination of qualitative and quantitative approaches is often mistakenly understood as a two-step procedure in which the 'explorative' qualitative data merely serve as an input for the design of quantitative surveys. In our study, however, we alternate back and forth between the two methods, aiming to clarify, illustrate and interpret the results from one method with the results from the other (also called 'complementary approach', see e.g. Greene et al., 1989). While the quantitative methods can complement our understanding by elucidating, for example, trends in physical land use changes or (quantitatively measurable) economic dynamics, the qualitative research sheds more light on the institutional context and the local perceptions of governance approaches, as well as on the motivations, feelings and opinions of the research participants. In-depth understanding also requires a lengthy stay in the field and a reasonable familiarity with the complex local settings. That is why we decided to focus on one specific region, which we regularly visited in the course of four years.

The research took place in the rural municipalities of Matiguás and Río Blanco, in the central department of Matagalpa, Nicaragua (Figure 1). We chose this area and the specific research sites for various reasons. In the first place, Nicaragua is one of the countries where deforestation is a major problem. The current loss in forest cover amounts to about 70,000 ha/year, corresponding to a 2.11 per cent annual net decrease, which is - next to the 2.16 per cent loss in Honduras - the highest in Central

America (FAO, 2010). Furthermore, between 60 and 88 per cent of forests in Nicaragua are privately owned, with the remaining areas mainly publicly or community-owned (FAO, 2010; INAFOR, 2009). The expansion of agricultural cropping areas and pastures for cattle is considered as still one of the main pressures on forested areas, especially in the central region where the agricultural frontier is steadily advancing eastward (Kaimowitz, 1996; Maldidier and Marchetti, 1996; Ruíz and Marín, 2005). National forestry policies, which have mainly centred on strict regulatory approaches such as the creation of protected areas and the issuing of strict forestry laws (Barahona, 2001; Ravnborg, 2010), have so far not been successful in halting further agricultural land expansion. The combination of these characteristics makes Nicaragua an interesting setting for experimenting with PES schemes. During the last decade an increasing number of (mainly small-scale) PES schemes have indeed been implemented throughout the country (see e.g. Kosoy et al., 2007; Pagiola et al., 2007, 2008).

Figure 1. Matiguás and Río Blanco in the department of Matagalpa, Nicaragua

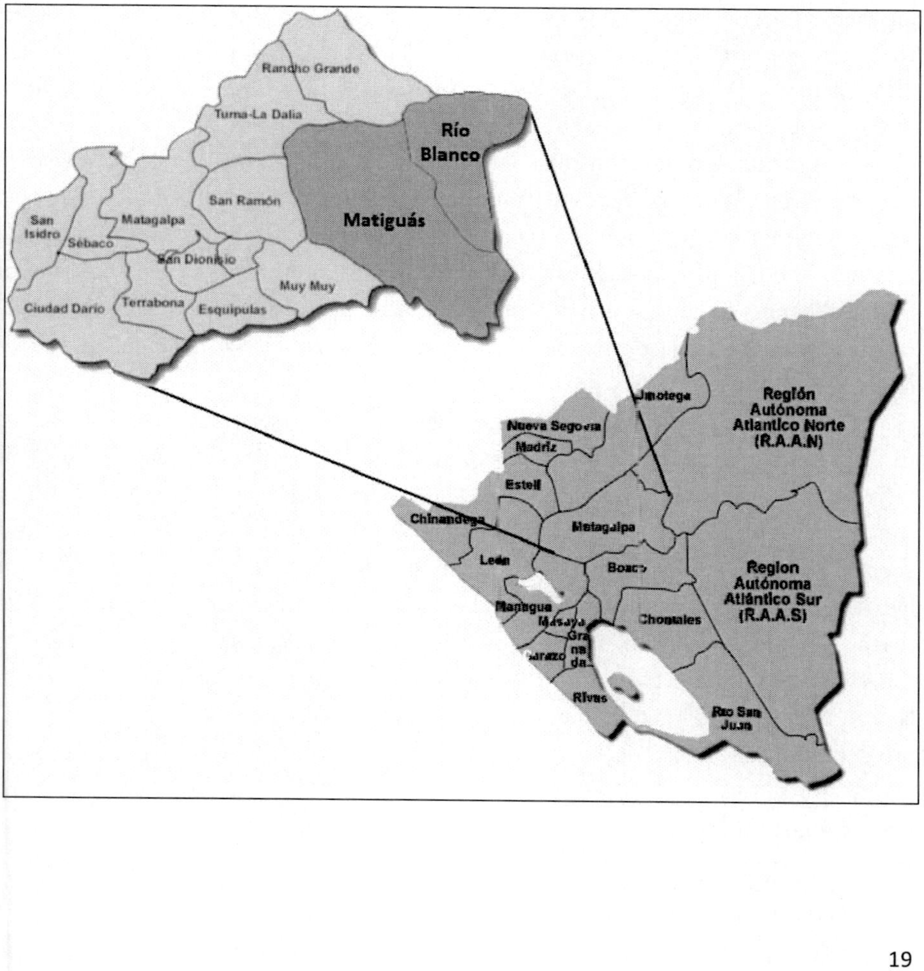

Secondly, the focus on Matiguás and Río Blanco is justified because of the typical land use dynamics in this region which reflect 'hard' conservation and development trade-offs. The region belongs to the so-called 'old agricultural frontier' (Maldidier and Marchetti, 1996; Ruíz and Marín, 2005), which has been characterised by a high rate of deforestation from the 1920s onwards, mainly by peasants in search of pasture land for their cattle. Since then, the region has gradually transformed into what is now popularly known as the '*cuenca lechera*' or 'dairy belt', encompassing the majority of dairy farms in Nicaragua (Polvorosa, 2007). As will be explained in chapter 3, mounting land prices and expanding dairy markets put increasing pressure on the few remaining forests in this area, and have driven an increasing number of farmers to expand their agricultural activities into zones pertaining to the region's two nature reserves (the Sierra Quirragua and the Cerro Musún).

Third, the Matiguás-Río Blanco area was part of an international PES pilot experiment in Central and Latin America: the GEF silvopastoral project, which took place in Colombia, Costa Rica and Nicaragua from 2002 until 2008. The project was aimed at promoting silvopastoral practices in degraded pasture areas through payments for environmental services (generated by these practices). The results of this study are discussed in chapter 3. Farmers in the neighbouring Quirragua region, an area that was excluded from the silvopastoral project, have increasingly taken over the project narrative and even organised themselves by starting a local conservation foundation, the main aim of which is to attract funds to invest in ecosystem payments to Quirragua farmers. The municipality of Matiguás has also shown interest in implementing a payment scheme in which upstream Quirragua farmers would be paid by downstream urban dwellers in Matiguás. An assessment of local willingness to pay for such a scheme is the subject of chapter 4. In short, it may be clear from this description that the idea and discourse of paying farmers for ecosystem protection is very present in this region.

And finally, for almost twenty years the region has been one of the focus areas of the Nicaraguan research and development institute Nitlapán[4], which is a long-term partner of the Antwerp Institute of Development Policy and Management (IOB). Our cooperation with this institute and the profound knowledge of the latter on this specific area proved, for various reasons, to be very beneficial to our study. Firstly, it allowed us to link our research with the local expertise and the institute's large research databases developed over the past two decades. Especially in the case of the silvopastoral project, in which Nitlapán was one of the two executing institutes in Nicaragua, our close institutional collaboration allowed us good access to the official project databases and their interpretation with the expert help of the local project coordinators. Secondly, it facilitated our entrance to the field research area, both from a logistical and from a 'networking' point of view. The local field technicians

[4] see http://www.nitlapan.org.ni

were well placed to indicate important key informants and to give us useful background information on local dynamics and on potential research participants. And thirdly, the association with Nitlapán allowed us to discuss our research results with local field experts, greatly benefitting the interpretation of the data we obtained.

5. STRUCTURE OF THE THESIS

In addition to the present general introduction, the thesis comprises four chapters. Chapter 1 provides the theoretical background on PES and gives an extensive review of the literature. It starts by framing the development of the PES concept within the broader literature on market-based conservation instruments, and shows how the ecosystem services metaphor is used as the legitimising framework underlying PES. It then enters into a general discussion of the environmental economics perspective to market-based PES, which has so far dominated the literature, and goes on to contrast the latter with two alternative views that have recently entered the PES literature. Through the elaboration of a simplified typology of PES perspectives, it indicates the main subjects of discussion dominating current PES debates, and points out how each of the remaining chapters of this thesis contributes to this debate. Chapter 2 provides a theoretical discussion on some of the main assumptions underlying market-based PES. From an institutional and political economy perspective, it qualifies the positive externality/ecosystem services framework underpinning PES and shows how this framework risks obfuscating some of the real political choices underlying environmental governance, which contains the risk of perpetuating and deepening regressive financing of global public goods by poor local communities.

Chapters 3 and 4 comprise the empirical research of the thesis. From a supply-side perspective, chapter 3 investigates the Nicaraguan component of the international GEF silvopastoral project, which piloted the use of PES schemes in Central and Latin America. Based on extensive field research, this chapter assesses farmers' motivation for adopting environmentally-sound land use practices and shows how the role of PES is mistakenly understood as a simple matter of financial incentives. It reveals how the project set-up failed to account for alternative factors and dynamics influencing farmers' motivation, and argues that PES approaches should be understood as part of a broader process of local institutional transformation rather than as a market-based alternative for allegedly ineffective government and/or community governance. Chapter 4, in turn, empirically investigates the under-researched demand-side aspects of PES by assessing local willingness to pay for water and watershed services in an upstream-downstream setting. It combines both quantitative and qualitative research approaches and shows how local perceptions of agricultural externalities and entitlements affect the feasibility of local PES schemes. From a broader institutional perspective, the chapter offers alternative and more plausible explanations for the ongoing socio-political interactions in the field, and argues that future research on PES should be much more sensitive to the local social structures and institutional arrangements.

REFERENCES

Baland, J.-M. and Platteau, J.-P. (1996) Halting degradation of natural resources: Is there a role for rural communities?, New York: Clarendon Press.

Barahona, T. (2001) "Protected Areas and Natural Resources: With or Without People?", *Revista Envío* 242.

Bulte, E.H., Lipper, L., Stringer, R. and Zilberman, D. (2008) "Payments for ecosystem services and poverty reduction: concepts, issues and empirical perspectives", *Environment and Development Economics* 13: 245-254.

Cleaver, F. (1998) "Incentives and informal institutions: Gender and the management of water", *Agriculture and Human Values* 15: 347-360.

Cleaver, F. (2002) "Reinventing Institutions and the Social Embeddedness of Natural Resource Management", *European Journal of Development Research* 14(2): 11–30.

Cleaver, F. (2005) "The Inequality of Social Capital and the Reproduction of Chronic Poverty", *World Development* 33(6): 893-906.

Corbera, E., Brown, K. and Adger, W.N. (2007a) "The equity and legitimacy of markets for ecosystem services", *Development and Change* 38(4): 587–613.

Corbera, E., Kosoy, N. and Tuna, M.M. (2007b) "Equity implications of marketing ecosystem services in protected areas and rural communities: Case studies from Meso-America", *Global Environmental Change* 17: 365-380.

Corbera, E., González Soberanis, C. and Brown, K. (2009) "Institutional dimensions of payments for ecosystem services. An analysis of Mexico's carbon forestry programme", *Ecological Economics* 68: 743–761.

Denzin, N.K. (1978) The research act: An introduction to sociological methods, New York: McGraw-Hill.

Dietz, T., Ostrom, E. and Stern, P.C. (2003) "The struggle to govern the commons", *Science* 302: 1907–1912.

Engel, S., Pagiola, S. and Wunder, S. (2008) "Designing payments for environmental services in theory and practice: an overview of the issues", *Ecological Economics* 65: 663–675.

Ervine, K. (2010) "Participation denied: the Global Environment Facility, its universal blueprint, and the Mexico-Mesoamerican biological corridor in Chiapas", *Third World Quarterly* 31(5): 773-790.

Food and Agriculture Organisation (FAO) (2009) *State of the World's Forests 2009*, Rome: FAO.

Food and Agriculture Organisation (FAO) (2010) *Global Forest Resources Assessment 2010 – Main Report*, Rome: FAO.

Ferraro, P.J. (2001) "Global Habitat Protection: Limitations of Development Interventions and a Role for Conservation Performance Payments", *Conservation Biology* 15(4): 1-12.

Ferraro, P.J. and Simpson, R.D. (2002) "The cost-effectiveness of conservation payments", *Land Economics* 78(3): 339-353.

Greene, J.C., Caracelli, V.J. and Graham, W.F. (1989) "Toward a conceptual framework for mixed-method evaluation designs", *Educational Evaluation and Policy Analysis* 11: 255-274.

Harvey C.A., Dickson, B. and Kormos, C. (2010) "Opportunities for achieving biodiversity conservation through REDD", *Conservation Letters* 3(1): 53-61.

Insituto Nacional Forestal (INAFOR) (2009) Resultados del Inventario Nacional Forestal: Nicaragua 2007-2008 (Results of the National Forest Inventory: Nicaragua 2007-2008), Managua, INAFOR.

Kaimowitz, D. (1996) Livestock and Deforestation in Central America in the 1980s and 1990s: A Policy Perspective, Bogor: CIFOR.

Kosoy, N., Martinez-Tuna, M., Muradian, R. and Martinez-Alier, J. (2007) "Payments for environmental services in watersheds: Insights from a comparative study of three cases in Central America", *Ecological Economics* 61: 446-455.

Kosoy, N., Corbera, E. and Brown, K. (2008) "Participation in payments for ecosystem services: Case studies from the Lacandón rainforest, Mexico", *Geoforum* 39: 2073-2083.

Landell-Mills, N. and Porras, I. (2002) Silver Bullet or Fools' Gold? A Global Review of Markets for Forest Environmental Services and Their Impact on the Poor, London: IIED.

Maldidier, C. and Marchetti, P. (1996) El Campesino-Finquero y el potencial económico del campesinado nicaragüense (The Peasant-Farmer and the Economic Potential of the Nicaraguan Peasantry), Managua, Nitlapán.

McAfee, K. (1999) "Selling nature to save it? Biodiversity and green developmentalism", *Environment and Planning D: Society and Space* 17(2): 133–154.

McAfee, K. and Shapiro, E.N. (2010) "Payment for Environmental Services in Mexico: Neoliberalism, Social Movements, and the State", *Annals of the Association of American Geographers* 100(3): 579-599.

McCauley, D.J. (2006) "Selling out on nature", *Nature* 443: 27-28.

Muñoz-Piña, C., Guevara, A., Torres, J.M. and Braña, J. (2008) "Paying for the hydrological services of Mexico's forests: Analysis, negotiations and results", *Ecological Economics* 65: 725-736.

Muradian, R., Corbera, E., Pascual, U., Kosoy, N. and May, P. (2010) "Reconciling theory and practice: An alternative conceptual framework for understanding payments for environmental services", *Ecological Economics* 69(6): 1202–1208.

North, D.C. (1990) Institutions, Institutional Change and Economic Performance, New York: Cambridge University Press.

Ostrom, E. (1990) Governing the Commons: The Evolution of Institutions for Collective Action, New York: Cambridge University Press.

Ostrom, E., Gardner, R. and Walker, J. (1994) *Rules, Games, and Common Pool Resources,* Michigan: The University of Michigan Press.

Ostrom, E., Dietz, T., Dolsak, N., Stern, P.C., Stonich, S. and Weber, E.U. (Eds.) (2002) *The drama of the commons*, Washington D.C.: National Academy Press.

Paavola, J. and Adger, N.W. (2005) "Institutional ecological economics", *Ecological Economics* 53: 353-368.

Paavola, J. (2007) "Institutions and environmental governance: a reconceptualization", *Ecological Economics* 63: 93-103.

Pagiola, S. and Platais, G. (2007) *Payments for Environmental Services: From Theory to Practice*, Washington D.C.: World Bank.

Pagiola, S., Bishop, J. and Landell-Mills, N. (eds.) (2002) Selling forest environmental services. Market-based mechanisms for conservation and development, London: Earthscan.

Pagiola, S., Ramírez, E., Gobbi, J., de Haan, C., Ibrahim, M., Murgueitio, E. and Ruíz, J. (2007) "Paying for the environmental services of silvopastoral practices in Nicaragua", *Ecological Economics* 64: 374–385.

Pagiola, S., Rios, A.R. and Arcenas, A. (2008) "Can the poor participate in payments for environmental services? Lessons from the Silvopastoral Project in Nicaragua", *Environment and Development Economics* 13(3): 299-325.

Pattanayak, S.K., Wunder, S. and Ferraro, P.J. (2010) "Show me the money: do payments supply environmental services in developing countries?" *Review of Environmental Economics and Policy* 4(2): 254-274.

Petheram, L. and Campbell, B.M. (2010) "Listening to locals on payments for environmental services", *Journal of Environmental Management* 91: 1139–1149.

Polvorosa, J.C. (2007) "Elección de contrato y estrategias de vida: estudio de caso de la cadena de la leche en Matiguás, Nicaragua (Contract Election and Livelihood Strategies: A Case Study of the Dairy Chain in Matiguás, Nicaragua)", *Encuentro* 78: 47-75.

Ravnborg, H.M. (2010) "From declaration to real protection: Biodiversity and local participation in the management of four protected areas in Nicaragua", Danish Institute for International Studies (DIIS) Report 2010:04. Copenhagen, DIIS.

Ravnborg, H.M., Damsgaard, M.G. and Raben, K. (2007) "Payments for Ecosystem Services. Issues and pro-poor opportunities for development assistance", DIIS Report 2007:6, Copenhagen: Danish Institute for International Studies.

Redford, K.H. and Adams, W.M. (2009) "Payments for Ecosystem services and the Challenge of Saving Nature", *Conservation Biology* 23: 785-787.

Robalino, J., Pfaff, A., Sánchez-Azofeifa, G.A., Alpízar, F., León, C. and Rodríguez, C.M. (2008) "Deforestation impacts of environmental services payments: Costa Rica's PSA Program 2000-2005", Discussion Paper 2008-24: Environment for Development.

Rubin, H.J. and Rubin, I.S. (2005) *Qualitative Interviewing: The Art of Hearing Data*, California: Sage Publications.

Ruíz, A. and Marín, Y. (2005) Tipología de los sistemas de producción y zonificación agro socioeconómica a la luz del Censo Agropecuario 2001 (Typology of production systems and agro-socioeconomic zoning on the basis of the 2001 agricultural census), Managua, Nicaragua: UCA-Nitlapán.

Slavíková, L., Kluvánková-Oravská, T. and Jílková, J. (2010) "Bridging theories on environmental governance: Insights from free-market approaches and institutional ecological economics perspectives", *Ecological Economics* 69: 1368-1372.

Strauss, A. and Corbin, J. (1990) Basics of Qualitative Research – Grounded Theory Procedures and Techniques, California: Sage Publications.

Uphoff, N. (1993) "Grassroots Organizations and NGOs in Rural Development: Opportunities with Diminishing States and Expanding Markets", *World Development* 21(4): 607-622.

Vatn, A. (2005a) "Rationality, institutions and environmental policy", *Ecological Economics* 55: 203-217.

Vatn, A. (2005b) *Institutions and the Environment*, Cheltenham: Edward Elgar.

Vatn, A. (2009) "An institutional analysis of methods for environmental appraisal", *Ecological Economics* 68: 2207-2215.

Vatn, A. (2010) "An institutional analysis of payments for environmental services", *Ecological Economics* 69(6): 1245–1252.

Wilson, E. (1992) *The Diversity of Life*, New York: W.W. Norton.

Wunder, S. (2005) "Payments for environmental services: some nuts and bolts", CIFOR Occasional Paper 42, Jakarta: CIFOR

Wunder, S. (2008) "Necessary Conditions for Ecosystem Service Payments", Paper presented at the Workshop on Economics and Conservation in the Tropics: a Strategy Dialogue, San Francisco, USA, 31 January–1 February, 2008.

Wunder, S. and Vargas, M.T. (2005) "Beyond "markets": why terminology matters", in Bayon, R., Nathaniel, C. and Hawn, A. (eds.), *The tale of two continents – Ecosystem services in Latin America and East and Southern Africa,* Ecosystem Marketplace.

Young, O.R. (2002a) The Institutional Dimensions of Environmental Change: Fit, Interplay and Scale, London: MIT Press.

Young, O.R. (2002b) "Institutional Interplay: The Environmental Consequences of Cross-scale Interactions", in: Ostrom, E., Dietz, T., Dolsak, N., Stern, P.C., Stonich, S. and Weber, E.U. (Eds.) *The Drama of the Commons*, Washington D.C.: National Academy Press.

CHAPTER 1

THE CONCEPTUAL UNDERPINNINGS OF PAYMENTS FOR ENVIRONMENTAL SERVICES

Note: Section 3 of this chapter is partly based upon Van Hecken, G. and Bastiaensen, J. (2010) "Payments for Ecosystem Services: A Political View of its Justification, or the Lack of it", *Environmental Science & Policy* 13(8): 785-792.

The chapter has benefited from useful comments and suggestions by Johan Bastiaensen, Bram Büscher, Frédéric Huybrechs, Griet Steel and Guido Van Hecken. The research was funded by a Ph.D. grant of the Flemish Interuniversity Council (VLIR-UOS). The usual disclaimers apply.

1. INTRODUCTION

Less than ten years ago, PES was still a fairly new theoretical concept. As such, it lacked a clear definition, so that it was difficult to distinguish it from other market-based conservation instruments. But already before the establishment of the PES terminology as it is known nowadays, an increasing number of conservation initiatives during the 1980s and 1990s reflected similar characteristics, which were later qualified under the common dominator of Payments or Markets for Environmental Services (MES)[5]. After Landell-Mills and Porras' (2002) review of almost 300 case studies on emerging conservation markets around the world and Wunder's (2005) first 'formal' definition of PES, this policy tool gained further ground in both academic and policy circles. Various authors, however, noted that the swift adoption of this new conservation paradigm is accompanied by rather limited empirical evidence (e.g. Redford and Adams, 2009). Moreover, a growing number of voices challenge the rather uncritical enthusiasm for these new institutional arrangements by referring to the potentially negative social and environmental consequences of the introduction of market mechanisms. In order to better understand the raison d'être of PES, and in order to distinguish advocacy from analysis, it is essential to dig deeper into the implicit and explicit assumptions and theoretical foundations underlying PES, and to contextualise the concept within the broader literature on environmental governance. In this chapter we will take up this challenge.

Section 2 therefore briefly frames the development of PES within the broader literature on the evolution of (economic) conservation instruments. From an environmental economics perspective it describes how conservation and economic thinking have embraced each other through the adoption of the stock-flow model of ecosystems and ecosystem services, which eventually laid the foundation of the PES concept. From the same environmental economics perspective, section 3 goes on to analyse in more detail the genesis of the PES concept, and the main implicit and explicit assumptions underlying this approach. This section also discusses Wunder's (2005) mainstream definition of PES, some major PES typologies encountered in the literature, and the scope of the instrument. Next, section 4 critically assesses some of the main arguments underlying market-based PES. Through the elaboration of a simplified typology, it contrasts the mainstream view with two emerging alternative perspectives; by doing so, it brings to the foreground the main subjects of discussion in the currently prevailing broader debates on the appropriateness of market-based environmental instruments. Finally, concluding section 5 will indicate how these debates frame the structure of this doctoral thesis.

---

[5] In section 3 of this chapter we will further elaborate on the conceptual difference between 'payments' and 'markets' for ES.

2. ECOSYSTEM SERVICES AS THE INTEGRATION OF CONSERVATION AND ECONOMIC THINKING

2.1. THE BIRTH OF THE ECOSYSTEM SERVICES CONCEPT

Especially after the 1972 UN Environment Conference in Stockholm, nature conservation moved from being a mainly isolated and individual concern to the centre of the political stage (Sayer, 1995). This growing attention from the political world initially manifested itself through the establishment of several international conventions[6], and through the exponential growth of protected areas during the 1970s. From the outset, this 'fences and fines' or 'command-and-control' (C&C) approach resulted in conflicts with local population and indigenous peoples, as the concern for the interests of local communities was virtually non-existent (Brockington et al., 2006; Wilkie et al., 2010). Conservationists became increasingly aware that this coercive approach could prove harmful to local livelihoods, and how this in turn undermined the effectiveness of protected areas in conserving nature. The rise of social movements and the emergence of the concept of sustainable development in the late 1970s and the 1980s gave birth to more participatory and inclusive approaches to conservation, broadly coined as community-based natural resource management (Blaikie, 2006; Dressler et al., 2010). The growing body of research and the political interest into the assumed positive correlation between poverty and environmental degradation (Durning, 1989) spawned so-called 'integrated conservation and development projects' (ICDPs), which were mainly implemented from the 1980s onwards (Wells and Brandon, 1992). The philosophy behind these projects was rooted in a strong belief that pressure on natural resources could be reduced by offering poor local communities alternative economic incomes not based on resource extraction (e.g. from ecotourism or intensified agriculture), which - it was hoped - could provide an alternative to environmentally damaging activities. Conservation would thus 'win', but only on condition of simultaneously addressing the 'development' of the economically deprived local people (Ervine, 2010).

Despite some ICDP successes, an increasing number of publications during the 1990s (e.g. Sayer, 1991; Wells et al., 1998) questioned the impacts of these projects on both conservation and development objectives. The authors attributed the perceived weakness of the approach to a general over-emphasis on the social agenda, with too little attention for effective conservation outcomes (MacKinnon, 2001). It is at this point that economists actively entered the conservation scene, as they attributed the perceived failure of many ICDP interventions to the 'lack of

[6] E.g. the 1973 Convention on International Trade in Endangered Species of Wild Fauna and Flora, and the 1979 Bonn Convention on the Conservation of Migratory Species of Wild Animals

linkage' between economic benefits and conservation (Martin et al., 2008). For these environmental economists it was obvious that the missing link could be bridged by assigning an exchange value to nature, which would allow conservationists, economists, governments and local communities to speak the same language: money (ibid: 3). In this logic, the main reason why society had been neglecting the 'real' value of nature for so long, was because this value had never been made explicit in monetary terms (Büscher, 2010). Once nature would acquire a universal and commensurable monetary value, it would finally 'earn its own right to survive in a world market economy' (McAfee, 1999: 134) and by reinventing itself, conservation would finally become politically acceptable (Büscher, 2008).

Already in the second half of the 20th century environmental economists started to expand their traditional research field by developing methods to value and assess economic impacts on the environment (Gómez-Baggethun et al., 2010). Mainly inspired by Pigou's (1920) theory on economic externalities, they argued that environmental degradation is primarily caused by nature's exclusion from the economy (Pearce, 1993; Pearce and Turner, 1990; Turner et al., 1994). This view resulted in new theories advocating that governments should play the central role in regulating the extractive economy, and - at the practical policy level - led to the introduction of market-based instruments, such as environmental taxes and subsidies, which were increasingly implemented in Western countries since the 1960s (Lemos and Agrawal, 2007). At the same time, this school of thought argued that further incorporation of the environment into economic and policy decision making could be facilitated by developing utility-based environmental appraisal methods (such as cost-benefit analysis and contingent valuation), which allowed the explicit allocation of monetary exchange values to intangible environmental assets (Balmford et al., 2002; Costanza et al., 1997; Freeman, 1993). The integration of conservation and economics proved to be a promising way for raising public interest for biodiversity conservation (Gómez-Baggethun et al., 2010). Ecosystems were no longer viewed as passive sinks and sources of the extractive economy, but were presented as active 'economic players' that produced valuable goods and services.

The economic and anthropocentric view of ecosystems as fixed capital stocks producing flows of benefits to human societies soon gave rise to the concept of ecosystem (or environmental) services (ES) (Costanza and Daly, 1992; Daily, 1997). These were broadly defined as the direct or indirect benefits that human populations derive from ecosystems, and - as depicted in Figure 2 - can be subdivided into provisioning, regulating, cultural, and supporting services. These services were often neglected in policy decisions, precisely because they were not defined in terms similar to 'traditional' economic services and manufactured capital (Costanza and Daly, 1992). In their famous and widely-discussed article in Nature, Costanza et al.

(1997) estimated the total value of global ES at about 33 trillion dollars per year. The article forcefully stressed the economic value of ES and catapulted the concept into mainstream environmental thinking. Economists and conservationists had finally discovered a convincing way to communicate nature's vital importance to society through the elaboration of the ES concept. During the 1990s the ES framework increasingly caught on, both in policy circles and in the scientific world (Fisher et al., 2009). The popularity was reached a climax with the publication of the Millennium Ecosystem Assessment in 2005 (MA, 2005). This assessment, carried out in cooperation with more than 1,000 scientists from around the world, unambiguously revealed how the ES communicative and 'eye-opening metaphor' had soon converted into a central and dominant framework for scientifically assessing ecosystem change (Norgaard, 2010).

Figure 2. The Ecosystem Services concept

<table>
<tr><th colspan="2">ECOSYSTEM SERVICES</th></tr>
<tr><td rowspan="3">Supporting
• Nutrient cycling
• Soil formation
• Primary production
• …</td><td>Provisioning
• Food
• Fresh water
• Wood and fiber
• Fuel
• …</td></tr>
<tr><td>Regulating
• Climate regulation
• Flood regulation
• Disease regulation
• Water purification
• …</td></tr>
<tr><td>Cultural
• Aesthetic
• Spiritual
• Educational
• Recreational
• …</td></tr>
</table>

Source: MA, 2005: 28

2.2. INTEGRATION OF ECOSYSTEM SERVICES IN MARKET THINKING

Once ecosystems had been recognised as valuable economic capital stocks, the next step consisted in creating the institutional mechanisms that would offer the right incentives to conserve the 'optimal' amount of nature. In the 1980s and 1990s, a growing number of economists started to criticise the 'traditional' economic instruments of government taxes and subsidies for being costly and inefficient

(Baumol and Oates, 1988; Engel et al., 2008; Pagiola and Platais, 2007). This critique paralleled more traditional debates on the appropriate treatment of social cost problems (externalities), either through government-regulated taxes and subsidies (Pigou, 1920) or through private negotiation between the involved parties (Coase, 1960). This latter position largely corresponds with the view of free-market economists that environmental problems are not caused by failing markets (since they have not been established yet), 'but the state, as the main leader, fails by blocking the evolution of the property right structure' (Block, 1990 and Raeder, 1998, as cited by Slavíková et al., 2010: 1370). Instead of influencing consumers' and producers' behaviour indirectly through government-regulated price modifications, the idea of creating new markets for (often intangible) environmental assets steadily emerged. The practice - by then standardised - of establishing monetary exchange value to natural assets allowed nature and its ES to be treated in much the same way as any other commodity. Moreover, in this scheme environmental degradation and crises could even be considered as sources of profit (Bakker, 2010). Various authors point out how this market perspective mainly emerged during the late 1980s, coinciding with the rise, expansion, and deepening of neoliberal economics (Brockington et al., 2008; McCarthy, 2005), which emphasised the potential efficiency gains of market regulation through the allocation of well-defined property rights and the pricing of nature's services or 'disservices' (Anderson and Leal, 2001).

In the mid 1990s, the United States pioneered this 'direct' approach through the creation of 'cap-and-trade' markets for sulphur dioxide (SO2) permits (Bayon, 2004). The US government pre-determined a total permissible amount of SO2 emissions, and emitted the property rights (permits) that enabled the market to work. The market, in turn, allocated the permits in the most efficient way (ibid). The relative success of this new approach spurred the development of similar commercial markets in the US, such as the trading of wetland ecosystem services through wetland mitigation banking (Robertson, 2004), or the trading of renewable energy credits (Bayon, 2004). It is important to note that these initiatives were not aimed at the active production of ecosystem services, but rather at limiting the production of negative externalities or environmental 'disservices'. Mainly within the framework of the United Nations Framework Convention on Climate Change (UNFCCC) and the Kyoto Protocol, various international greenhouse gas emission markets, such as the Clean Development Mechanism (CDM) and the EU emission trading system, soon followed suit (Corbera and Brown, 2008). The emergence of voluntary markets, such as the Chicago Climate Exchange, also stimulated the global trade of greenhouse gas emission reductions, and has attracted key players from countries as different as Canada, the United States, Brazil and Mexico (ibid). Markets for limiting environmental disservices have become a well-established phenomenon. In 2009 global carbon markets transacted about 8.7 billion tonnes of carbon dioxide equivalent, which was valued at US$ 144 billion (Hamilton et al., 2010). Madsen et al. (2010) found 39 functioning compensatory biodiversity mitigation programmes around the world, representing a minimum market size of about US$ 1.8-2.9 billion.

International market opportunities have also motivated several national governments in developing countries to experiment with different types of conditional payments for the delivery of positive ecosystem services linked to environmentally-friendly land use management in agriculture and forestry. The best-known example is Costa Rica's country-wide Pagos por Servicios Ambientales (PSA) or PES programme, in which land users receive government money for the adoption or protection of certain land uses believed to be beneficial to the production of various ES, such as carbon sequestration, hydrological services or biodiversity protection (Pagiola, 2008). Other government-financed programmes can be found in Mexico, China and South Africa (Muñoz-Piña et al., 2008; Pagiola et al., 2005). Corbera and Brown (2008: 1958) frame this evolution by stating that state-based PES schemes 'are not actual markets but rather economic transfers through which governments in developing countries aim to increase the capacity of local project developers and enable their participation in international markets'. Local communities in developing countries have also increasingly started to experiment with local PES schemes (see e.g. Landell-Mills and Porras, 2002, Ravnborg et al., 2007 or Wunder et al., 2008, for an overview).

The development of (and pilot experimentation with) additional international trading mechanisms which provide positive compensations for environmental management and avoided environmental degradation, such as payments for 'Reducing Forest Degradation and Deforestation' (REDD), the inclusion of which in the post-Kyoto framework is now widely accepted, constitute evidence of how market solutions, and more specifically PES, have steadily moved to centre stage in the international climate change debate (Angelsen, 2008). REDD involves the principle that industrialised countries mobilise financial resources in order to provide positive financial incentives to developing countries for reducing greenhouse gas emissions, mainly through reducing deforestation and forest degradation. The more recent REDD+ also includes sustainable forest management activities, forest conservation activities in protected areas or indigenous reserves, and the enhancement of forest carbon stocks (Clements, 2010). As noted by Farley et al. (2010), an important argument in favour of international PES mechanisms has been the fact that 'international law recognizes a nation's sovereign right to use its own natural resources as it wishes, which rules out penalties, prescription, and externally mandated changes in property rights'. International payments schemes thus tend to 'impose fewer threats to sovereignty and are likely to be welcomed by low-income nations' (ibid: 2075). At the international level, payments across borders may therefore turn out to be the only functioning mechanism if the country where the environmental resource is located is not willing to accept an externally-imposed obligation (Vatn, 2010). REDD then offers the possibility to integrate local and nationwide PES mechanisms and the growing mitigation efforts associated with climate change (Angelsen et al., 2009; Blom et al., 2010; Clements, 2010; Huberman, 2009).

It is within this general context that we now turn to the discussion of PES, a concept that has gradually developed into one of the leading instruments in hybridised economic and environmental thinking.

3. PAYMENTS FOR ENVIRONMENTAL SERVICES: UNDERLYING PHILOSOPHY AND PRACTICAL EXPERIENCES

In this section we will outline the more 'traditional' - and what we could still call 'mainstream' - approach to PES, typified by Wunder's (2005) famous definition. This definition and the corresponding framework of analysis are largely - though not exclusively - based on an environmental economics approach (see e.g. Engel et al., 2008; Pagiola et al., 2002; Pattanayak et al., 2010; Wunder, 2005), which is rooted in economic perspectives that mainly emphasise the potential efficiency gains that can be obtained by harnessing market forces and offering individual price incentives. More specifically, the greater part of the literature on PES often refers to the famous 'Coase theorem', which asserts that on the condition of sufficiently low transaction costs and clearly defined and enforced property rights, individual and voluntary bargaining through the market will lead to the most efficient allocation of externalities (Coase, 1960). The underlying philosophy of PES can therefore best be understood if we examine the emergence of the policy tool against this conceptual background[7]. In what follows, we will briefly sketch the underpinnings leading to the genesis of PES. We will then discuss Wunder's definition, some of the main typologies of PES in the relevant scientific literature, and the scope of the instrument. And finally, we will summarise the main practical PES experiences in the field.

3.1. UNDERLYING PHILOSOPHY: EXTERNALITIES, MISSING MARKETS AND COASEAN NEGOTIATIONS

Figure 3 represents the basic logic of PES, illustrated in a typical upstream-downstream watershed context. It shows how upstream farmers and foresters tend to gain few private benefits from ecologically sound and socially more optimal land use. Hence, such behaviour is not competitive with privately more attractive, but ecologically destructive, land uses such as croplands or pastures. Since ecosystem services such as carbon sequestration, biodiversity maintenance or watershed protection are mostly public or club goods[8], i.e. externalities or unintended by-products of economic activity for which there is usually no market, so that

[7] The aim of this section, however, is not to try to neatly classify PES as belonging to one clearly-defined school of economic thought. PES have grown out of various other conceptual approaches, such as new institutional economics (North, 1990), free-market economics (Anderson and Leal, 2001) and contract theory (Bolton and Dewatripont, 2005). Yet, most of the literature on PES uses a Coasean framework to explain and legitimise PES.

[8] Public goods, such as carbon sequestration, are non-excludable (users cannot be prevented from benefiting from it) and non-rival (consumption by one user does not affect consumption by another). Club goods, such as watershed services, are similar to public goods, as they can be consumed by many individuals (the members of the 'club') without affecting the consumption of the others, but consumption by non-members can be prevented. (Engel et al., 2008: 665-666).

beneficiaries only rarely pay, and society is systematically underprovided with these services (Engel et al., 2008; Pagiola et al., 2002; Pattanayak et al., 2010). However, the costs of 'environmentally-bad' land management imposed on downstream populations (or broader society) can be higher than the upstream land users' conservation opportunity cost. Should this be the case, payments by the service users can be the right incentive for making conservation the more attractive option for upstream land users (Engel et al., 2008). From the same perspective, Wunder and Wertz-Kanounnikoff (2009) explain that PES are thus the most adequate for situations with hard 'trade-offs' between the environment and the landowners' economic self-interest, resulting in clear win-lose or lose-win scenarios. They exemplify this as follows:

> '...Without any PES, the land user residing in the upper watershed may find it more profitable to gradually deforest his land for agricultural purposes than to conserve it, which could ultimately have negative impacts on residents of the lower watershed, due to the lost water regulation benefits from forest cover. While land users in the upper watershed "win", residents in the lower watershed "lose". On the other hand, the downstream municipalities could enforce an environmental regulation that prohibits the upstream landowners from deforesting. Here, the land manager "loses", while the broader society and the environment "win". In these conflict situations, PES can help bridging gaps through compensations.' (ibid: 573).

In this philosophy, PES can - under certain circumstances - create parallel markets where service providers could sell the positive externalities of managing their land 'adequately'. As such, the PES approach moves beyond the Pigovian philosophy of taxing negative or subsidising positive externalities within existing commodity markets. In theory it creates new market transaction mechanisms that pay separately for the provision of positive ES. The PES approach therefore defines the problem not as a 'mere' pollution problem, but rather as a social cost problem (Salzman, 2005). It attempts 'to put in practice the Coase theorem, which stipulates that the problems of external effects can, under certain conditions, be overcome through private negotiation between affected parties' (Coase, 1960, as cited by Engel et al., 2008). In this way the mechanism shifts the governance of natural resources from states to autonomous actors, responding individually to monetary incentives (McAfee and Shapiro, 2010; Muradian et al., 2010).

Figure 3. The main underpinning of PES

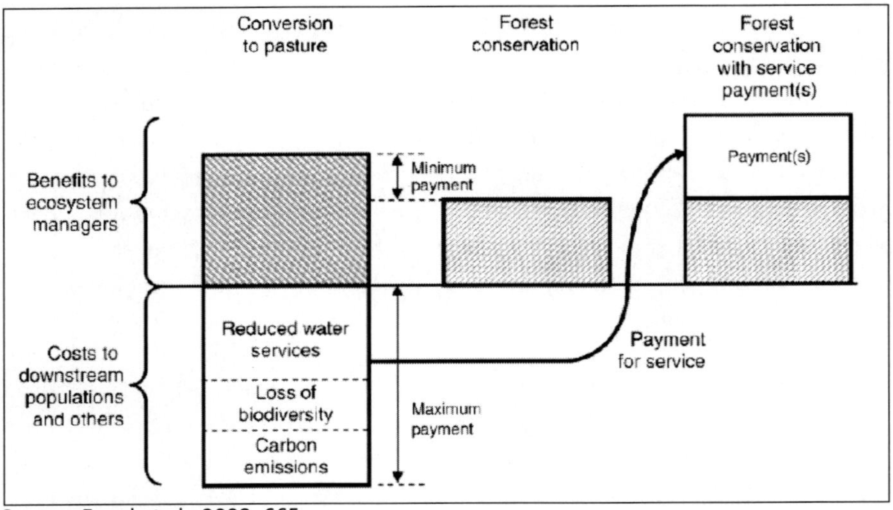

Source: Engel et al., 2008: 665

The explicit focus on positive externalities results in a shift from the commonly applied 'Polluter Pays Principle' (PPP) to a 'Beneficiary Pays Principle' (BPP) (Pagiola et al., 2002; Pearce, 2004) or 'Provider Gets Principle' (PGP) (Huberman and Leipprand, 2006). Land users are now seen not as polluters, but as potential service providers who are presented with an opportunity to add an ES to their production portfolio. Furthermore, reliance on direct payments should secure the basic economic premise of efficiency optimisation of scarce conservation funds (Ferraro, 2001; Ferraro and Simpson, 2002; Pagiola et al., 2002), by taking advantage of the land users' knowledge of the cost of ES provision and seeking out the low-cost providers (Engel et al., 2008) or concentrating on the higher-benefit cases (Pagiola et al., 2005).

Poverty alleviation is usually not the main objective of PES schemes. This follows from the Coasean perspective, which maintains that Pareto efficiency requires determining which party could change behaviour most cheaply (Vatn and Bromley, 1997). From this perspective, 'what really matters is the aggregate gains and losses by different economic agents and not how they are distributed in society' (Pascual et al., 2010: 1237). Nevertheless, the revenue flow made possible by selling ES is believed to contribute to local development and thus poverty alleviation, prompting some researchers to devote more attention to the important 'pro-poor side-effects' of PES (Grieg-Gran et al., 2005; Landell-Mills and Porras, 2002; Pagiola et al., 2005, Pagiola et al., 2008; Wunder, 2008a). The purported pro-poor potentials make PES an attractive way of achieving a double dividend, meeting both social and environmental objectives, making it increasingly popular among international aid agencies and private donors (Bulte et al., 2008b), but also with national governments who often need to justify government expenditure on environmental programmes in economic and social terms (Chisholm, 2010). Empirical evidence on poverty alleviation, however, still remains very limited, and many of the available data suggest that PES programmes are not always capable of simultaneously addressing both poverty and environmental issues (Pattanayak et al., 2010; Wunder, 2008a; Zilberman et al., 2008).

3.2. DEFINITION AND TYPOLOGY

In order to distinguish it from other market-based conservation instruments, Wunder (2005) defines PES as:

> 'a voluntary transaction where a well-defined ES (or a land use likely to secure that service) is being "bought" by a (minimum one) ES buyer from a (minimum one) ES provider if and only if the ES provider secures ES provision (conditionality)' (ibid: 3).

In order for a transaction to qualify as PES under this 'mainstream' definition, several essential criteria must be met. In the first place, the voluntary nature of the transaction presupposes that from a supply side perspective ES providers have *de facto* or real land-use options, and thus can choose to either respond or not to the monetary incentives provided by the potential purchaser of the ES. This characteristic distinguishes the transaction on the supply side from command-and-control approaches, where choice is restricted by force or by consensus (Wunder, 2005; Ravnborg et al., 2007). Given the difficulty of organising the market on the demand side, it is often necessary for the state (usually with the support of international donors) or a local authority or other governance body to assume the role of the minimally required one buyer and to act as the representative expression of public demand (Vatn, 2010). From the demand side, the criterion of voluntariness is thus difficult to comply with in practice. Even if a government, communities or other outside organisations finance PES, it remains a market-based governance model, as the supply response stems from individual decision making mediated by price incentives (Kosoy and Corbera, 2010; Van Hecken and Bastiaensen, 2010a; Uphoff, 1993).

Secondly, the ES, or at least the land-use proxy that is likely to result in its provision, must be well-defined, which implies that it should be measurable. Wunder (2005) recognises that, in this sense, the definition can be problematic, especially as the lack of scientific knowledge on the complex relationships between a proxy and its real ES-providing effect can undermine the sustainability of the transaction[9]. Thirdly, a PES scheme requires a transfer of (monetary or in-kind) resources from buyer to provider, possibly via an intermediary (e.g. a water utility or NGO). It is in this respect that the PES approach is particularly innovative: rather than to focus on indirect conservation actions (such as in the case of ICDPs), it ties the payments directly to the investment goals (Ferraro and Simpson, 2002). Finally, the hardest but most important requirement to meet, according to Wunder, is the conditionality criterion of the scheme, which in practice implies the establishment of a baseline and the monitoring of compliance by the buyers or intermediaries, which may generate prohibitive transaction costs. So although Wunder's definition presents the PES approach as a rather simple and straightforward mechanism, closer scrutiny of each of the criteria to be fulfilled compels him to concede that very few 'true' PES schemes exist in the field (Wunder, 2005).

Within the growing volume of literature on PES, several categorisations of PES programmes have emerged, mostly depending on which underlying criteria are used to distinguish different schemes within the PES family. Landell-Mills and Porras (2002), for example, distinguish payment schemes by focusing on the resource contents of the service (biodiversity, carbon, water, and landscape beauty). Ravnborg et al. (2007) further elaborate on this distinction and make a characterisation of ES according to the degree of spatial boundedness of the beneficiaries of the ecosystem service (see Table 1). In this context, it is important to note that the 'location-bounded' nature of some ES (e.g. hydrological services in an upstream-downstream context) often implies that buyers do not really have the choice whom to buy from. Spatial boundedness of ES often also implies the need for collective action between the sellers of ES; one non-cooperating upstream farmer could jeopardise the efforts of all other suppliers and therefore the credibility of the whole PES scheme. As argued by Ravnborg et al. (2007), and as will be seen in the empirical case study in chapter 4, this characteristic may reduce consumers' willingness to pay for ES.

Van Hecken and Bastiaensen (2010b) recognise that this distinction has important implications for the institutional arrangements between buyers and sellers of the service and categorise PES schemes on the basis of the type of buyers within these geographical areas; they distinguish between 'locally-financed' PES schemes (e.g. downstream water users paying upstream farmers), and 'globally-financed' schemes (e.g. global funds going to ES providers in developing countries, also called international PES or IPES, see e.g. Huberman, 2009).

[9] In chapter 2 we will devote more specific attention to some of the complexities involved in measuring ES stocks and flows.

Table 1. Types of ecosystem services and their spatial dimensions

Category of ES	Examples of ES	Spatial boundedness of ES beneficiaries and potential buyers		
		Local (beneficiaries within area where ES is produced)	**Regional** (beneficiaries distant from area where ES is produced)	**Global** (beneficiaries anywhere on the globe)
Hydrological services	Water (quality and quantity)	X	X	
	Erosion and landslide prevention	X	X	
	Micro-climate regulation	X	X	
Landscape beauty	Eco-tourism	X	X	X
Biodiversity conservation	Habitat protection			X
	Gene-pool conservation			X
Carbon sequestration	Vegetative carbon sequestration			X

Source: Adapted from Ravnborg et al., 2007: 11

Another commonly used distinction, which is also based on the types of buyers is between 'government-financed' schemes, in which the buyers of the ES are a third party acting on behalf of service users (typically a government agency or an international financial or conservation institution) and 'user-financed' schemes, in which the buyers are (part of) the actual users of the ES (e.g. downstream water users paying upstream farmers) (Engel et al., 2008). Wunder (2005), on the other hand, bases a possible categorisation on the nature of the conservation practice: conservation (paying for the net opportunity costs of conservation) versus asset-building schemes (paying for the costs of restoration activities)[10]. Wunder also

[10] Note that the recurrence to the concept of opportunity costs in the PES literature mainly is a consequence of the many problems associated with the quantification and valuation of ES. As noted by Van Hecken and Bastiaensen (2009: 34) the intangible character of most ES indeed complicates their valuation. In the context of existing PES schemes, this problem is generally solved by implicitly or explicitly basing the monetary value on the farmers' opportunity costs of the main alternative land uses (Pagiola et al., 2007). The use of opportunity costs, however, does not always imply their full remuneration, accentuated by the 'tipping the balance' argument in the PES literature (i.e. calculating the payment net of the opportunity cost of the promoted land use (Pagiola et al., 2005)). This rather arbitrary juggling with opportunity cost and 'tipping the balance' concepts is at least theoretically confusing, but more importantly undermines the use of the term payments for

distinguishes between cash and in-kind payments (e.g. infrastructural benefits). Finally, another common distinction can be made by splitting the schemes into 'output-based' PES programmes, in which payments are directly based on the ES provided, and the more commonly occurring 'input-based' or 'area-based' schemes, which focus on land use proxies for ES (Engel et al., 2008; Wunder, 2005).

3.3. SCOPE OF THE INSTRUMENT

Although the discussion in the previous sections may have created the impression that PES are the silver bullet for all types of environmental problems, PES scholars clearly indicated the limitations of their instrument. They stress that the scope for application of PES is 'to a narrow set of problems: those in which ecosystems are mismanaged because many of their benefits are externalities from the perspective of ecosystem managers' (Pagiola and Platais, 2007, as cited by Engel et al., 2008: 665). This means that in the case of privately-beneficial internalisations of externalities, in which land managers themselves reap the benefits, PES are not an adequate policy tool (Wunder and Wertz-Kanounnikoff, 2009). Moreover, 'among the threatened externalities, there will only be payments for those that are most valuable, with the condition that ES buyers' willingness to pay has to exceed ES sellers' willingness to accept' (ibid: 578).

Wunder (2008b) mentions other necessary preconditions for the functioning of PES schemes, relating to cultural (e.g. social appropriateness of cash or in-kind payments), institutional (e.g. existence of trust between service users and providers), and informational characteristics (e.g. transaction costs should be manageable). In order to fulfil its promises of superiority over other instruments, PES should also demonstrate compliance with various generally-accepted (efficiency-related) principles, such as additionality (i.e. payments should only be made for activities that would not have occurred otherwise), conditionality (i.e. payments should only be made on the condition of 'contract' fulfilment), and non-leakage (i.e. payments for activities in a specific area should not lead to the shifting of environmentally-damaging activities to elsewhere in space) (Engel et al., 2008; Wunder, 2005). In practice, however, most existing PES experiences operate in the real and 'messy' world, where these preconditions and criteria are difficult to verify and are only rarely all or all simultaneously fulfilled.

---

environmental services; the ES as such are not actually paid for, but payments are rather directed to cover part of the opportunity costs of economically more, but often ecologically less attractive practices.

3.4. PES EXPERIENCES AND RESEARCH IN PRACTICE

Interest in PES has soared in recent years. Landell-Mills and Porras (2002) reported 287 examples of PES-like mechanisms worldwide, and the number of additional examples has grown since (Pattanayak et al., 2010; Porras et al., 2008; Ravnborg et al., 2007). But until two or three years ago, discussion of PES mechanisms remained confined largely to the 'grey literature' (Engel et al., 2008: 664), motivating journals such as Ecological Economics, Environment and Development Economics and the Journal of Sustainable Forestry to dedicate a number of special issues and sections to the review and systemisation of PES experiences worldwide (Bulte et al., 2008b; Rebelo, 2009; Wunder et al., 2008). A whole range of other journals have also increasingly dedicated space to the publication of PES or PES-related articles. Discussing all the experiences would take us too far, and therefore we will limit ourselves to some general observations.

The first of these concerns the geographical range of PES programmes. Costa Rica and Mexico's first nation-wide PES programmes at the end of the 1990s and the beginning of the 2000s respectively (Muñoz-Piña et al., 2008; Pagiola, 2008) can be considered as the starting point for further dissemination of PES throughout Latin America and the rest of the world. Today PES schemes are taking place around the globe, from Africa (Ferraro, 2009) to Latin America (Grieg-Gran et al., 2005; Southgate and Wunder, 2009), and from Asia (Huang et al., 2009) to Europe and North America (Appleton, 2002; Perrot-Maître, 2006). But the great majority of current PES experiments and research is concentrated in developing countries, and more specifically in Latin America (Landell-Mills and Porras, 2002; Ravnborg et al., 2007). Pattanayak et al. (2010) explain the focus on developing countries by underlining that most forests and biodiversity (and thus many potential critical ecosystem services providers) are located in developing countries. They also indicate that coercive approaches tend to fail in developing countries, most of which also have weak governments; this, according to the authors, poses 'a special test for market-based solutions to conservation like PES' (ibid: 255). They also explain the widespread advocacy for PES in developing countries by referring to the potential win-win approach resulting from the simultaneous reduction of poverty and ecosystem degradation. The main reason for the specific interest in Latin America, however, could be the high dependence of that region's population on the environmental services and the protection provided by natural ecosystems, which became starkly evident after the devastating effects of Hurricane Mitch in 1998 (Pagiola et al., 2005).

A second observation relates to the types of ecosystem services generally covered in existing PES initiatives. Most schemes are targeted at either carbon sequestration (Corbera et al., 2009; Grieg-Gran et al., 2005), biodiversity conservation[11] (Asquith et al., 2008; Pagiola et al., 2004), and hydrological services (Muñoz-Piña et al., 2008; Porras et al., 2008; Southgate and Wunder, 2009; Wunder and Albán, 2008). Other objectives of PES can be landscape beauty (Villamor and Lasco, 2009), and wildlife protection (Bulte et al., 2008a; Frost and Bond, 2008). A literature review by Ravnborg et al. (2007) gives an idea of the 'popularity' of the different types of ES; out of a total of 167 PES references dealing with specific ES, almost two-thirds concern hydrological services, while around one half deal with biodiversity conservation and carbon sequestration and 21 per cent with landscape beauty. The same authors note that these numbers add up to more than one hundred per cent, which reflects the frequent 'bundling' and 'layering' of ecosystem services, by which a specific geographical area in a PES programme is considered to produce a combination of multiple marketable ecosystem services[12]. One example is the silvopastoral project in Nicaragua, Costa Rica and Colombia discussed in chapter 3, with explicit payments for both the biodiversity and carbon services provided by the introduction of silvopastoral practices (Pagiola et al., 2007; Van Hecken and Bastiaensen, 2010a). The combination of various ES can help access additional funding and make the protection of the area a more competitive land use option (Wunder and Wertz-Kanounnikoff, 2009).

Our third observation concerns the presumed effectiveness and efficiency of different types of PES programmes. A recent overview by Wunder et al. (2008), assessing various case studies with respect to design, costs, environmental effectiveness and other outcomes, concluded that existing PES programmes often differ substantially from each other, especially when they are compared on the basis of funding characteristics. According to the authors, user-financed programmes (currently primarily focused on local watershed protection) are 'much more likely to be efficient than government-financed ones', as they are usually 'better targeted, more closely tailored to local conditions and needs, [have] better monitoring and a greater willingness to enforce conditionality, and [have] far fewer confounding side objectives than government-financed programmes' (ibid: 851), such as poverty alleviation or employment creation. These findings - though contested by some

[11] It could be argued that biodiversity conservation is not an ecosystem service as such, as it only indirectly enhances or decreases the production of other specific services (e.g., specific biodiversity 'levels' could enable or disable an ecosystem to deliver specific hydrological services). Nevertheless, much of the literature on PES distinguishes ES on the basis of the resource contents of the service, assuming that biodiversity protection leads to a better environmental state. As will be argued in chapter 2, this confusion mainly emanates from the need to find 'marketable' products that are attractive to the public.

[12] The terminology is adapted from marketing theory. 'Bundling' refers to the selling of different services from the same plot to the same single buyer, while 'layering' refers to the combination of payments from different service buyers to promote the joint delivery of various services from the same plot (Wunder and Wertz-Kanounnikoff, 2009). An additional strategy is called 'piggybacking', and refers to the integration of a less-popular or less-marketable service (e.g. biodiversity conservation) into PES schemes providing more-popular services (e.g. watershed services), without explicitly paying for the less-popular service (ibid).

authors (e.g. Blackman and Woodward, 2010) - have spurred the expansion of user-financed PES programmes. Furthermore, although Wunder et al.'s (2008) review devotes special attention to the presumed effects that funding characteristics may have on the efficiency of PES programmes in the supply of ES, they largely neglect the ethical consequences of the close relationship between user-financed and locally-financed PES; they avoid the more difficult political question of how the costs of these programmes should be met (Van Hecken and Bastiaensen, 2010b), something we will further discuss in chapters 2 and 4.

A fourth and last observation relates to the research topics and the methodologies applied in PES studies. PES research until now has been largely confined to supply-side related aspects, mostly motivated by a strong - though perhaps sometimes implicit - normative Coasean emphasis on efficiency gains that can be obtained by reducing transaction costs through a range of 'technical' and mostly quantitative optimisation instruments. This focus mainly translates into research on economic models of contract design and bargaining processes (Ferraro, 2008); specific property right structures (Engel and Palmer, 2008; Landell-Mills, 2002); spatial targeting for the selection of ES providers (Alix-Garcia et al., 2008; Engel and Palmer, 2008; Wünscher et al., 2008); cross-farm cooperation incentives among ES providers (Horan et al., 2008; Parkhurst and Shogren, 2007); and the potential pro-poor effects among ES providers (Antle and Stoorvogel, 2008; Pagiola et al., 2005; Zilberman et al., 2008). Despite these efforts, the empirical basis for attributing measurable environmental and/or social impacts to PES programmes remains limited (Greenstone and Gayer, 2009; Pattanayak et al., 2010; Vaessen and Van Hecken, 2009). Some studies suggest that the impacts of PES may in reality be very limited because of the lack of additionality (e.g. payments to landholders already committed to forest conservation, or payments in areas with low deforestation risk; see e.g. Kosoy et al., 2007; Muñoz-Piña et al., 2008; and Robalino et al., 2008) or because of the confusion of PES with pre-PES incentives (e.g. reforestation subsidies; see Daniels et al., 2010). In many cases it will therefore be very difficult to demonstrate the efficiency gains of PES (Muradian et al., 2010). The lack of clear and straightforward empirical evidence has prompted some authors to argue for more experimental and quasi-experimental PES impact evaluations, which should 'credibly eliminate rival explanations for observed outcomes' (Pattanayak et al., 2010: 261)[13].

The largely economic-inspired quantitative research agenda on PES has been complemented recently by a limited - but growing - number of published studies devoting explicit and trans-disciplinary attention to local perceptions and socio-institutional context specificity (Börner et al., 2010; Corbera et al., 2009; Kosoy et al.,

[13] One of the few pilot programmes attempting to apply an experimental approach to PES will be assessed in chapter 3.

2008), to fairness and distributional aspects (Corbera et al., 2007a, 2007b; Karsenty, 2007; Sommerville et al., 2010), and to ecological sustainability (Kosoy et al., 2007). This recent research shift from mainly technical-economic efficiency to broader socio-institutional and political economy dimensions parallels the different perspectives in the ongoing PES debate, which is the subject of the next section.

4. TOWARDS A RECONCEPTUALISATION OF PES?

For some time now, the original concept of Coasean or market-based PES schemes has been the subject of criticism from various angles. Some authors are either largely rejecting PES (see e.g. Büscher et al., forthcoming; McAfee and Shapiro, 2010; McCauley, 2006; Robertson, 2004), while others are rather drawing attention to some of its limitations and conceptual flaws, and are therefore advocating conceptual modifications to the traditional PES approach (see e.g. Corbera et al., 2009; Farley and Costanza, 2010; Muradian et al., 2010; Vatn, 2010). These different views are probably best understood if they are framed in three broader perspectives on PES. With the risk of oversimplification, Table 2 sketches a descriptive typology of different PES approaches. It is partly based on parallel conflicts between conventional environmental economics and ecological economics, as described by Farley and Costanza (2010). We will start from Farley and Costanza's terminology, but complement their conceptualisation by qualifying and expanding some of the main underlying assumptions in each approach. This exercise should not be interpreted as an attempt at an all-encompassing and ideal-type format of the different PES concepts, but rather as a useful tool for positioning and contextualising ongoing critiques and debates surrounding PES. It will also allow us to frame our next chapters' contribution to the broader PES debate.

4.1. THE TENSION BETWEEN COASEAN AND PES-SCEPTICISM PERSPECTIVES

At the right-hand side of Table 2, we find the environmental economics or Coasean perspective, which could be considered the 'traditional' approach to PES. As already indicated in the previous sections, it is largely from this perspective that the PES idea and logic emerged. The approach prioritises economic efficiency within a positive externality framework, and mainly focuses on Coasean principles and conditions for the design of PES (clearly-defined property rights, low transaction costs, and private negotiations, leading to Pareto-efficiency). It largely does so by forcing (or at least theoretically conceptualising) ecosystem services into the welfare-based market model (Farley and Costanza, 2010), and therefore assumes that individual price signals are the most appropriate incentive to induce pro-environmental behavioural change. It also devotes increasing attention to the potential of PES for poverty alleviation, though often only on condition that inclusion of the poor does not imply efficiency losses[14] (Bulte et al., 2008b; Engel et al., 2008; Pagiola et al., 2005).

[14] An increasing number of authors, however, recognises that PES can have both direct and indirect effects on the poor, for example through changes in food prices, wages and land access, which implies an ethical obligation to take poverty effects into account, even if poverty alleviation is not the priority of PES (Bulte et al., 2008b)

Table 2. Typology of PES approaches

	PES-scepticism perspective	Institutional ecological economics perspective	Environmental economics/ Coasean bargain
Main research focus	• PES and ES concept as commodity fetishism (commodification of nature) and 'rollout' neoliberalism • PES as inappropriate ecological fix of extractive capitalist expansion	• Critical role of equity and ecological sustainability in developing PES • PES not restricted to markets • ES concept as potential eye-opener • PES as part of a policy mix in a broader rural development strategy	• PES as efficient solution to missing markets or market failure • Emphasis on economic value of ES, as non-accounted for economic externalities • Focus on Coasean negotiation through the market
Main underlying conceptual framework	(Neo-)Marxism and social constructivism	Institutional ecological economics and political economy	Environmental economics, Coasean institutional economics and free market environmentalism
Principal assumptionshu man behaviour	Human beings not primarily motivated by self-interest and profit-maximization	Individualistic and collective approach: role of institutions in developing (individual) motivations to cooperate	Individualistic approach: people as self-interested, profit-maximizing and autonomous rational human beings
Principal assumptionseco systems/ nature	Capitalist markets have deep-rooted ecological contradictions that make them inherently anti-ecological	Besides their intrinsic value, ecosystems are, also as producers of ES, beneficial to human society (but not necessarily measurable in monetary terms)	As producers of ES, ecosystems are beneficial to human society (theoretically measurable in monetary terms)
Main publications	Büscher et al., forthcoming Kosoy & Corbera, 2010 McAfee & Shapiro, 2010 Robertson, 2004	Corbera et al., 2009 Farley & Costanza, 2010 Muradian et al., 2010 Vatn, 2010	Engel et al., 2008 Pagiola & Platais, 2007 Pattanayak et al., 2010 Wunder, 2005

Source: Author's own elaboration

At the opposite side are the PES sceptics, who largely reject PES, and even the notion of ecosystem services, as improper commodification[15] processes that attempt to cash ecosystem services on new markets. This PES-sceptical approach is mainly

[15] Commodification refers to the reduction of all value dimensions to exchange values (Vatn, 2009: 2211).

rooted in a still-expanding body of literature focusing on the consequences of 'neoliberal conservation' or 'green neoliberalism' (e.g. Bakker, 2005; Büscher, 2010; Castree, 2003; McAfee, 1999), and describes PES and the concept of ES as phenomena that are firmly within the neoliberal project. Although there is no clear and coherent consensus of the exact meaning of 'neoliberalism' in this context, and whether it is indeed the appropriate terminology to describe the ongoing market-based processes of conservation (Bakker, 2010; Castree, 2006), the concept is broadly understood as an ideology that 'largely discounts the state as a viable environmental administrator' (McCarthy, 2005: 1007) and that aims to reconfigure political, social and ecological governance to 'self-regulating' capitalist market dynamics (Büscher, 2008; McCarthy, 2005). This perspective associates the growing popularity of PES with the rise of neoliberal discourse in supranational environmental policy-making institutions, such as the World Bank and the Global Environment Facility (GEF), and some of the most influential conservation NGOs, such as the International Union for the Conservation of Nature (IUCN) and the World Wildlife Fund (WWF) (Ervine, 2010; McAfee, 1999). Through the elaboration of a one-size-fits-all universal blueprint, which a priori defines the causes of biodiversity loss in market terms, these institutions are believed to peddle market-based approaches as universal solutions to environmental problems (Büscher et al., forthcoming; Ervine, 2010).

Some authors (e.g. Brockington et al., 2008; McCarthy, 2005; Tickell and Peck, 2003), however, qualify this rather broad 'neoliberalisation' process by referring to the shift from 'rollback' neoliberalism of the 1980s, which was characterised by 'undisguised hostility towards the state and efforts to roll it back in various ways during neoliberalism's first control over state apparatuses during the 1980s' (McCarthy, 2005: 998), to a hybrid 'rollout' neoliberalism from the mid-1990s onwards. The latter recognises the need for the state, but in more neoliberal forms, resulting in 'public-private partnerships organised according to market models, a discursive focus on empowering local governments rather than on slashing the central government, and reforms framed as technocratic searches for best practices rather than as the enactment of rigid ideological principles' (ibid: 998). From this perspective, the PES concept also perfectly ties in with the ruling development paradigms, which emphasise processes of decentralisation, capacity-building and community empowerment as the new guiding principles in development policy. McCarthy (2005: 999) and Ervine (2010), for example, illustrate how different actors perceive PES as a new opportunity to promote decentralised environmental governance and create 'market citizenship', by asserting a close cooperative relationship between markets and civil societies or communities, which are both 'the aggregate results of free individuals voluntarily entering into contracts and associational life, free of coercion from the sovereign' (McCarthy, 2005: 999).

The main critiques that emanate from this sceptical approach to PES can be encapsulated in three major points. Firstly, market-based PES are perceived to be inappropriate and even perverse as it purports to present a solution to environmental problems which - ironically - capitalism has played a role in creating (Bakker, 2010; Brockington et al., 2008; McAfee, 1999). It purposely uses popular win-win discourses on the compatibility of economic growth and environmental protection and thereby creates the belief that the underlying ecological contradiction of capitalism can be resolved through the same mode of operation that produced it in the first place (Büscher et al., forthcoming). In this way, PES are thus not so much about saving nature, but rather about finding new arenas for markets to operate in (ibid). It creates the belief that we can reach a sustainable economy through marginal 'quick ecological fixes' without major structural change (Lohmann, 2009; Norgaard, 2010). In this context, Büscher et al. (forthcoming) use the term 'ideological blinkers', referring to the process of converting conservation, an inherently deeply political undertaking, into a technical and apolitical design process. The use of economic language and market-based blueprints stimulate the image that political and moral decision making can be guided by simple economic trade-offs in the form of standard cost-benefit analyses (Van Hecken and Bastiaensen, 2010b). Clements (2010) and Redford and Adams (2009) underline the risk that a single economic justification for nature conservation may outweigh non-economic justifications and thus can make nature vulnerable to conversion to other more profitable land-uses, changes in carbon prices or international politics. In this way, commodification and monetary compensations entail the risk of eroding the cultural basis for conservation (Heyman and Ariely, 2004; Martin et al., 2008).

Secondly, the ecosystem services approach and the associated commodification of nature (McCauley, 2006) disguise the inherent complex nature of ecosystems, which contains a number of social and ecological risks (Norgaard, 2010). The economic view of ecosystems as producers of marketable benefits to human society implicitly ignores the intrinsic value of nature, as it requires that a single and uniform exchange value is adopted for making nature's value explicit to human beings (Castree, 2003; Kosoy and Corbera, 2010). The impression is thus created that ecosystem protection is only important in as far as it directly sustains human economic development[16] (Swart, 2003). Furthermore, the 'itemisation' (Vatn, 2005), 'iconification' (Brockington et al., 2008) or 'cutting up' of connections and relationships within and between ecosystems, in order to produce, sell and consume

[16] Note that this human welfare-based view also implies that the optimal amount of environmental protection does not necessarily mean an increase in environmental protection. Demand and supply will regulate the optimal amount of nature conservation in society at the most efficient cost. In other words, 'if individuals in the society do not demand high quality of the environment, it is not (and should not be) provided' (Slavíková et al., 2010: 1369). In this same philosophy, command-and-control approaches can in certain circumstances lead to over-control, whereby society is receiving too much 'conservation', which can be 'Pareto-inefficient' (see e.g. Oates et al., 1989).

their constituent elements in the form of ES, creates the illusion that, instead of being complex flows of information, ecosystems and their ES are easily convertible into separate entities (Brockington et al., 2008; Büscher et al., forthcoming). Indeed, the fragmented focus on single-service provision has already led to the creation of novel ecosystems conceived for delivering specific critical services (such as carbon sequestration), at times even to the detriment of additional services (such as biodiversity and watershed protection) (Caparrós et al., 2010; Chisholm, 2010; German et al., 2009; Kareiva et al., 2007; Lohman, 2006). Büscher (2010) goes even further and refers to the concept of 'derivative nature', whereby nature and 'the poor' are the underlying assets upon which marketable images and perceptions are built in order to attract interested buyers[17]. The focus on assets reflecting idealised representations of nature and poverty (rather than their true nature) constitutes a significant risk; these idealised assets are susceptible to become the focus of speculation, making them vulnerable to bubbles and crashes (Lohmann, 2010)[18]. The implication is that 'localised realities of nature and poverty are allowed to be alienated and forgotten as complex and contradictory spaces that deserve actual long-term engagement, human interaction and critical understanding' (Büscher, 2010: 272).

This leads us to the third major critique, which relates to the potentially unequal social consequences of PES mechanisms. Kosoy and Corbera (2010) explain this by referring to the concept of 'commodity fetishism', which they understand as 'the masking of the social relationships underlying the process of production' (Marx, 1867, as cited by Kosoy and Corbera, 2010: 1229). Rather than delivering on its pro-poor promises (see e.g. Pagiola et al., 2005), the fetishist character of PES conceals underlying power asymmetries masking important issues concerning global environmental justice likely to contribute to the reproduction of existing inequalities in the access to natural resources (Corbera et al., 2007b; Kosoy and Corbera, 2010; Van Hecken and Bastiaensen, 2010b). At the local level, this can result in increased competition for control over valuable flows of services and the ecosystems that provide them (Redford and Adams, 2009). Market creation will favour those with economic and social power (McAfee, 1999; O'Neill, 2001; Vatn, 2010) and harm the poor, as the latter are in a disadvantaged position because access to these services is largely mediated through property rights and other institutional means (Kosoy and Corbera, 2010). Markets of any kind are indeed 'social constructs in which participants are positioned differently, with divergent assets, interests and negotiating power' (ibid: 1234). This strengthens the fear among some authors that

[17] This closely resembles the political ecologists' argument that strict distinctions between the natural and the social are becoming increasingly artificial (Nygren and Rikoon, 2008).

[18] Lohmann (2010) exemplifies this by referring to carbon off-set markets, which soon became 'playgrounds for speculative investment', mainly by disembedding climate change problems from their historically and political context, and 're-embedding' them in neoclassical economics and property law.

PES could eventually lead to a 'tragedy of enclosure' (Ervine, 2010; Peterson et al., 2010), with further dispossession of poor indigenous communities (Hall and Lovera, 2009). This reconstruction of development and conservation as market goods could thus very well result in the addition of 'layers of governance that simply complicate being poor' (Dressler et al., 2010: 13). At a more global level, the fetishist character of PES also disguises structural poverty issues, as the so-called 'lower cost of conservation' economic argument (see e.g. Stern, 2006) offers the opportunity to buy conservation at a bargain price in developing countries, where local populations are compensated according to their current poverty level (Karsenty, 2007)[19]. Payments for 'renouncing development' among 'the poor who sell cheap' (Martínez-Alier, 2004) raise important fundamental ethical questions that compromise potential win-win synergies of PES at both the development and the conservation levels (see also chapter 2).

Finally, the middle column of table 2 depicts the institutional ecological economics approach to PES. As will be explained in detail in the next section, this approach neither rejects PES as a purely neoliberal tool on a priori ideological grounds, nor does it merely embrace the mainstream market-based approach to PES. It rather offers alternative conceptualisations of PES, embedding it in a broader institutional context, and thus pointing to a number of important avenues that need to be further investigated in future PES research. Starting from a broader institutional analytical framework, it argues that PES should explicitly be considered as a complementary part of a policy mix in a broader rural development strategy, instead of positing it as a market-based alternative for allegedly ineffective government and/or community governance.

4.2. BEYOND MARKET RHETORIC: IS THERE SCOPE FOR SYNERGIES?

Discourses among PES sceptics generally boil down to one central recurring theme - that of the perverse consequences of applying a neoliberal market philosophy to environmental and development problems. The sceptics' perspective can therefore be conceived as an intellectual Polanyian-type countermovement of societal resistance against unrestrained commodification processes in the realm of capitalist expansion (Polanyi, 1944). The tension between both the Coasean and sceptics' perspectives may thus give the impression that debates on PES are mainly restricted to (ideological) arguments in favour or against markets and commodification, with little room for synergies from a scientific or policy point of

[19] Karsenty (2007: 512) further notes that 'this mechanism risks imposing the role of biodiversity reservoirs on the poorest forested countries. This is certainly in exchange for some rent, but only a "poor man's rent" since the latter is calculated according to the "lowest cost" based on compensations in under-developed countries and regions'.

view. Most sceptics tend to demonise the mainstream approach by depicting PES as a capitalist stooge in the hands of the neoliberal demon who uses the PES instrument as a Trojan horse to take neoliberal ideas to new niches. This radical characterisation is further nourished by the discursive claims of many PES advocates that unattractive regulated nature conservation should be converted into alluring business transactions (e.g. Wunder and Wertz-Kanounnikoff, 2009). By using the neoliberal market vision of PES as a paradigmatic reference, sceptics have put forward many crucial points that doubtlessly deserve further critical discussion, and have cautioned us against the potential detrimental outcomes of 'pure market' approaches. At the same time, however, they have been rather unsuccessful in taking their case beyond the battlefield of (theoretical) discourses. After all, 'there are real costs to providing ecosystem services, and we must develop suitable mechanisms for paying for them' (Farley and Costanza, 2010: 2066). A constructive debate on the potential and appropriateness of (certain elements of) PES is, however, only possible if one manages to steer clear of some of the caricatured (and mainly ideologically-inspired) representations of mainstream PES theory. This may not be easy, as the underlying conceptual underpinnings of PES are often framed in many different ways, depending on the context and the audience (Wunder and Vargas, 2005).

Although the underlying Coasean discourse may seem to suggest the opposite, in practice, most PES programmes are not confined to free markets where nature or ecosystem services are consecutively 'commoditised', priced and traded according to the rules of demand and supply. Wunder's (2005) mainstream PES definition, for example, is clearly based on market principles, referring, as it does, to suppliers, buyers, services, transactions and conditionality. Yet, in other publications the same Wunder asserts that 'a frequent misunderstanding is that PES requires "markets" to function', while in fact 'markets and competition are neither necessary nor sufficient preconditions for PES' (Wunder, 2008b: 3-4). PES, therefore, do not necessarily depend on the creation of markets, yet it is often framed in market terms as it makes the concept more attractive to market enthusiasts and thus is 'a fashionable term that helps "sell" programs' (Engel et al., 2008: 664). On other occasions, when the market discourse is likely to invoke ideological resistance rather than support, PES might be made 'politically palatable' by using non-market semantics, such as 'compensations' or 'rewards' instead of 'payments' for ES (Swallow et al., 2009; Wunder and Vargas, 2005). In other words, the use of the PES terminology within or outside a market context is often a strategic choice and not necessarily rooted in a strong belief in free market environmentalism. PES should thus not be seen as a substitute to command-and-control mechanisms (Börner et al., 2010), but rather as a new paradigm of 'contractual conservation' (Wunder, 2008b), which - through its focus on conditionality - may be able to indicate a more efficient alternative for the use of existing conservation funds (Ferraro and Kiss, 2002), and - through its focus on the integration of supply and demand sides - can potentially generate sustainable funding (Pagiola and Platais, 2007). Yet, even though the dominant PES literature does not consider markets and private property rights as strictly necessary conditions[20] (Wunder, 2005), it depicts them - at least theoretically - as the ideal scenario in which PES would flourish (Gómez-Baggethun et al., 2010; Wunder et al., 2008), and it generally uses the market as the model legitimising PES (Vatn, 2010).

The conceptual and practical confusion created by this ambiguous stance to PES has been increasingly recognised and criticised in the literature. A growing number of authors acknowledge some of the potential strengths of (certain elements of) PES, but they simultaneously stress the need for clarification of many points raised by PES sceptics (see e.g. Farley and Costanza, 2010; Muradian et al., 2010; Vatn, 2010). Furthermore, they point out that the Coasean approach largely overlooks other important questions and observations. How can it, for example, explain the participation of ES suppliers, even though most payments in existing schemes do not cover land users' opportunity cost and might thus be considered economically inefficient from an individual point of view (Kosoy et al., 2007)? Or how can it conceptualise the transfer of resources between ES providers and beneficiaries in the absence of clearly-defined commodities (Corbera et al., 2007b)? And also: why are PES mechanisms defined as voluntary transactions, while in fact many PES schemes clearly lack this condition (Sommerville et al., 2009)?[21] The integration of these and other critiques into PES theory requires a broader framework than the currently dominant Coasean conceptualisation (Muradian et al., 2010; Farley and Costanza, 2010). This has resulted in the emergence of a new perspective to PES, mainly inspired by insights from 'institutional ecological economics' (IEE), as schematised in the middle column of Table 2.

In our introductory chapter we already indicated the main conceptual underpinnings of IEE, and how it explicitly prioritises ecological sustainability and social justice over market efficiency (Paavola, 2007; Paavola and Adger, 2005; Slavíková et al., 2010). In the context of PES, this approach looks for common ground by avoiding to reduce the debate to an ideologically-based dichotomy between, on the one hand, conservation approaches as market promotion versus, on the other hand, government intervention or other forms of public governance. Instead, it focuses on how PES can play a useful complementary role in a broader policy mix or

[20] In many cases, private property rights are indeed very difficult to establish for some types of resources, particularly flow resources, such as environmental services (Bakker, 2010; Vatn, 2009).

[21] Typical examples include payments for watershed services in local communities, where water users are generally not even aware of the higher water fees for PES that they are charged by the intermediary water utility (Kosoy et al., 2007). Neither do, from the supply side perspective, service providers necessarily have the choice whether or not to provide the service, for example when threatened that their land will be incorporated into protected areas if they do not participate in a PES scheme (Kosoy et al., 2007; see also Sommerville et al., 2009).

governance structure, and it explicitly takes up the challenge of redefining PES within a broader framework. It mainly criticises the Coasean approach for being overly restrictive and for its prioritisation of efficiency over equity considerations and its implicit adherence to weak instead of strong sustainability[22] (Farley and Costanza, 2010; Muradian et al., 2010; Pascual et al., 2010).

Corbera and Brown (2008) and Corbera et al. (2009) - partly inspired by Young (2002a, 2002b) - explain how a more explicit and interdisciplinary institutional approach to PES can contribute to understand a broad range of important issues that the Coasean literature has largely overlooked or failed to explain. By referring to the analytical domains of institutional design, performance and interplay, and to the crosscutting dimensions of capacity and scale (see Table 3), they show how an institutional approach can contribute

> 'to reveal the tensions between PES design rules and resource managers' practices, any likely controversies over who owns and should benefit from payments, and it can emphasise the way in which PES schemes attribute a value to ES and plan to monitor their outcomes' (Corbera et al., 2009: 744).

Furthermore, this framework can also

> 'reveal the extent to which PES influence local ecosystem management practices and cultural values, strengthening or increasing beneficiaries' interest in ecosystem conservation, in addition to discuss any likely contradictions between PES and other existing policies for land-use management' (ibid: 744).

An IEE approach may also be able to shed more light on notions of justice and fairness, not only among (potential) ES providers, but also among ES buyers, an issue that has largely been neglected in the Coasean-inspired literature. It can also help to dispel the false dichotomy of markets versus states, as it recognises that PES are not necessarily confined to the functioning of markets and the strict commodification of nature, but that in practice PES reflect socially-constructed situations in which governments play an intermediary role (Corbera et al., 2007b: 366). Vatn (2010) complements this by stating that PES are thus not necessarily about shifting public policies to market allocations; 'it is more about a reconfiguration of state-market-community relationships' (ibid: 1251).

[22] Proponents of weak sustainability believe that human-made and natural capital are substitutable in the long term whilst followers of strong sustainability believe they are not (Neumayer, 2003).

Table 3. Institutional approach to PES: Analytical domains and key research questions

Analytical domain and dimensions	Guiding research questions
Institutional design Are rules conductive to achieve goals?	• Why are PES proposed as a policy tool? • Which actors shape the rule-design process and how are their interests represented in the final rules? • How and why do design rules change over time?
Institutional performance Is an institution achieving its goals?	• How do PES schemes affect the beneficiaries of direct payments, the services they attempt to conserve, and the ecosystems providing such services? • How do PES schemes affect the buyers of the targeted services? • Why do beneficiaries decide to participate in PES? • How do PES schemes measure and monitor the provision of ES, and account for changes?
Institutional interplay How do institutions affect each other?	• How do PES schemes account for other institutions in their design and implementation? • Which institutional synergies and conflicts exist as a result of institutional interactions?
Organisational capacity How does capacity affect performance?	• Has PES design or implementation been hampered by a lack of organisational capacities across involved actors?
Scale How does scale affect PES design and performance?	• Is there an optimal scale of governance for the provision of each ES? • Have there been any cross-scale institutions created to address problems of interplay? • How do cross-scale institutions benefit PES design and performance?

Source: Adapted from Corbera et al., 2009: 746

It is important to note how this IEE focus differs from the Coasean approach to PES. Coase's theory, in fact, is often considered as one of the founding blocks of new institutional economics (North, 1990; Williamson, 1985) and much of the Coasean-inspired PES research has explicitly dedicated attention to the design of formal institutions with clearly-defined boundaries (see e.g. Landell-Mills and Porras, 2002, and Wunder et al., 2008). From this perspective, the limitations of most existing PES schemes can be explained by 'design failures' or 'institutional failures' (e.g. weak institutions or lack of property rights) (e.g. Pattanayak et al., 2010). However, rather than trying to adapt the real world to a Coasean world of zero transaction costs and clearly-defined property rights, the IEE approach explicitly recognises how PES systems are not created in an institutional vacuum (Vatn, 2010) and how their outcomes are not predictable as they result 'from a combination of institutional factors, some of which are extrinsic to institutional design' (Corbera et al., 2009; see also Cleaver, 2002). Moreover, it advocates adapting (economic) institutions to the physical characteristics of the (natural) world it is dealing with, and not the other way around (Farley and Costanza, 2010; Vatn, 2009). Indeed, the services that PES are dealing with are often public goods[23], and this usually implies that their provision entails the solution to a problem of collective action (or social rationality), rather than to a dilemma of individual rational choice. It is, therefore, 'problematic to use methods based on individual rationality for decision concerning common goods' (Vatn, 2009: 2210). Since the role of institutions is to signal which rationality is expected (ibid), it may thus 'make more sense for collective institutions to take the lead, supplemented by more market-based approaches where possible' (Farley and Costanza, 2010: 2065). Rather than promoting PES as a value-articulating tool that would correct the inefficient outcomes of regulatory or development-based approaches - and therefore limit research on institutional design to structures capable of enabling commodity trading and contractual relationships between supply and demand (Corbera and Brown, 2008) -, the IEE perspective argues that PES should be explicitly considered as part of an integrated and multi-purpose rural governance strategy, which cannot simply be reduced to an 'isolated' efficiency problem (Muradian et al., 2010). The emphasis of PES should therefore move from the 'internalisation of externalities' to 'incentives for collective action' (ibid). This expanded view devotes much more attention to the way different practices, institutions and hybrid governance structures can strengthen (or weaken) each other by taking into account the non-economic cognitive-motivational dimensions, as well as the social and political relations that shape environmental governance (Cleaver, 2002, 2005; Ravnborg, 2003; Uphoff, 1993).

4.3. A NEW DEFINITION AND RESEARCH AGENDA FOR PES

The recognition that institutional settings of PES implementation in practice are characterised by high levels of uncertainty, imperfect and asymmetric information, and therefore high transaction costs (Muradian et al., 2010), inspired a number of scholars to abandon Wunder's (2005) restrictive and normative definition, and to

[23] As discussed in section 4.1, it is only within the conceptualisation as single and isolated items that they can be conceived as commodities. As processes, however, they are common goods, implying also a common responsibility (Vatn, 2009).

propose a new definition for PES, which explicitly recognises that PES can be applied in a wide variety of complex institutional contexts (Sommerville et al., 2009). Muradian et al. (2010) have proposed to more broadly define 'PES as a transfer of resources between social actors, which aims to create incentives to align individual and/or collective land use decisions with the social interest in the management of natural resources' (ibid: 1205). This definition does not impose a normative claim on the way PES should be designed. It is useful to cite the authors' explanation at length:

> 'Such transfers (monetary or non-monetary) are embedded in social relations, values and perceptions, which are decisive in conditioning PES design and outcomes. The transfers may thus take place through a market (or something close to one), as well as through other mechanisms like incentives or public subsidies defined by regulatory means. Therefore, not all PES are market transactions and even those that may be considered as such tend indeed to be rather imperfect on the ground. These considerations and the definition presented above translate into the existence of a large diversity of PES initiatives which can be clustered according to three criteria, namely the importance of the economic incentive, the directness of the transfer and the degree of commodification of environmental services ... [T]he proposed definition and classification of PES schemes goes beyond the dichotomy between state-driven and private-driven schemes and does not distinguish between 'genuine' and 'PES-like' interventions. This approach allows a wide diversity of possible institutional settings and permits to identify a large variety of cases as determined by the combination of our three main criteria, from schemes that could meet the conditions of market transactions (fitting into the Coasean definition) to more complex institutional arrangements for dealing with the management of common-pool natural resources, where economic transfers play a role in facilitating the coordination between participants.' (ibid: 1205-1206).

This continuous and more hybrid classification of PES recognises the institutional complexity in which PES schemes operate, and it opens a whole new research agenda which allows to address more explicitly the research questions formulated in Table 3. From this broader perspective, various empirical and theoretical studies have already inquired into the analytical and empirical lacunae that still need to be clarified. Corbera et al. (2007a), for example, explicitly deal with fairness and distributional aspects, and indicate how payments for carbon forestry are largely mediated by land entitlements and local political conflicts, potentially leading to the exclusion of poor minorities from PES programmes. Similarly, Pascual et al. (2010) and Sommerville et al. (2010) emphasise the role of the institutional setting in determining the prevailing fairness and/or efficiency criteria in PES schemes, and call for further research on power relationships between buyers and sellers of environmental services. Blackman and Woodward (2010), Kosoy et al.

(2008) and Miranda et al. (2007), in turn, show how people's willingness to participate in payment schemes is not only dependent on economic incentives, but can be influenced by social rules and cultural perspectives, as well as by the communication 'skills' between the involved actors. The role of intermediary agents is thereby increasingly recognised (see also Pham et al., 2010). Corbera et al. (2007b) and Kosoy et al. (2007) emphasise that non-financial incentives, such as forest management training and agricultural extension support might induce participation in PES schemes, and that successes of PES schemes, in terms of efficiency and equity, largely depend on the institutional context and other 'intangibles', such as the levels of trust and understanding between the involved actors. Greiner and Gregg (2011) and Kosoy et al. (2007) suggest that monetary compensations through PES can provide moral incentives for conservation actions, but may not necessarily improve economic efficiency and sustainability of conservation actions. Some authors even caution that monetary compensations may 'crowd out' non-profit-based motivations for environmental governance (Bowles, 2008; Corbera et al., 2007a; Vatn, 2010). In short, most of these (still largely inconclusive) studies call for further multidisciplinary research on the social embeddedness of PES and the social and environmental transformations this instrument may trigger, as well as for further research on how PES can be formulated in ways that lead to the strengthening of cooperative will and the inducement of a commitment to long-term conservation.

5. CONCLUSION: THE STUDY'S CONTRIBUTION TO THE BROADER PES DEBATE

This chapter discussed how the conceptualisation of environmental problems within an ES framework has steadily paved the way to a new conservation paradigm: that of creating payments and markets for ES. It illustrated the mushrooming of practical experiences with PES, but found that the enormous popularity of this new conservation tool has, however, not always been accompanied by sufficient critical research on its socio-ecological outcomes. Most PES research has indeed largely been inspired by Coasean institutional design principles, with a constrained research focus on possible ways to achieve maximum efficiency gains by adapting and 'designing' the study site to resemble as much as possible an ideal world with low transaction costs and clearly-defined property rights. Farley and Costanza (2010), however, nimbly note that the mere fact that 'PES schemes are possible does not mean that they are desirable' (ibid: 2066). Indeed, little critical thought has been given to the appropriateness of PES. In the course of the last three to five years, however, the tendency is changing. On the one hand, there is the emergence of a growing body of literature actively opposing PES, depicting it as a perverse and fetishist instrument of 'roll-out' neoliberalism. Authors pertaining to this school of thought have indicated many important limitations of payments and markets for nature conservation, but their 'radical' vision has somewhat foreclosed a more constructive debate on PES. On the other hand, another fledging school of thought is advocating a reconceptualisation of PES rather than a complete rejection. Mainly inspired by institutional ecological economics, it criticises Coasean PES for being insensitive to institutional contexts and for prioritising market-based efficiency criteria over other equally or even more important considerations, such as equity and sustainability. This alternative and novel theoretical perspective has launched a new and more multidisciplinary research agenda on the potential of PES as one element of a broader and hybrid environmental governance framework.

The aim of this doctoral thesis is to contribute to this expanded research agenda by investigating several of the important questions raised in Table 3 (the most important of which were also formulated in the introductory chapter). It also aims to complement the still limited empirical research that has been conducted on this new PES perspective, and seeks to add to the growing body of knowledge in this field. In the following chapters we will investigate the potential and limitations of market-based PES through different case studies. Table 4 gives an overview of the next three chapters, and shows how each chapter will cover different aspects and dimensions of PES, both from a theoretical (chapter 2) and from an empirical perspective (chapters 3 and 4). The empirical chapters will elucidate the PES story from two important angles: chapter 3 will focus on the supply side aspects, and chapter 4 will investigate the largely under-researched demand side aspects.

Chapter 2 qualifies some of the main theoretical assumptions underlying market-based PES. More specifically, it critically assesses the externality framework underpinning Coasean PES from an institutional and political economy perspective. It focuses on two important aspects: the hidden political ambiguities of using the externality framework and the risk that PES, especially if user-funded, may perpetuate and deepen the regressive financing of global commons by poor local communities. The analysis will show that these considerations have been largely overlooked in the PES literature, which generally assumes that externality and financing issues are mere technical matters subject to socio-economic engineering, and therefore neglect the fact that they are much more closely linked with social perceptions about property rights and entitlements. Just as the ES conceptualisation risks to mask the inherent complexity of ecosystems (Norgaard, 2010), the externality framework entails the danger of obfuscating the very real political choices underlying environmental governance. The theoretical reflections and insights that will be discussed in this chapter will serve as an input for the interpretation of some of the findings in the empirical chapters.

Chapter 3 investigates the supply-side dimensions of PES schemes through the analysis of the Nicaraguan component of the international GEF silvopastoral PES pilot project, which took place in Colombia, Costa Rica and Nicaragua. Based on an extensive field study, this chapter inquires into the motivational aspects underlying farmers' adoption of silvopastoral practices. The empirical research, which was partly based on official project survey data, but also on additional qualitative fieldwork, suggests that a mixture of economic and non-economic factors determines farmers' motivation to adopt the envisaged silvopastoral practices and that the actual role of PES is mistakenly understood as a simple matter of financia incentives. It shows how additional factors, such as technical assistance and changing local perceptions ensuing from new opportunities and local discourses have played an - at least equally - important role in adopting more environmentally-friendly land use practices. A Coasean approach might thus not be able to explain adequately the dynamics that are taking place, nor does it automatically contribute to effective and sustainable improvements in ES provision. The research shows that PES approaches should be understood as part of a broader process of local institutional transformation rather than as a market-based alternative for allegedly ineffective government and/or community governance.

Table 4. Scope of the following chapters and contribution to the PES debate

	Chapter 2: Theoretical reflections	Chapter 3: Empirical supply	Chapter 4: Empirical demand
Research scope			
• Case study theme	Qualification of assumptions underlying market-based PES	Supply side aspects GEF silvopastoral PES project	Demand side aspects local watershed PES feasibility study
• Research topics	Political implications of Coasean PES framework for different geographical governance scales	Motivational factors influencing adoption of silvopastoral practices	Institutional embeddedness of willingness to pay for local watershed services
• Main institutional dimensions	Institutional interplay and performance across geographical scales	Institutional interplay and performance	Institutional interplay and performance
• Research questions	What fairness implications can PES have on local communities? Does an optimal scale of governance exist?	What factors influence the adoption of environmentally-friendly land use changes? How do they interact with PES?	What factors influence willingness to pay for local watershed services?
• Main positions	1) Market-based PES externality framework mediated by political factors 2) Market-based PES may lead to regressive financing of global commons	1) Besides financial rewards, land users have other (and at least equally important) motivations to engage in land use changes 2) Payments may 'crowd out' intrinsic motivation	1) Local people's willingness to finance PES is mediated by institutional, political and cultural factors 2) Willingness to pay depends on prior building of trust and cognitive synergies
• Research methods	Theoretical reflections from an institutional/ political economy perspective	Quantitative analysis (Quasi-experimental research & survey data) Qualitative analysis (qualitative in-depth interviews & observations)	Quantitative analysis (Contingent valuation & survey data) Qualitative analysis (qualitative in-depth interviews & observations)
• Research site	N.A.	Rural Matiguás-Río Blanco (central Nicaragua)	Urban-rural Matiguás (central Nicaragua)

Finally, chapter 4 inquires into the under-researched demand-side aspects of PES by assessing local willingness to pay (WTP) for water and watershed services in an upstream-downstream setting. Based on extensive fieldwork in Matiguás,

Nicaragua, and using both qualitative and quantitative research approaches, it demonstrates how urban dwellers are very aware of upstream-downstream interdependencies and have a positive WTP for improved water services, suggesting potential for a 'Coasean' water-related PES scheme. Contrary to expectations, the feasibility of such a locally-financed PES system is, however, undermined by prevailing local perceptions of agricultural externalities and entitlements, questioning the fairness of such payments. Low levels of mutual trust also seem to undermine the credibility of the PES framework. From a broader institutional perspective, the chapter thus offers alternative and more plausible explanations for the ongoing socio-political interactions in the field, and argues that future research on PES ought to be much more sensitive to the local social structures and institutional arrangements. It also suggests that this is best achieved by adopting a multidisciplinary research approach, expanding the use of traditional economic cost-benefit instruments to more participative and deliberative procedures in environmental decision making.

REFERENCES

Alix-Garcia, J., De Janvry, A. and Sadoulet, E. (2008) "The role of deforestation risk and calibrated compensation in designing payments for environmental services", *Environment and Development Economics* 13: 375-394.

Anderson, T.L. and Leal, D.R. (2001) *Free Market Environmentalism*, New York: Palgrave.

Angelsen, A. (ed.) (2008) Moving ahead with REDD: Issues, options and implications, Bogor, Indonesia: CIFOR.

Angelsen, A., Brockhaus, M. Kanninen, M., Sills, E., Sunderlin, W. and Wertz-Kanounnikoff, S. (Eds.) (2009) *Realizing REDD: National Strategy and Policy Options*, Bogor, Indonesia: CIFOR.

Antle, J.M. and Stoorvogel, J.J. (2008) "Agricultural Carbon Sequestration, Poverty and Sustainability", *Environment and Development Economics* 13: 327-352.

Appleton, A. (2002) "How New York City Used an Ecosystems Services Strategy Carried Out Through an Urban-Rural Partnership to Preserve the Pristine Quality of its Drinking Water and Save Billions of Dollars", Forest Trends.

Asquith, N.M., Vargas, M.T. and Wunder, S. (2008), "Selling two environmental services: in-kind payments for bird habitat and watershed protection in Los Negros, Bolivia", *Ecological Economics* 65: 675-684.

Bakker, K. (2005) "Neoliberalizing nature? Market environmentalism in water supply in England and Wales", *Annals of the Association of American Geographers* 95(3): 542–565.

Bakker, K. (2010) "The limits of 'neoliberal natures': Debating green neoliberalism", *Progress in Human Geography*, doi: 10.1177/0309132510376849.

Balmford, A., Bruner, A., Cooper, P., Costanza, R., Farber, S., Green, R.E., Jenkins, M., Jefferiss, P., Jessamy, V., Madden, J., Munro, K., Myers, N., Naeem, S., Paavola, J., Rayment, M., Rosendo, S., Roughgarden, J., Trumper, K. and Turner, R.K. (2002) "Economic reasons for conserving wild nature", *Science* 297: 950-953.

Baumol, W.J. and Oates, W.E. (1988) *The Theory of Environmental Policy*, Second edition, Cambridge: Cambridge University Press.

Bayon, R. (2004) Making Environmental markets work: lessons from early experience with sulfur, carbon, wetlands, and other related markets, Washington D.C.: Forest Trends.

Blackman, A. and Woodward, R.T. (2010) "User financing in a national payments for environmental services program: Costa Rican hydropower", *Ecological Economics* 69: 1626-1638.

Block, W.E. (1990) "Environmental problems, private property rights solutions", in: Block, W.E. (ed.), *Economics and the Environment: A Reconciliation* (pp.281-318), Vancouver, Canada: The Fraser Institute.

Blom, B., Sunderland, T. and Murdiyarso, D. (2010) "Getting REDD to work locally: lessons learned from integrated conservation and development projects", *Environmental Science & Policy* 13: 164-172.

Bolton, P. and Dewatripont, M. (2005) *Contract Theory*, Cambridge, Massachusetts: MIT Press.

Börner, J., Wunder, S., Wertz-Kanounnikoff, S., Rügnitz Tito, M., Pereira, L. and Nascimento, N. (2010) "Direct conservation payments in the Brazilian Amazon: Scope and equity implications", *Ecological Economics* 69(6): 1272-1282.

Bowles, S. (2008) "Policies designed for self-interested citizens may undermine 'the moral sentiments': evidence from economic experiments", *Science* 320: 1605-1609.

Brockhaus, M. and Botoni, E. (2009) "Ecosystem services - local benefits, global impacts", *Rural 21: The International Journal for Rural Development* 43(1): 8-11.

Brockington, D., Igoe, J. and Schmidt-Soltau, K. (2006) "Conservation, Human Rights, and Poverty Reduction", *Conservation Biology* 20(1): 250-252.

Brockington, D., Duffy, D. and Igoe, J. (2008) Nature Unbound. Conservation, Capitalism and the Future of Protected Areas, London: Earthscan.

Bulte, E.H., Boone, R.B., Stringer, R. and Thornton, P.K. (2008a) "Elephants or onions? Paying for nature in Amboseli, Kenya", *Environment and Development Economics* 13: 395-414.

Bulte, E.H., Lipper, L., Stringer, R. and Zilberman, D. (2008b) "Payments for ecosystem services and poverty reduction: concepts, issues and empirical perspectives", *Environment and Development Economics* 13: 245-254.

Büscher, B. (2008) "Conservation, Neoliberalism, and Social Science: a Critical Reflection on the SCB 2007 Annual Meeting in South Africa", *Conservation Biology* 22(2): 229-231.

Büscher, B. (2010) "Derivative Nature: interrogating the value of conservation in 'Boundless Southern Africa'", *Third World Quarterly* 31(2): 259-276.

Büscher, B, Neves, K., Sullivan, S., Brockington D. and Igoe, J. (forthcoming) "Towards a Consolidated Critique of Neoliberal Conservation", *Capitalism, Nature Socialism.*

Caparrós, A., Cerdá, E., Ovando, P. and Campos, P. (2010) "Carbon Sequestration with Reforestations and Biodiversity-scenic Values", *Environmental and Resource Economics* 45: 49-72.

Castree, N. (2003) "Commodifying what nature?", *Progress in Human Geography* 27(3): 273–297.

Castree, N. (2006) "From neoliberalism to neoliberalization: Consolations, confusions, and necessary illusions", *Environment and Planning A* 38(1): 1-6.

Chisholm, R.A. (2010) "Trade-offs between ecosystem services: Water and carbon in a biodiversity hotspot", *Ecological Economics* 69: 1973-1987.

Cleaver, F. (2002) "Reinventing Institutions and the Social Embeddedness of Natural Resource Management", *European Journal of Development Research* 14(2): 11-30.

Cleaver, F. (2005) "The Inequality of Social Capital and the Reproduction of Chronic Poverty", *World Development* 33(6): 893-906.

Clements, T. (2010) "Reduced Expectations: the political and institutional challenges of REDD+", *Oryx* 44(3): 309-310.

Coase, R.H. (1960) "The problem of social cost", *Journal of Law and Economics* 3: 1-44.

Corbera, E. and Brown, K. (2008) "Building Institutions to Trade Ecosystem Services: Marketing Forest Carbon in Mexico", *World Development* 36(10): 1956-1979.

Corbera, E., Brown, K. and Adger, W.N. (2007a) "The equity and legitimacy of markets for ecosystem services", *Development and Change* 38(4): 587-613.

Corbera, E., Kosoy, N., Martínez Tuna, M. (2007b) "Equity implications of marketing ecosystem services in protected areas and rural communities: Case studies from Meso-America", *Global Environmental Change* 17(3-4): 365-380.

Corbera, E., González Soberanis, C. and Brown, K. (2009) "Institutional dimensions of payments for ecosystem services. An analysis of Mexico's carbon forestry programme", *Ecological* Economics 68: 743–761.

Costanza, R. and Daly, H.E. (1992) "Natural Capital and Sustainable Development", *Conservation Biology* 6: 37-46.

Costanza, R., d'Arge, R., de Groot, R., Farber, S., Grasso, M., Hannon, B., Limburg, K., Naeem, S., O'Neill, R.V., Paruelo, J., Raskin, R.G., Sutton, P. and van den Belt, M. (1997) "The value of the world's ecosystem services and natural capital", *Nature* 387: 253–260.

Daily, G.C. (1997) Nature's Services: Societal Dependence on Natural Ecosystems, Washington, D.C.: Island Press.

Dressler, W., Büscher, B., Schoon, M., Brockington, D., Hayes, T., Kull, C., McCarthy, J. and Streshta, K. (2010) "From Hope to Crisis and Back? A Critical History of the Global CBNRM Narrative", *Environmental Conservation* 37(1): 5-15.

Durning, A. (1989) "Poverty and the environment: reversing the downward spiral", Worldwatch Paper 92, Washington, D.C.: Worldwatch Institute.

Engel, S. and Palmer, C. (2008) "Payments for environmental services as an alternative to logging under weak property rights: the case of Indonesia", *Ecological Economics* 65: 799-809.

Engel, S., Pagiola, S. and Wunder, S. (2008) "Designing payments for environmental services in theory and practice: an overview of the issues", *Ecological Economics* 65: 663–675.

Ervine, K. (2010) "Participation denied: the Global Environment Facility, its universal blueprint, and the Mexico-Mesoamerican biological corridor in Chiapas", *Third World Quarterly* 31(5): 773-790.

Farley, J. and Costanza, R. (2010) "Payments for ecosystem services: from local to global", *Ecological Economics* 69: 2060-2068.

Farley, J., Aquino, A., Daniels, A., Moulaert, A., Lee, D. and Krause, A. (2010) "Global mechanisms for sustaining and enhancing PES schemes", *Ecological Economics* 69: 2075-2084.

Ferraro, P.J. (2001) "Global Habitat Protection: Limitations of Development Interventions and a Role for Conservation Performance Payments", *Conservation Biology* 15(4): 1-12.

Ferraro, P.J. (2008) "Asymmetric information and contract design for payments for environmental services", *Ecological Economics* 65(4): 810-821.

Ferraro, P.J. (2009) "Regional Review of Payments for Watershed Services - Sub-Saharan Africa", *Journal of Sustainable Forestry* 28: 525-550.

Ferraro, P.J. and Kiss, A. (2002) "Direct payments for biodiversity conservation", *Science* 298: 1718-1719.

Ferraro, P.J. and Simpson, R.D. (2002) "The cost-effectiveness of conservation payments", *Land Economics* 78(3): 339-353.

Fisher, B., Turner, R.K. and Morling, P. (2009) "Defining and classifying ecosystem services for decision making", *Ecological Economics* 68: 643-653.

Fisher, B., Kulindwa, K., Mwanyoka, I., Turner, R.K. and Burgess, N. (2010) "Common pool resource management and PES: Lessons and constraints for water PES in Tanzania", *Ecological Economics* 69(6): 1253-1261.

Freeman, A.M. (1993) The measurement of environmental and resource values: Theory and methods, Washington, D.C.: Resources for the Future.

Frost, P.G.H. and Bond, I. (2008) "The CAMPFIRE programme in Zimbabwe: payments for wildlife services", *Ecological Economics* 65: 777-788.

German, L., Villamor, G., Twine, E., Velarde, S.J. and Kidane, B. (2009) "Environmental Services and the Precautionary Principle: Using Scenarios to Reconcile Conservation and Livelihood Objectives in Upper Catchments", *Journal of Sustainable Forestry* 28: 368-394.

Gómez-Baggethun, E., de Groot, R., Lomas, P.L. and Montes, C. (2010) "The history of ecosystem services in economic theory and practice: from early notions to markets and payment schemes", *Ecological Economics* 69(6): 1209-1218.

Greenstone, M. and Gayer, T. (2009) "Quasi-experimental and experimental approaches to environmental economics", *Journal of Environmental Economics and Management* 57: 21-44.

Greiner, R. and Gregg, D. (2011) "Farmers' intrinsic motivations, barriers to the adoption of conservation practices and effectiveness of policy instruments: Empirical evidence from northern Australia", *Land Use Policy* 28: 257-265.

Grieg-Gran, M., Porras, I. and Wunder, S. (2005) "How can market mechanisms for forest environmental services help the poor? Preliminary lessons from Latin America", *World Development* 33(9): 1511-1527.

Hall, R. and Lovera, S. (2009) *REDD Realities: How strategies to reduce emissions from deforestation and forest degradation could impact on biodiversity and Indigenous Peoples in developing countries*, Asunción, Paraguay: Global Forest Coalition.

Hamilton, K., Sjardin, M., Peters-Stanley, M. and Marcello, T. (2010) *Building Bridges: State of the Voluntary Carbon Markets 2010,* Ecosystem Marketplace and Bloomberg New Energy Finance.

Heyman, J. and Ariely, D. (2004) "Effort for payment: a tale of two markets", *Psychological Science* 15(11): 787-793.

Horan, R.D., Shogren, J.F. and Gramig, B.M. (2008) "Wildlife conservation payments to address habitat fragmentation and disease risks", *Environment and Development Economics* 13: 415-439.

Huang, M., Upadhyaya, S.K., Jindal, R. and Kerr, J. (2009) "Payments for Watershed Services in Asia: A Review of Current Initiatives", *Journal of Sustainable Forestry* 28: 551-575.

Huberman, D. (2009) "World Heritage Sites and the Integration of Biodiversity into an international PES framework", *Journal of Sustainable Forestry* 28: 456-480.

Huberman, D. and Leipprand, T. (2006) "Developing International Payments for Ecosystem Services: A Technical Discussion" (Background paper) Geneva: UNEP-ETB.

Kareiva, P., Watts, S., McDonald, R. and Boucher, T. (2007) "Domesticated Nature: Shaping Landscapes and Ecosystems for Human Welfare", *Science* 316: 1866-1869.

Karsenty, A. (2007) "Questioning rent for development swaps: new market-based instruments for biodiversity acquisition and the land-use issue in tropical countries", *International Forestry Review* 9(1): 503-513.

Kosoy, N. and Corbera, E. (2010) "Payments for ecosystem services as commodity fetishism", *Ecological Economics* 69(6): 1228-1236.

Kosoy, N., Martinez-Tuna, M., Muradian, R. and Martinez-Alier, J. (2007) "Payments for environmental services in watersheds: Insights from a comparative study of three cases in Central America", *Ecological Economics* 61: 446-455.

Kosoy, N., Corbera, E. and Brown, K. (2008) "Participation in payments for ecosystem services: Case studies from the Lacandón rainforest, Mexico", *Geoforum* 39: 2073-2083.

Landell-Mills, N. (2002) "Developing markets for forest environmental services: an opportunity for promoting equity while securing efficiency?" *Philosophical transactions – Royal Society. Mathematical, physical and engineering sciences* 360: 1817-1825.

Landell-Mills, N. and Porras, I. (2002) Silver Bullet or Fools' Gold? A Global Review of Markets for Forest Environmental Services and Their Impact on the Poor, London: IIED.

Lemos, M.C. and Agrawal, A. (2006) "Environmental Governance", *Annual Review of Environment and Natural Resources* 31: 297-325.

Lohman, L. (Ed.) (2006) *Carbon Trading: A Critical Conversation on Climate Change, Privatisation and Power*. Uppsala, Sweden: Dag Hammarskjöld Foundation - Durban Group for Climate Justice and the Corner House.

Lohmann, L. (2009) "Climate as investment", *Development and Change* 40(6): 1063-1083.

Lohmann, L. (2010) "Uncertainty markets and carbon markets: variations on polanyian themes", *New Political Economy* 15(2): 225-254.

Millennium Ecosystem Assessment (MA) (2005) *Millennium Ecosystem Assessment. Ecosystems and Human Well-being*, Washington, D.C.: Island Press.

MacKinnon, K. (2001) "Integrated conservation and development projects - can they work?", *Parks* 11(2): 1-5.

Madsen, B., Carroll, N. and Moore Brands, K. (2010) State of Biodiversity Markets Report: Offset and Compensation Programs Worldwide, Ecosystem Marketplace.

Martin, A., Blowers, A. and Boersema, J. (2008) "Paying for environmental services: can we afford to lose a cultural basis for conservation?", *Environmental Sciences* 5(1): 1-5.

Martínez-Alier, J. (2004) The Environmentalism of the Poor: A Study of Ecological Conflicts and Valuation, New Delhi: Oxford University Press.

Marx, K. (1867) *Capital: Volume 1,* New York: Penguin Books.

McAfee, K. (1999) "Selling nature to save it? Biodiversity and green developmentalism", *Environment and Planning D: Society and Space* 17(2): 133–154.

McAfee, K. and Shapiro, E.N. (2010) "Payment for Environmental Services in Mexico: Neoliberalism, Social Movements, and the State", *Annals of the Association of American Geographers* 100(3): 579-599.

McCarthy, J. (2005) "Devolution in the woods: Community forestry as hybrid neoliberalism", *Environment and Planning A* 37(6): 995-1014.

McCauley, D.J. (2006) "Selling out on nature", *Nature* 443: 27-28.

Miranda, M., Dieperink, C. and Glasbergen, P. (2007) "Voluntary agreements in watershed protection in Costa Rica", *Environment, Development and Sustainability* 9: 1-19.

Muñoz-Piña, C., Guevara, A., Torres, J.M. and Braña, J. (2008) "Paying for the hydrological services of Mexico's forests: Analysis, negotiations and results", *Ecological Economics* 65: 725-736.

Muradian, R., Corbera, E., Pascual, U., Kosoy, N. and May, P. (2010) "Reconciling theory and practice: An alternative conceptual framework for understanding payments for environmental services", *Ecological Economics* 69(6): 1202–1208.

Neumayer, E. (2003) Weak versus strong sustainability: Exploring the limits of two opposing paradigms, Cheltenham: Edward Elgar Publishing.

Norgaard, R. (2010) "Ecosystem services: From eye-opening metaphor to complexity blinder", *Ecological Economics* 69(6): 1219–1227.

North, D.C. (1990) Institutions, Institutional Change and Economic Performance, New York: Cambridge University Press.

Nygren, A. and Rikoon, S. (2008) "Political Ecology Revisited: Integration of Politics and Ecology Does Matter", *Society and Natural Resources* 21: 767-782.

O'Neill, J. (2001) "Property, care, and environment", *Environment and Planning C: Government and Policy* 19: 695–711.

Oates, W.E., Portney, P.R. and McGartland A.M. (1989) "The Net Benefits of Incentive-Based Regulation: A Case Study of Environmental Standard Setting", *American Economic Review* 79: 1233-1243.

Paavola, J. (2007) "Institutions and environmental governance: a reconceptualization", *Ecological Economics* 63: 93-103.

Paavola, J. and Adger, N.W. (2005) "Institutional ecological economics", *Ecological Economics* 53: 353-368.

Pagiola, S. (2008) "Payments for environmental services in Costa Rica", *Ecological Economics* 65: 712-724.

Pagiola, S. and Platais, G. (2007) *Payments for Environmental Services: From Theory to Practice*, Washington D.C.: World Bank.

Pagiola, S., Bishop, J. and Landell-Mills, N. (eds.) (2002) Selling forest environmental services. Market-based mechanisms for conservation and development, London: Earthscan.

Pagiola, S., Agostini, P., Gobbi, J., de Haan, C., Ibrahim, M., Murgueitio, E., Ramírez, E., Rosales, M. and Ruíz, J.P. (2004) "Paying for biodiversity conservation services in agricultural landscapes", Environment Department Paper, vol. 96. Washington D.C.: World Bank.

Pagiola, S., Arcenas, A. and Platais, G. (2005) "Can payments for environmental services help reduce poverty? An exploration of the issues and the evidence to date from Latin America", *World Development* 33(2): 237-253.

Pagiola, S., Ramírez, E., Gobbi, J., de Haan, C., Ibrahim, M., Murgueitio, E. and Ruíz, J. (2007) "Paying for the environmental services of silvopastoral practices in Nicaragua", *Ecological Economics* 64: 374–385.

Pagiola, S., Rios, A.R. and Arcenas, A. (2008) "Can the poor participate in payments for environmental services? Lessons from the Silvopastoral Project in Nicaragua", *Environment and Development Economics* 13(3): 299-325.

Parkhurst, G.M. and Shogren, J.F. (2007) "Spatial incentives to coordinate contiguous habitat", *Ecological Economics* 64: 344-355.

Pascual, U., Muradian, R., Rodríguez, L.C. and Duraiappah, A. (2010) "Exploring the links between equity and efficiency in payments for environmental services: a conceptual approach", *Ecological Economics* 69: 1237-1244.

Pattanayak, S.K., Wunder, S. and Ferraro, P.J. (2010) "Show me the money: do payments supply environmental services in developing countries?" *Review of Environmental Economics and Policy* 4(2): 254-274.

Pearce, D. (1993) *Economic Values and the Natural world*, London: Earthscan.

Pearce, D. (2004) "Environmental market creation: saviour or oversell?", *Portuguese Economic Journal* 3(2): 115–144.

Pearce, D. and Turner, R. (1990) *Economics of Natural Resources and the Environment*, New York and London: Harvester.

Perrot-Maître, D. (2006) "The Vittel Payments for Ecosystem Services: a 'Perfect' PES Case?", Project Paper No.3, London: IIED.

Peterson, M.J., Hall, D.M., Feldpausch-Parker, A.M. and Peterson, T.R. (2010) "Obscuring Ecosystem Function with Application of the Ecosystem Services Concept", *Conservation Biology* 24(1): 113-119.

Pham, T.T., Campbell, B.M., Garnett, S., Aslin, H. and Hoang, M.H. (2010) "Importance and impacts of intermediary boundary organizations in facilitating payment for environmental services in Vietnam", *Environmental Conservation* 37: 64-72.

Pigou, A.C. (1920) *The Economics of Welfare*, London: MacMillan.

Polanyi, K. (1944) The Great Transformation: The Political and Economic Origins of Our Time, New York: Rhinehart.

Porras, I., Grieg-Gran, M. and Neves, N. (2008) *All that glitters: A review of payments for watershed services*, London: International Institute for Environment and Development (IIED).

Raeder, L.C. (1998) "Liberalism and the common good - a Hayekian perspective on communitarianism", *The Independent Review* II(4): 519-535.

Ravnborg, H.M. (2003) "Poverty and Environmental Degradation in the Nicaraguan Hillsides", *World Development* 31(11): 1933–1946.

Ravnborg, H.M., Damsgaard, M.G. and Raben, K. (2007) "Payments for Ecosystem Services. Issues and pro-poor opportunities for development assistance", DIIS Report 2007:6, Copenhagen: Danish Institute for International Studies.

Rebelo, C. (2009) "Financing for Forest Conservation; Payments for Ecosystem Services in the Tropics Yale ISTF Conference, March 2007", *Journal of Sustainable Forestry* 28: 279-284.

Redford, K.H. and Adams, W.M. (2009) "Payments for Ecosystem services and the Challenge of Saving Nature", *Conservation Biology* 23: 785-787.

Richards, M. (2000) "Can sustainable tropical forestry be made profitable? The potential and limitations of innovative incentive mechanisms", *World Development* 28(6): 1001–1016.

Robertson, M.M. (2004) "The neoliberalization of ecosystem services: wetland mitigation banking and problems in environmental governance", *Geoforum* 35: 371-373.

Salzman, J. (2005) "Creating markets for ecosystem services: notes from the field", *New York University Law Review* 80: 870–961.

Sayer, J.A. (1991) *Rainforest Buffer Zones: Guidelines for Protected Area Management*, Gland, Switzerland: IUCN.

Sayer, J.A. (1995) "Science and International Nature Conservation", Occasional Paper No.4, Bogor, Indonesia: CIFOR.

Slavíková, L., Kluvánková-Oravská, T. and Jílková, J. (2010) "Bridging theories on environmental governance: Insights from free-market approaches and institutional ecological economics perspectives", *Ecological Economics* 69: 1368-1372.

Sommerville, M., Jones, J.P.G., Milner-Gullard, E.J. (2009) "A Revised Conceptual Framework for Payments for Environmental Services", *Ecology and Society* 14(2): 34.

Sommerville, M., Jones, J.P.G., Rahajaharison, M. and Milner-Gulland, E.J. (2010) "The role of fairness and benefit distribution in community-based Payment for Environmental Services interventions: A case study from Menabe, Madagascar", *Ecological Economics* 69(6): 1262–1271.

Southgate, D. and Wunder, S. (2009) "Paying for Watershed Services in Latin America: A Review of Current Initiatives", *Journal of Sustainable Forestry* 28: 497-524.

Stern, N. (2006) The economics of climate change: *Stern Review on the Economics of Climate Change*, London: UK Treasury.

Swallow, B.M., Kallesoe, M.F., Iftikhar, U.A., van Noordwijk, M., Bracer, K., Scherr, S.J., Raju, K.V., Poats, S.V., Duraiappah, A.K., Ochieng, B.O., Mallee, H. and Rumley, R. (2009) "Compensation and Rewards for Environmental Services in the Developing World: Framing Pan-Tropical Analysis and Comparison", *Ecology and Society* 14(2): 26.

Swart, J.A.A. (2003) "Will direct payments help biodiversity?" *Science* 299: 1981.

Tickell, A. and Peck, J. (2003) "Making global rules: globalization or neoliberalization?", in: Peck, J. and Yeung, H. (eds.), *Remaking the Global Economy: Economic-Geographical Perspectives* (pp.163-181), London: Sage, pp 163-181.

Turner, R.K., Pearce, D. and Bateman, I. (1994) *Environmental Economics. An Elementary Introduction*, United Kingdom: Prentice Hall Press.

Uphoff, N. (1993) "Grassroots Organizations and NGOs in Rural Development: Opportunities with Diminishing States and Expanding Markets", *World Development* 21(4): 607-622.

Vaessen, J. and Van Hecken, G. (2009) "Assessing the potential for experimental evaluation of intervention effects: The case of the Regional Integrated Silvopastoral Approaches to Ecosystem Management Project", GEF Impact Evaluation Report, Washington D.C.: GEF Evaluation Office.

Van Hecken, G. and Bastiaensen, J. (2010a) "Payments for Ecosystem Services in Nicaragua: Do Market-based Approaches Work?", *Development and Change* 41(3): 421-444.

Van Hecken, G. and Bastiaensen, J. (2010b) "Payments for Ecosystem Services: A Political View of its Justification, or the Lack of it", *Environmental Science & Policy* 13(8): 785-792.

Vatn, A. (2005) "Rationality, institutions and environmental policy", *Ecological Economics* 55: 203-217.

Vatn, A. (2009) "An institutional analysis of methods for environmental appraisal", *Ecological Economics* 68: 2207-2215.

Vatn, A. (2010) "An institutional analysis of payments for environmental services", *Ecological Economics* 69(6): 1245–1252.

Vatn, A. and Bromley, D.W. (1997) "Externalities - A market model failure", *Environmental and Resource Economics* 9: 135-151.

Villamor, G.B. and Lasco, R.D. (2009) "Rewarding Upland People for Forest Conservation: Experience and Lessons Learned from Case Studies in the Philippines", *Journal of Sustainable Forestry* 28: 304-321.

Wells, M. and Brandon, K. (1992) *People and Parks: Linking Protected Area Management with Local Communities*, Washington, D.C.: The International Bank for Reconstruction and Development/The World Bank.

Wells, M., Guggenheim, S., Khan, A., Wardojo, W. and Jepson, P. (1998) *Investing in Biodiversity: a Review of Indonesia's Integrated Conservation and Development Projects*, Washington, D.C.: World Bank.

Wilkie, D.S., Redford, K.H. and McShane, T.O. (2010) "Taking of Rights for Natural Resource Conservation: A Discussion About Compensation", *Journal of Sustainable Forestry* 29: 135-151.

Williamson, O.E. (1985) *The Economic Institutions of Capitalism*, New York: Free Press.

Wunder, S. (2005) "Payments for environmental services: some nuts and bolts", CIFOR Occasional Paper 42, Jakarta, CIFOR.

Wunder, S. (2008a) "Payments for environmental services and the poor: concepts and preliminary evidence", *Environment and Development Economics* 13: 279-297.

Wunder, S. (2008b) "Necessary Conditions for Ecosystem Service Payments", Paper presented at the Workshop on Economics and Conservation in the Tropics: a Strategy Dialogue, San Francisco, USA, 31 January–1 February, 2008.

Wunder, S. and Albán, M. (2008) "Decentralized payments for environmental services: the cases of Pimampiro and PROFAFOR in Ecuador", *Ecological Economics* 65(4): 685-698.

Wunder, S. and Vargas, M.T. (2005) "Beyond "markets": why terminology matters", in Bayon, R., Nathaniel, C. and Hawn, A. (eds.), *The tale of two continents – Ecosystem services in Latin America and East and Southern Africa,* Ecosystem Marketplace.

Wunder, S. and Wertz-Kanounnikoff, S. (2009) "Payments for ecosystem services: a new way of conserving biodiversity in forests", *Journal of Sustainable Forestry* 28: 576-596.

Wunder, S., Engel, S. and Pagiola, S. (2008) "Taking stock: A comparative analysis of payments for environmental services programs in developed and developing countries", *Ecological Economics* 65: 834-852.

Wünscher, T., Engel, S. and Wunder, S. (2008) "Spatial targeting of payments for environmental services: a tool for boosting conservation benefits", *Ecological Economics* 65: 822-833.

Young, O.R. (2002a) The Institutional Dimensions of Environmental Change: Fit, Interplay and Scale, London: MIT Press.

Young, O.R. (2002b) "Institutional Interplay: The Environmental Consequences of Cross-scale Interactions", in: Ostrom, E., Dietz, T., Dolsak, N., Stern, P.C., Stonich, S. and Weber, E.U. (Eds.) *The Drama of the Commons*, Washington D.C.: National Academy Press.

Zilberman, D., Lipper, L. and McCarthy, N. (2008) "When could payments for environmental services benefit the poor?", *Environment and Development Economics* 13(3): 255-278.

CHAPTER 2

EXTERNALITIES, ENTITLEMENTS AND FUNDING OF PES – A THEORETICAL DISCUSSION

Note: This chapter is based upon Van Hecken, G. and Bastiaensen, J. (2010) "Payments for Ecosystem Services: A Political View of its Justification, or the Lack of it", *Environmental Science & Policy* 13(8): 785-792.

The chapter has benefited from useful comments and suggestions by Johan Bastiaensen and two anonymous reviewers. The research was funded by a Ph.D. grant of the Flemish Interuniversity Council (VLIR-UOS). The usual disclaimers apply.

1. INTRODUCTION

The previous chapter already argued that while the Coasean conceptualisation of PES is attractive at first sight, further reflection on its theoretical foundations and practical consequences is warranted. Recent contributions to the more critical PES literature already indicated some important issues that tend to be overlooked in a Coasean perspective. More specifically, payments and markets for ES are often represented as apolitical - and therefore potentially more sustainable - alternatives for engaging in environmental conservation (e.g. Pattanayak et al., 2010; Wunder, 2008). This view has been contested from various angles (Kosoy and Corbera, 2010; Muradian et al., 2010; Vatn, 2010). An explicit focus on distributional aspects is undertaken by Corbera et al. (2007a, 2007b) and Pascual et al. (2010), who refer to important interdependencies between efficiency and equity concepts in PES schemes. They argue that distributional aspects of payments are mostly subordinated to the efficiency criterion, and emphasise the role of the politico-institutional setting in determining the prevailing fairness criterion. Their analyses focus primarily on the participation of and distribution of payments among ES providers. The analysis presented in this chapter will broaden these critical political economy perspectives and will also explicitly focus on potential distributional consequences for ES buyers.

More specifically, the chapter focuses on two interconnected issues. The first (section 2) relates to the 'backbone' of PES approaches: its underlying externality framework. Closer scrutiny of the positive externality focus reveals how the 'technical' shift from a traditional focus on 'negative' externalities to 'positive' externalities is in fact based on real political choices (with real political consequences) - which are often overlooked in the PES debate (Vatn, 2010), or masked behind technical arguments related to efficiency optimisation. This 'positive' approach also entails important distributional consequences related to the funding characteristics of PES schemes. And this leads to the second issue: section 3 will argue that the focus on beneficiaries of ES contains the risk of perpetuating regressive financing of global commons by poor local communities. It underlines the importance of further reflections on global policy options and the cross-scale institutional design of PES schemes. These two issues for discussion in this chapter pave the way to the subsequent empirical chapters, which draw upon several of the (theoretical) insights that will now be articulated.

2. EXTERNALITIES AND ENVIRONMENTAL ENTITLEMENTS: TRICKY POLITICAL ISSUES

As has been indicated in chapter 1, positive externalities lie at the core of the PES approach. In particular, PES adherents propose that farmers should be regarded not as 'polluters' or 'destroyers of the environment', but rather as potential or unrecognised ES providers. This change of perspective is, however, not politically neutral. As will be argued further, it entails a conceptual shift with significant and largely undiscussed implications. At a more fundamental level, though, it should first of all be recalled that epistemologically the framing of environmental issues in terms of externalities tends to lock-in both problems and solutions (Vatn, 2005, 2009; Vatn and Bromley, 1997). According to the externality framework, it is indeed almost inevitable that the inexistence of appropriate price signals (for externalities) causes inappropriate individual actions leading to further environmental degradation. Unsurprisingly, the solution is found in PES. In this context, McAfee (1999: 151) warns that an exclusive reliance on the externality framework implicitly depoliticises environmentalism and that the creation of environmental markets 'offers a rationale for the illusion that biological diversity can be "saved" without fundamental changes in present distributions of political power' (see also Bakker, 2010; or Brockington et al., 2008). Fortunately, the realisation that environmental issues are not necessarily correctly understood in a 'simple' externality framework is gaining terrain, including among proponents of the Coasean PES approach, who argue that PES should be seen not as a stand-alone solution, but rather as an integral part of a broader policy approach that comprises a diversity of market and non-market interventions (Börner et al., 2010; Engel et al. 2008; Wunder, 2008).

Still, even with regard to the market-related aspects of such a broader policy approach, the externality framework itself leaves ample room for contradictory views. Important outstanding issues are, for example, how an externality should be defined, whether society should focus on positive or negative externalities, and the direct and indirect consequences this choice may entail. The PES approach argues that farmers switching to more environmentally sustainable land-use practices should be compensated for the positive externalities they provide to society. A first thing to note, however, is that an externality only exists if a third party is affected by it and if it is found to originate in a specific (economic) practice or activity. This, of course, depends on the appreciation of the relationship between human activity and its ecological/economic consequences. Therefore, whether a farmer is regarded as a polluter or an 'environmentalist' depends in the first place on our understanding of the effects of his or her economic actions on the surrounding ecosystem. The complex relationships between ecosystem functions (Kareiva et al., 2007), their context dependency (Kremen, 2005), and the still limited knowledge of their mutual interactions (Swift et al., 2004), make the existence of an externality and its assessment as positive or negative mainly subject to local perceptions, which are more often than not based on unproven local popular discourses (Rojas and Aylward, 2003). In the absence of unequivocal scientific evidence, the internalisation of one externality may then even lead to the creation of a new externality. The plantation of carbon sequestering tree species, for example, may increase carbon sequestration but simultaneously reduce biodiversity (Caparrós et al., 2010; Chisholm, 2010). These observations underline the important role of environmental science in informing society about the existence of certain externalities, and warn against the potentially perverse consequences of pseudo-scientific discourses (see below).

A second important question is how to qualify externalities as either positive or negative. In the context of land-use practices and from a Coasean PES perspective, Engel et al. (2008) recognise that both negative and positive externalities exist, but they implicitly claim that the focus of environmental programmes on positive or negative externalities is mainly an objective, technical condition, dictating where PES programmes should be concentrated in order to achieve maximum ecological impact per unit of funding. The key issue, however, is that the identification - or rather the definition - of the externality and its positive or negative characteristics is anything but a technical matter. As the following example illustrates, it may not be clear a priori whether externalities are positive or negative. Consider a farmer whose farm is geared entirely to the production of agricultural crops and who decides to replant the boundary hedges that have over the years been destroyed and replaced with barbed wire. Should the farmer be compensated for making a positive contribution to the environment? Or should one argue instead that farmers have a socially-limited entitlement over their land[24], which includes a moral and social duty to meet certain minimum environmental standards in the management of their farms? In the latter case, taxes might be imposed to compensate for the negative externalities generated by those falling short of the standard. In our example, the farmer may be granted a tax reduction or even exemption on the basis of the investment made in the hedges. According to this logic, PES to farmers could be seen as a 'bribe' by society in order to secure the supply of the service in question (Hanley et al., 1998), thereby extending rights to them that they arguably would never have had under existing

[24] With this term we refer to Sen's approach to entitlements, who defines entitlements as 'the set of alternative commodity bundles that a person can command in a society using the totality of rights and opportunities that he or she faces' (Sen, 1984: 497). In this context the term entitlements (and property rights) are thus used in a broad sense, indicating the 'real' set of rights that land owners have over their land (and over the natural resources present within the boundaries of their property), depending on formal and informal rules and norms, as well as social practices. In the context of environmental governance, a more specific definition can be obtained from Leach et al. (1999), who refer to environmental entitlements as the 'alternative sets of utilities derived from environmental goods and services over which social actors have legitimate effective command and which are instrumental in achieving wellbeing' (ibid: 233).

regulations. Moreover, from an efficiency point of view, it is often argued that, in order to maximise the environmental impact of PES, priority should be given to the most seriously degraded farms (Engel et al., 2008). This, however, effectively converts the 'Provider Gets Principle' into a 'Pay the Polluter Principle' (Hanley et al., 1998), which could be normatively disturbing, to say the least (Salzman, 2005).

So what is the most appropriate policy approach: to punish polluters or to pay providers? For a long time now, these issues have been at the centre of traditional economic debates between Coasean and Pigovian economists, provoking disagreements on the different policy implications of both positions. Pigou's (1920) analysis of externalities mainly leads to the conclusion that the state has an active corrective role to play by punishing the perpetrators of social disservices (Pigovian taxes) or by paying a bounty to actors that take measures to prevent the production of negative externalities (Pigovian subsidies). Coase (1960), on his turn, criticises the use of Pigovian taxes and subsidies and argues in his famous article that Pigovian measures do not lead to socially-optimal situations (ibid: 41-42). According to Coase, Pigovian analysis fails to recognise that externality problems have a reciprocal nature. He explains this by stating that:

> 'The question is commonly thought of as one in which A inflicts harm on B and what has to be decided is: how should we restrain A? But this is wrong. We are dealing with a problem of a reciprocal nature. To avoid the harm to B would inflict harm on A. The real question that has to be decided is: should A be allowed to harm B or should B be allowed to harm A?' (ibid: 2).

This important insight laid the foundation for the famous Coase theorem which states that in the presence of externalities, private negotiations between parties will lead to optimal social outcomes, independently of the initial allocation of property rights (ibid: 19). Vatn (2010), however, asserts that the policy implications of the Coase approach are not really relevant: 'As low transaction costs are illusory for most environmental goods, the Coasean model is relevant only for a very small number of cases' (ibid: 1247).

Moving beyond the traditional economic arguments, and expanding our analysis to other disciplinary perspectives, the broader academic literature suggests that either strategy (rewarding or punishing) is defensible to some extent, and that the categorisation of externalities - which will largely determine which policy is applied - is fundamentally based on the historical and socio-institutional evolution of entitlements, in particular property rights over land. Law scholars, such as for example Ellickson (1973), propose the 'normalcy' concept, whereby externalities are categorised by reference to a socially accepted norm or 'zero-reference' state. In this way, one can classify deviations from the reference state as either harmful (negative) or beneficial (positive) and determine the corresponding environmental entitlements. Young et al. (2003) - and later Earl et al. (2010) - further elaborate this concept in a duty-of-care approach, where land users have the obligation to 'take all reasonable and practical steps to prevent harm arising from their activities' (Young et al., 2003: 4). The social imperative of the duty-of-care principle partially substitutes for an approach based upon the internalisation of externalities, as it makes little sense to provide monetary incentives for what is regarded to be a social obligation. However, at the same time both approaches leave room for 'grey' areas of mixed responsibilities in between the two extremes: land users should be punished by society if management falls below the socially desirable level and rewarded if their management produces benefits above the minimum duty of care (Bromley and Hodge, 1990, as cited by Young et al., 2003).

Still from a legal perspective, but drawing again on the (social) cost efficiency criterion, Wittman (1984) points out that externality problems are inherently symmetric, implying that they can be viewed as either positive or negative and treated correspondingly, resulting in either the provision of subsidies or the imposition of taxes. Nonetheless, he claims that the existence of administrative (or transaction) costs tied to governance structures calls for a 'negative', minimum standard approach, since 'there would be low administrative costs if [a land owner] were charged only for acting inefficiently, a type of behaviour rare in comparison to acting efficiently' (ibid: 61). His implicit assumption, however, is that most people will comply with the minimum standard, such that positive payments would have to be made in numerous instances. In the case of the currently desired minimum environmental standards, this seems far from guaranteed. In fact, under certain conditions, Wittman's argument could convert itself into an argument in favour of the 'positive' approach, especially in settings (e.g. in remote regions in developing countries) where the imposition and enforcement of minimum standards by a capable and independent state is a far cry from reality. Hence, in the short run, the question of which is the more efficient approach would appear to be a simple empirical matter. In the longer term, however, one must also consider the issue of 'motivation crowding-out', i.e. the danger that monetary payments for actions that are to be regarded as 'normal' and 'to be expected from any full member of society' could contribute to the erosion of existing social norms (Frey and Oberholzer-Gee, 1997; Kosoy and Corbera, 2010; Van Hecken and Bastiaensen, 2010; on this issue see also chapter 3). If most people violate the socially desired minimum standards, it might indeed be more efficient to treat contributions to the environment that are well above those standards as positive externalities. However, this does of course raise fundamental questions about any dynamic effects on the public's respect for the minimum standards, and consequently also about the long-term efficiency of the approach. Paying for activities that are below the minimum standard - and are thus to be expected as a matter of routine - could eventually lead to implicit endorsement of the lower standards as *de facto* entitlements (Bénabou and Tirole, 2003).

Recognising that the efficiency criterion is just one among many others, the externality discussion can be elevated to yet another level. More specifically, the fairness perspective[25] gives rise to the important question of whether, or to what extent, it is fair to ask 'environmental service users' to pay for services they used to get 'for free', especially if those users contribute neither directly nor indirectly to environmental degradation. Is affordable access to clean water and air, for example, not the normal 'zero-reference' situation? In order to clarify this important point, it may be useful to consider another - simple yet illustrative - example. Suppose farmer A has two hectares of land, subdivided into one hectare of forest and one hectare of pasture on which is kept one cow. Further downstream live two urban dwellers (B and C), who are dependent for the provision of clean water on good upstream land stewardship. For A, deforestation of the one hectare would generate the extra income from one additional cow. Application of the positive externalities policy, which assesses the one hectare of forest as a form of land use creating positive externalities, would require the two urban dwellers jointly to pay the equivalent opportunity cost of the income of one cow to A in order to 'save' the forest and assure clean water provision. The distribution of the costs could then be proportional to the quantity of water consumed by each of urban dwellers A and B (in fact, this methodology is often used in hydrological PES schemes; see for example Kosoy et al., 2007 or Porras et al., 2008). Suppose B consumes 100 litres of water and C 200 litres. B would then be required to pay A the cow income equivalent of 0.33 cows, whereas C would have to pay A the income equivalent of 0.66 cows. But what if B is a carnivore and a heavy milk consumer, while C is a vegetarian or even a vegan? Is it then fair to expect a higher contribution from C, simply because he consumes more water? In fact, it could be argued that it would be fairer to charge a fee to the producer (farmer A), thereby forcing B - whose meat/milk consumption is driving the expansion of cattle raising (and thus deforestation) - to contribute more in compensation through increased meat and dairy prices[26]. Furthermore, in the likely case that demand for dairy is partially driven by world markets, this approach would

[25] Although 'fairness' is often related to 'equity', the two concepts are often confused. According to Corbera et al. (2007b: 589) 'equity relates to the distribution of socio-economic factors and goods in a society according to an agreed set of principles or criteria'. As De Herdt and D'Exelle (2009: 152) assert: '"*Fair*" is something we ask others to be. It is an injunction to act in a particular way.' It has to do with accepted and acceptable behaviour according to certain social rules, like, for example, the right to a reward proportional to your efforts or the duty not to impose harm on others.

[26] The example refers to a user-financed PES system, but a similar reasoning can obviously be applied to government-financed systems, where it is the taxpayer who finances the compensation.

spread the cost of the externality over additional numbers of foreign meat and dairy consumers.

In the example, therefore, the positive externality approach does not seem to address the core of the problem, but would rather appear to be looking for solutions at a level that is detached from the actual drivers of the environmental problem. Usually, the PES approach searches for demand-side funding, based on who benefits the most from the ES, while ignoring the fact that fairness might dictate that the funding issue should be addressed at the level of the driving forces, i.e. by considering who is directly or indirectly responsible for the undersupply of the ES. In this respect, a negative Pigovian externality-cum-tax approach would be a fairer conservation tool, at least if it were possible to properly and universally tie it to the commodities that (indirectly) cause the negative public externality. This last principle would allow one to raise environmental funds, irrespective of the exact nature of the public services the particular piece of forest offers to society. This would at least partly resolve the free-riding problem (see chapter 1) that is artificially created by a focus on impacts rather than on drivers of environmental degradation. These insights also underline the potential perverse effects of using or promoting institutional mechanisms that capitalise on individual rationality for making decisions concerning public goods (Vatn, 2009).

Summarising the above arguments, we note that the implementation of PES mechanisms has important implications on the *de facto* legitimacy of the underlying actions (see also Corbera et al., 2007a). The key issue lies with the social limits of private property rights. Determining the appropriate characterisation of an externality is therefore not so much an objective, technical assignment as a tricky political and moral question. Salzman (2005) therefore concludes that the categorisation of externalities 'turns less on biophysical measures or ecological modelling than on our sense of what the allocation and definition of entitlements ought to look like and how they should change over time. These questions, in the end, are value judgements' (ibid: 960, emphasis added, see also Vatn and Bromley, 1997 and Farley and Costanza, 2010)[27]. The prioritisation of certain criteria above others is, in other words, a largely subjective matter, even if it is often deceitfully naturalised as a scientific truth or instance of common sense. Such a representation corresponds to the view of (institutional) ecological economists, who argue that the superiority of institutional solutions for all sorts of environmental degradation, based solely on efficiency criteria, is in fact an ideological claim (Bromley, 1990; Paavola and Adger, 2005; Vatn, 2005, 2009). Such naturalisations and black-boxing indeed

[27] In fact, Coase himself also argued that the choice among different social arrangements should not be confined to analyses in strict efficiency terms, but 'must ultimately dissolve into a study of aesthetics and morals' (Coase, 1960: 43).

constitute the ideological basis of the power vested in particular institutional structures in society (Bourdieu, 1990).

3. PES: A LOCAL BILL FOR A GLOBAL FREE LUNCH?

The positive externality approach of PES also entails both a need and an opportunity to find and exploit hitherto unclaimed private funds for environmental conservation and restoration (Pagiola and Platais, 2007; Pattanayak et al., 2010). Again, though, this is not as innocent a proposition as it appears. In a way, the PES approach emphasises that it is unsustainable, inefficient and possibly unfair from an ethical point of view to place the burden of conservation entirely upon local land users by 'expropriating' or 'attenuating' part of their property rights. As indicated above, such a privatisation of society's natural resources is far from evident and warrants explicit political discussion, whereby due account must be taken of the income level and social status of the land users concerned. Whether or not based upon social considerations relating to the relative affluence or poverty of the land-user providing the ES (Landell-Mills and Porras, 2002; Pagiola et al., 2005), PES adherents argue that the beneficiaries of the positive externalities ought to pay for their provision (Engel et al., 2008; Wunder, 2005).

Simultaneously it is recognised that, by pushing conservation into a 'conditional' market context, PES programmes generally require ongoing rather than finite payments[28] (Pagiola et al., 2002). As such, the short-term-project nature of most current, usually government-funded, PES schemes leads to unsustainable outcomes, so that additional long-term funding must be secured in order to turn current pilot projects into longer-term sustainable PES systems. One promising avenue for achieving this goal is through negotiations with interested private service users (Engel et al., 2008; Pagiola et al., 2007; Wunder et al., 2008). Those who directly benefit from the ES, not the government as a proxy for the users, should bear the cost. As ES are supplied at different spatial scales, it seems fair that global services, such as biodiversity protection and carbon sequestration, should be globally funded, while local benefits, such as watershed services or scenic beauty, should be financed locally. But there is the rub.

Private funding opportunities are still very unbalanced across different geographical scales (Balmford and Whitten, 2003; Farley et al., 2010). Budget-constrained governments in developing countries allocate only very limited funds to natural resource protection (Balmford et al., 2003). At a more global level, funding options are also limited. Existing funding mechanisms are currently mainly restricted to voluntary markets and some scarce examples of forestry projects financed through the Clean Development Mechanism (CDM) (Pagiola et al., 2007; Thomas et

[28] It should be noted that there are exceptions to this rule, especially if promoted land uses are privately profitable for the land user, as for example in the case of silvopastoral practices, which generally enhance farm productivity in the longer term (see chapter 3).

al., 2010). As further noted by Pagiola et al. (2007) other international structures, such as the Global Environment Facility (GEF) and environmental NGOs also tend to have limited financial means and generally only provide short-term funding. Nevertheless, increasing efforts are focused on establishing additional global funding systems through the concept of international payments for environmental services (IPES), the main aim of which is 'to build compensation mechanisms for ES whose benefits are enjoyed by those far removed from the place that generates the services' (UNEP-IUCN, 2006, as cited in Huberman, 2009: 458). The main idea of IPES is to complement the currently limited ES market initiatives by 'a scaling-up of the core "upstream-downstream" PES model to fit into a "North-South" approach', mainly in the realm of biodiversity conservation (Huberman, 2009: 458). Although this conceptual idea is gaining global momentum (manifested most clearly in the ongoing negotiations on international payments for REDD under the United Nations Framework Convention on Climate Change), the perspectives of finding sustainable long-term global funding for ES still look bleak, especially in the short term. Clements (2010), for example, indicates some of the difficulties in establishing REDD:

> 'Successful establishment of the REDD mechanism is dependent on the willingness of developed countries to pay for REDD, or willingness to establish markets for REDD credits ... At the same time the challenge for developing countries is to put together credible institutions to manage and implement REDD, including transfer of incentives to appropriate local stakeholders. Institutional reform is likely to be a slow process and should be driven by developing countries.' (ibid: 310).

Other studies have also indicated the many difficulties in establishing global funding mechanisms, and refer to barriers such as political struggles, limited human and technical capacity, restricted funding, high transaction costs and strict rules and conditionality tied to funding (e.g. Farley et al., 2010; Krey, 2004; Thomas et al., 2010). Furthermore, voluntary markets, such as the Chicago Climate Exchange, are promising avenues for international funding, but are currently largely restricted to the trade in greenhouse gas emissions.

As a consequence, expectations for new and sustainable 'fund-raising' in the context of PES are often focused on local communities. Budget and transfer constraints often oblige PES implementers to focus on potential local funds, and hence on local demand (Pagiola et al., 2007). Moreover, recent publications have argued that such local user-financed mechanisms would be more efficient and sustainable than government-financed schemes (Engel et al., 2008; Pagiola et al., 2007; Wunder et al., 2008), and would also be less vulnerable to volatile national and international political conditions (Blackman and Woodward, 2010; Pattanayak et al., 2010; Wunder, 2008). Wunder et al. (2008), for example, in their broad overview of current PES initiatives, observe an increasing tendency to transform government-financed PES programmes into user-financed programmes, which 'are attempting to develop additional financing sources from individual ES users to complement their public financing' (ibid: 851). According to Blackman and Woodward (2010), the World Bank is currently supporting the expansion of the user-financed components of national PES programmes in several Latin American countries. This local focus often directs attention to watershed services (as opposed to carbon or biodiversity services), since these offer the clearest and most valued locally-perceived benefits (Engel et al., 2008; Pagiola et al., 2007; Porras et al., 2008). Continuous and qualitative water provision to water users then 'constitutes a convenient lasting payment vehicle' that would allow other more global benefits such as biodiversity conservation 'to piggyback on these more marketable forest services' (Wunder and Wertz-Kanounnikoff, 2009: 585).

In conjunction with the promotion of the positive externality approach, this increasing search for and growing faith in local funding raises concerns in terms of the potential dispossession of local communities, especially if located in poor countries. Expecting poor local households, irrigating farmers or small businesses to pay for locally-generated upstream ES because of the (temporary) absence of international funding makes a dangerously biased and arbitrary abstraction of the 'joint production and consumption' nature of different ecosystem benefits. The complex relationships within and between different ecosystems (Kareiva et al., 2007; Kremen, 2005; Swift et al., 2004) make it practically impossible to meaningfully segregate or 'unbundle' different ES in order to sell them as separate services on different markets (Brockington et al., 2008; Vatn, 2009). The fact that a PES scheme can hardly ever take into account and provide compensation for all the ES provided seems indeed to be problematic. While it may well be the case that a forest is responsible for local people's water provision, the same forest inevitably also offers other global externalities, such as biodiversity and carbon sequestration, and a whole range of other services that even scientists are probably not aware of. In Mexico's national PES programme, for example, Corbera et al. (2009) note that 'what constitutes an ES has been influenced by the preferences of those actors involved in PES design' (ibid: 757). This would seem to indicate once again that the economic concept of externalities is misleading and ultimately based on political choices. If sheer reliance on local demand of arbitrarily chosen ES is applied to guarantee ecosystem conservation, then the extraction of funds out of the local community threatens widening the existing regressive financing of local conservation efforts that contribute to global benefits (Balmford and Whitten, 2003; Barrett et al., 2001). The internalisation of some environmental values but not others, may not only have potential detrimental impacts for ecosystems (Caparrós et al., 2010; Chisholm, 2010), but is thus also likely to generate important negative social consequences.

Moreover, in order to kindle the necessary interest of private funders, PES programmes often draw on so-called 'spectacles' (Igoe, 2010) or certain pseudo-scientific representations of nature, which tend to offer rather populist explanations of the way certain land uses result in the production of specific ecosystem benefits. Especially in the promotion of local watershed schemes, a recurring narrative is that forest cover contributes to the 'production' of improved water quality and quantity (Wilk, 2000). However, recent scientific contributions challenge these popular discourses, and clearly indicate that the precise effects of forest cover on water quality and quantity are very unpredictable and highly site-specific (Bruijnzeel et al., 2005; Grip et al., 2005). Nevertheless, and despite the absence of good empirical data, many (international) NGOs and other project implementers often legitimise their environmental projects by referring to watershed benefits as a major argument for conserving large areas of upland forests (Rojas and Aylward, 2003; Kosoy et al., 2007; Sayer, 1995).

The promotion of locally-funded PES systems on the basis of uncertain ES arguments therefore risks discarding global responsibility and making poor local people pay for a number of uncertain ES to which hitherto they enjoyed free, if perhaps limited, access. Clearly one cannot ethically expect local people in developing countries, who are often already struggling to survive, to bear the financial burden of conservation simply because they happen to have a need for a specific local ES. It seems unjustifiable to arbitrarily select locally-created externalities and ask local people to pay for the opportunity cost of conserving an ecosystem merely on the basis of the (perhaps even incorrect) argument that they are the principal beneficiaries of those few 'hand-picked' ES among many other - unidentified or even identified - simultaneously generated services. The promotion of such localised user-financed PES systems would actually boil down to dispossessing local communities of their natural resources, while maintaining or even increasing global free-riding on local efforts. Of course, matters would be quite different in a situation where the PES come from rich global ES users and the payments are transferred to a host of smaller-scale, poor ES providers, particularly if this were to result in the bundling or layering of different ES in synergetic local and global markets. However, the predominant market discourse in PES and its focus on (the price of) the ES as such, and not so much on the social nature of the ES buyers, contributes to the danger of misappropriation of the PES and the further dispossession of the poor. The question of who pays and who benefits clearly needs to be addressed as a priority when evaluating proposals for the organisation of PES schemes, or in the words of Corbera et al., 2007a):

> 'In focusing on markets in resource situations such as multiple use forests, it is important that the legitimacy and equity dimensions of these actions are made central

to discussions that affect large-scale environmental changes and significant marginalized populations. Otherwise, emerging markets may only contribute to reinforcing existing inequalities in access to environmental resources and decision making' (ibid: 608-609).

4. CONCLUSION

The notion of environmental externalities and the realisation of a need to correct ensuing market failures are at the centre of the PES approach. They give rise to an argument for the creation of markets or quasi-markets in ES, so that externalities would be internalised and private benefits brought more in line with social shadow prices. In practice, PES mechanisms focus on payments for positive externalities, i.e. for ES that are provided by land-users, who might otherwise prefer not to generate them at all. On closer scrutiny, there is, however, nothing innocent about these simple and attractive ideas. It is indeed not a priori clear whether the provision of an ES should be regarded as the generation of 'additional' positive externalities or merely as inherent in observing one's duty as a caretaker of society's natural resources. It depends largely on one's view on property rights and entitlements, and to what extent these entail the right to unfettered exploitation of available natural resources, even beyond sustainability levels. The key question is how to determine the 'zero-reference' situation in this respect. This will ultimately dictate who must pay for the ES: the ES user, for the benefit enjoyed from its production, or the ES provider, for the right not to provide it. If one does not expect land-users to observe (minimal) environmental standards, then all of the ES provided may be regarded as positive externalities to be rewarded. This is the position that most PES applications seem to adopt, with occasional reference being made to the poverty of the ES providers. In the name of maximising impact, one even ends up rewarding precisely those who have already destroyed most of the natural resources. Closer examination shows that this option involves an implicit, but very real political choice, which obviously needs to be discussed in a transparent fashion and should not be hidden behind the technical façade of environmental impact maximisation per unit of funding.

What applies to the funding of the supply side of the ES also holds with regard to the origin of the funding. This is not just a technical matter of finding sources of sustainable funding for PES schemes and their impact on the environment. In particular, the 'spontaneous' tendency towards locally-funded PES schemes for apparent operational reasons is quite questionable, since it boils down to denying local ES users continued free access to previously freely available ES, while maintaining or even increasing global free-riding on the environmental investment of local communities. This also raises important questions on what are the precise motives behind the creation of local PES schemes. While we would not go so far as to claim that all PES efforts are consciously created with the aim of piggybacking on local communities' efforts, we do, however, want to stress that due attention should be devoted to avoiding such dynamics, especially if they are legitimised by unproven assertions on the link between certain land use practices and ecosystem benefits.

Processes of decentralisation - especially if they are motivated by market logic - might then lead to a world in which the 'burden of conservation' is increasingly carried by the poor (Muradian et al., 2010).

To be sure, PES schemes (and their associated focus on rewarding positive externalities) have the potential to make a valuable contribution to both the environment and social justice, especially if they can be organised in such a way that rich ES users from the developed world - who are, for that matter, historically responsible for most ES depletion on a planetary scale - contribute to supporting poor ES providers in the developing world. However, - and especially in the absence of well-functioning global financing mechanisms -, framing the problem as a technical externality issue of matching supply of and demand for virtually-created ES as isolated items in separated markets is not helpful for avoiding unwanted social distortions that could lead to the dispossession of the poor and further free-riding by the rich. Instead, it should be acknowledged that payments and markets for ES are not 'objective' or 'neutral' tools that merely fulfil the job of capturing conservation funds and spending them in the most efficient way; they are based on real political decisions and therefore they need to be recognised and openly discussed as such.

REFERENCES

Bakker, K. (2010) "The limits of 'neoliberal natures': Debating green neoliberalism", *Progress in Human Geography*, doi: 10.1177/0309132510376849.

Balmford, A. and Whitten, T. (2003) "Who should pay for tropical conservation, and how could the costs be met?", *Oryx* 37(2): 238-250.

Balmford, A., Gaston, K.J., Blyth, S., James, A. and Kapos, V. (2003) "Global variation in conservation costs, conservation benefits, and unmet conservation needs", *Proceedings of the National Academy of Sciences, USA* 100(3): 1046-1050.

Barrett, C.B., Brandon, K., Gibson, C. and Gjertsen, H. (2001) "Conserving tropical biodiversity amid weak institutions", *BioScience* 51(6): 497-502.

Bénabou, R. and Tirole, J. (2003) "Intrinsic and extrinsic motivation", *Review of Economic Studies* 70: 489-520.

Blackman, A. and Woodward, R.T. (2010) "User financing in a national payments for environmental services program: Costa Rican hydropower", *Ecological Economics* 69: 1626-1638.

Blaikie, P. (2006) "Is small really beautiful? Community-based natural resource management in Malawi and Botswana", *World Development* 34(11): 1942-1957.

Börner, J., Wunder, S., Wertz-Kanounnikoff, S., Rügnitz Tito, M., Pereira, L. and Nascimento, N. (2010) "Direct conservation payments in the Brazilian Amazon: Scope and equity implications", *Ecological Economics* 69(6): 1272-1282.

Bourdieu, P. (1990) *The Logic of Practice*, Cambridge: Polity Press.

Brockington, D., Duffy, D. and Igoe, J. (2008) Nature Unbound. Conservation, Capitalism and the Future of Protected Areas, London: Earthscan.

Bromley, D.W. (1990) "The ideology of efficiency: Searching for a theory of policy analysis", *Journal of Environmental Economics and Management* 19: 86-107.

Bromley, D.W. and Hodge, I. (1990) "Private property rights and presumptive policy entitlements: reconsidering the premises of rural policy", *European Review of Agricultural Economics* 17: 197-214.

Bruijnzeel, L.A., Bonell, M., Gilmour, D., and Lamb, D. (2005) "Forests, water and people in the humid tropics: an emerging view", in: Bonell, M. and Bruijnzeel, L. (eds.) *Forests, Water and People in the Humid Tropics,* Cambridge and Paris: Cambridge University Press/UNESCO.

Caparrós, A., Cerdá, E., Ovando, P. and Campos, P. (2010) "Carbon Sequestration with Reforestations and Biodiversity-scenic Values", *Environmental and Resource Economics* 45: 49-72.

Chisholm, R.A. (2010) "Trade-offs between ecosystem services: Water and carbon in a biodiversity hotspot", *Ecological Economics* 69: 1973-1987.

Clements, T. (2010) "Reduced Expectations: the political and institutional challenges of REDD+", *Oryx* 44(3): 309-310.

Coase, R.H. (1960) "The problem of social cost", *Journal of Law and Economics* 3: 1-44.

Corbera, E., Brown, K. and Adger, W.N. (2007a) "The equity and legitimacy of markets for ecosystem services", *Development and Change* 38(4): 587-613.

Corbera, E., Kosoy, N., Martínez Tuna, M. (2007b) "Equity implications of marketing ecosystem services in protected areas and rural communities: Case studies from Meso-America", *Global Environmental Change* 17(3-4): 365-380.

Corbera, E., González Soberanis, C. and Brown, K. (2009) "Institutional dimensions of payments for ecosystem services. An analysis of Mexico's carbon forestry programme", *Ecological Economics* 68: 743–761.

De Herdt, T. and D'Exelle, B. (2009) "Fairness", in J. Peil and I. Van Staveren (eds.), *Handbook of Economics and Ethics* (pp. 152-158), Cheltenham U.K.: Edward Elgar.

Earl, G., Curtis, A. and Allan, C. (2010) "Towards a duty of care for biodiversity", *Environmental Management* 45: 682-696.

Ellickson, R.C. (1973) "Alternatives to zoning: Covenants, nuisance rules, and fines as land use controls", *The University of Chicago Law Review* 40(4): 681-781.

Engel, S., Pagiola, S. and Wunder, S. (2008) "Designing payments for environmental services in theory and practice: an overview of the issues", *Ecological Economics* 65: 663–675.

Farley, J. and Costanza, R. (2010) "Payments for ecosystem services: from local to global", *Ecological Economics* 69: 2060-2068.

Farley, J., Aquino, A., Daniels, A., Moulaert, A., Lee, D. and Krause, A. (2010) "Global mechanisms for sustaining and enhancing PES schemes", *Ecological Economics* 69: 2075-2084.

Frey, B.S. and Oberholzer-Gee, F. (1997) "The cost of price incentives: An empirical analysis of motivation crowding-out", *American Economic Review* 87: 746–755.

Grip, H., Fritsch, J.M. and Bruijnzeel, L. (2005) "Soil and Water Impacts during Forest Conversion and Stabilization to New Land Use", in: Bonell, M. and Bruijnzeel, L. (eds.) *Forests, Water and People in the Humid Tropics,* Cambridge and Paris: Cambridge University Press/UNESCO.

Hanley, N., Kirkpatrick, H., Simpson, I. and Oglethorpe, D. (1998) "Principles for the provision of public goods from agriculture: Modelling Moorland Conservation in Scotland", *Land Economics* 74(1): 102-113.

Huberman, D. (2009) "World Heritage Sites and the Integration of Biodiversity into an international PES framework", *Journal of Sustainable Forestry* 28: 456-480.

Igoe, J.J. (2010) "The Spectacle of Nature in the Global Economy of Appearances: Anthropological Engagements with the Spectacular Mediations of Transnational Conservation", *Critique of Anthropology* 30(4).

Kareiva, P., Watts, S., McDonald, R. and Boucher, T. (2007) "Domesticated Nature: Shaping Landscapes and Ecosystems for Human Welfare", *Science* 316: 1866-1869.

Kosoy, N. and Corbera, E. (2010) "Payments for ecosystem services as commodity fetishism", *Ecological Economics* 69(6): 1228–1236.

Kosoy, N., Martinez-Tuna, M., Muradian, R. and Martinez-Alier, J. (2007) "Payments for environmental services in watersheds: Insights from a comparative study of three cases in Central America", *Ecological Economics* 61: 446-455.

Kremen, C. (2005) "Managing ecosystem services: what do we need to know about their ecology?", *Ecology Letters* 8: 468-479.

Krey, M. (2004) "Transaction Costs of CDM Projects in India – An Empirical Survey", HWWA Report 238, Hamburg: Hamburg Institute of International Economics.

Landell-Mills, N. and Porras, I. (2002) Silver Bullet or Fools' Gold? A Global Review of Markets for Forest Environmental Services and Their Impact on the Poor, London: IIED.

Leach, M., Mearns, R. and Scoones, I. (1999) "Environmental entitlements: Dynamics and institutions in community-based natural resource management", *World Development* 27(2): 225-247.

McAfee, K. (1999) "Selling nature to save it? Biodiversity and green developmentalism", *Environment and Planning D: Society and Space* 17(2): 133–154.

Muradian, R., Corbera, E., Pascual, U., Kosoy, N. and May, P. (2010) "Reconciling theory and practice: An alternative conceptual framework for understanding payments for environmental services", *Ecological Economics* 69(6): 1202–1208.

Paavola, J. and Adger, N.W. (2005) "Institutional ecological economics", *Ecological Economics* 53: 353-368.

Pagiola, S. and Platais, G. (2007) *Payments for Environmental Services: From Theory to Practice*, Washington D.C.: World Bank.

Pagiola, S., Bishop, J. and Landell-Mills, N. (eds.) (2002) Selling forest environmental services. Market-based mechanisms for conservation and development, London: Earthscan.

Pagiola, S., Arcenas, A. and Platais, G. (2005) "Can payments for environmental services help reduce poverty? An exploration of the issues and the evidence to date from Latin America", *World Development* 33(2): 237-253.

Pagiola, S., Ramírez, E., Gobbi, J., de Haan, C., Ibrahim, M., Murgueitio, E. and Ruíz, J. (2007) "Paying for the environmental services of silvopastoral practices in Nicaragua", *Ecological Economics* 64: 374–385.

Pascual, U., Muradian, R., Rodríguez, L.C. and Duraiappan, A. (2010) "Exploring the links between equity and efficiency in payments for environmental services: a conceptual approach", *Ecological Economics* 69: 1237-1244.

Pattanayak, S.K., Wunder, S. and Ferraro, P.J. (2010) "Show me the money: do payments supply environmental services in developing countries?" *Review of Environmental Economics and Policy* 4(2): 254-274.

Pigou, A.C. (1920) *The Economics of Welfare*, London: MacMillan.

Porras, I., Grieg-Gran, M. and Neves, N. (2008) *All that glitters: A review of payments for watershed services*, London: International Institute for Environment and Development (IIED).

Robalino, J., Pfaff, A., Sánchez-Azofeifa, G.A., Alpízar, F., León, C. and Rodríguez, C.M. (2008) "Deforestation impacts of environmental services payments: Costa Rica's PSA Program 2000-2005", Discussion Paper 2008-24: Environment for Development.

Rojas, M. and Aylward, B. (2003) "What are we learning from experiences with markets for environmental services in Costa Rica? A review and critique of the literature", Markets for Environmental Services N°2, London: International Institute for Environment and Development.

Salzman, J. (2005) "Creating markets for ecosystem services: notes from the field", *New York University Law Review* 80: 870–961.

Sayer, J.A. (1995) "Science and International Nature Conservation", Occasional Paper No.4, Bogor, Indonesia: CIFOR.

Sen, A.K. (1984) Resources, Values and Development, Oxford: Blackwell.

Swift, M.J., Izac, A.-M.N. and van Noordwijk, M. (2004) "Biodiversity and ecosystem services in agricultural landscapes – Are we asking the right questions?", *Agriculture, Ecosystems and Environment* 104: 113-134.

Thomas, S., Dargusch, P., Harrison, S. and Herbohnet, J. (2010) "Why are there so few afforestation and reforestation Clean Development Mechanism projects?", *Land Use Policy* 27(3): 880–887.

Van Hecken, G. and Bastiaensen, J. (2010) "Payments for Ecosystem Services in Nicaragua: Do Market-Based Approaches Work?" *Development and Change* 41(3): 421-444.

Vatn, A. (2005) "Rationality, institutions and environmental policy", *Ecological Economics* 55: 203-217.

Vatn, A. (2009) "An institutional analysis of methods for environmental appraisal", *Ecological Economics* 68: 2207-2215.

Vatn, A. (2010) "An institutional analysis of payments for environmental services", *Ecological Economics* 69(6): 1245-1252.

Vatn, A. and Bromley, D.W. (1997) "Externalities – A market model failure", *Environmental and Resource Economics* 9: 135-151.

Wilk, J. (2000) "Local perceptions about forests and water in two tropical catchments", *GeoJournal* 50: 339-347.

Wittman, D. (1984) "Liability for harm or restitution for benefit?", *Journal of Legal Studies* 13: 57-80.

Wunder, S. (2005) "Payments for environmental services: some nuts and bolts", CIFOR Occasional Paper 42, Jakarta, CIFOR.

Wunder, S. (2008) "Necessary Conditions for Ecosystem Service Payments", Paper presented at the Workshop on Economics and Conservation in the Tropics: a Strategy Dialogue, San Francisco, USA, 31 January–1 February, 2008.

Wunder, S. and Wertz-Kanounnikoff, S. (2009) "Payments for ecosystem services: a new way of conserving biodiversity in forests", *Journal of Sustainable Forestry* 28(3-5): 576-596.

Wunder, S., Engel, S. and Pagiola, S. (2008) "Taking stock: A comparative analysis of payments for environmental services programs in developed and developing countries", *Ecological Economics* 65: 834-852.

Young, M., Shi, T. and Crosthwaite, J. (2003) *Duty of care: An instrument for increasing the effectiveness of catchment management*. Department of Sustainability and Environment, State of Victoria, Melbourne.

CHAPTER 3

A CRITICAL ASSESSMENT OF SUPPLY SIDE CHARACTERISTICS IN PES – THE RISEMP CASE IN MATIGUÁS-RÍO BLANCO, NICARAGUA

Note: This chapter is based upon Van Hecken, G., and Bastiaensen, J. (2010) "Payments for Ecosystem Services in Nicaragua: Do Market-based Approaches Work?", *Development and Change* 41(3): 421-444; and Van Hecken, G. and Bastiaensen, J. (2009) "The Potential and Limitations of Markets and Payments for Ecosystem Services in Agricultural Landscape Restoration: Critical Reflections Inspired by an Assessment of the RISEMP Program in Matiguás-Río Blanco, Nicaragua", IDPM-UA Discussion Paper 2009-02, Antwerp: Institute of Development Policy and Management.

The chapter has benefited from useful comments and suggestions by Johan Bastiaensen, Kathleen McAfee, Jos Vaessen, and two anonymous reviewers. It has also benefited from fruitful discussions with participants at the Study Day of the Belgian Latin Americanist Association (Leuven, December 2008), the Institute of Development Policy and Management (IOB) Doctoral Seminar (Antwerp, December 2008), the Annual Meeting of the Association of American Geographers (Washington D.C., April 2010), and the Workshop on Microfinance and Environment: Informal and Formal Financing of Ecosystem Services for Poverty Alleviation (Oxford, December 2010). The research was funded by a Ph.D. grant of the Flemish Interuniversity Council (VLIR-UOS). Our gratitude also goes to the Nitlapán staff for their collaboration. Special thanks go to Arturo Grigsby, Elías Ramírez, Yuri Marín, Omar Dávila and Alfredo Woo for providing us with detailed project information and constructive comments during the process of our field research. The usual disclaimers apply.

1. INTRODUCTION

This first empirical chapter assesses PES from a supply side perspective, and investigates the motivational aspects underlying farmers' adoption of environmentally-sound land use practices. It is based on an extensive field study of the Nicaraguan component of the recently concluded 'Regional Integrated Silvopastoral Ecosystem Management Project' (RISEMP), implemented from 2002 until 2008 in three Latin American countries (Nicaragua, Costa Rica and Colombia) under the auspices of the Global Environment Facility (GEF) and the World Bank. The project used PES to induce adoption of silvopastoral practices among farmers, and can be considered as one of the main pioneering pilot attempts to quantitatively investigate the potential of direct financial incentives in agricultural landscape restoration. Through an experimental approach the project attempted to separate the intervention's impact from confounders[29]; this, it was hoped, would contribute to the understanding of the effect of specific variables (mainly payments and technical assistance) on pro-environmental behaviour. The project formed part of a broader PES portfolio of the GEF and the World Bank (GEF, 2007a; World Bank, 2010), who both assumed a central role in the development of payment schemes for environmental services of global scope[30] (Gutman and Davidson, 2007).

Focusing primarily on efficiency and market considerations and assuming that human behaviour is mainly underpinned by profit-maximising motives, RISEMP presents a clear example of the 'environmental economics' or Coasean approach to PES. This central assumption was translated in the applied randomised experimental research set-up, which is useful for investigating the correlation between a specific (and therefore limited) set of variables and which, in the case of RISEMP, concentrated on the effect of payments with and without technical assistance. An initial assessment of the experimental data of the Nicaraguan component of the project (Pagiola et al., 2007) claimed to have found evidence of the positive role of financial incentives in the adoption of the envisaged silvopastoral practices and suggested that technical assistance may have played only a limited role. As will be explained below, regrettable but possibly inevitable flaws in the implementation of

[29] In the experimental literature, confounders 'are factors or events that also affect the measured outcomes and are correlated with the intervention' (Pattanayak et al., 2010: 261). 'Confounding can be caused by contemporaneous changes in conditions that affect outcomes, or by participants differing from non-participants in economic or psychosocial factors that affect the outcomes' (ibid: 261).

[30] Some authors attribute the World Bank's and the GEF's interest in developing PES to the central role that these multilateral organisations (should) play in international funding for the environment (e.g. Gutman and Davidson, 2007). They argue that these organisations should therefore play an active role in the development of and experiments with new funding mechanisms for the provision of globally important environmental services. Other authors (e.g. McAfee, 1999; Ervine, 2010) attribute the interest of these organisations in developing PES to the underlying neoliberal philosophy which typically characterises these organisations.

the experiment, however, do not allow to unequivocally attribute the observed changes to 'payments' only. Our reassessment from a broader institutional perspective will qualify Pagiola et al.'s claims and broadens the analysis by bringing in additional explanatory variables that may have played an at least equally important role in changing farmers' behaviour as the monetary incentives. Thus we hope to demonstrate how a broader institutional approach to PES (and environmental governance in general) can help to come to grips with some of the broader dynamics that have taken place, and to link PES design and performance to a broader rural development strategy.

After this introduction, the next section describes the main characteristics of the RISEMP and its Nicaraguan pilot site and participants, as well as the methodology used. The main results of the project are discussed in section 3, which first presents the 'official' land use data, and then reassesses the most important land use changes from a number of additional perspectives, as well as the farmers' main motivations for these changes. Section 4 places the empirical results in a broader theoretical framework. More specifically, it focuses on the potential of PES in stimulating cross-farm cooperation and on the effects of market-based institutions on different types of motivation. Empirical and theoretical reflections will both lead to some important conclusions that seem to confirm our central proposition on the need for a reconceptualisation of PES within a broader institutional framework.

2. THE RISEMP IN MATIGUÁS-RÍO BLANCO

2.1. PROJECT DESCRIPTION AND SITE CHARACTERISTICS

The RISEMP started in July 2002 and was concluded in January 2008. The project, a GEF/World Bank initiative, was an innovative pilot experiment aimed at promoting silvopastoral practices[31] in degraded pasture areas through PES (generated by these practices) and technical assistance (TA). The targeted ES were biodiversity conservation and carbon sequestration. At a later stage, hydrological services were also included. The project took place in Nicaragua, Costa Rica and Colombia, and was managed by the World Bank. Country sites were managed by local non-governmental organisations. For the three countries, the project had an estimated total budget of US$ 8.7 million, of which US$ 4.8 million was financed by a GEF grant and US$ 3.9 million through co-financing[32] (GEF, 2007b; Vaessen and Van Hecken, 2009; World Bank, 2002).

Despite their long-term on-site private benefits, silvopastoral practices tend to be unattractive to farmers (Pagiola et al., 2007). The main barriers to the adoption of more environmentally-friendly silvopastoral practices are the requirement of substantial capital and labour investments, and the long time-lag between investment and productivity increase (Dagang and Nair, 2003). The main objectives of the RISEMP were to demonstrate and to measure (1) the effects of the introduction of PES on the adoption by farmers of integrated silvopastoral farming systems in degraded pasture lands; and (2) the resulting improvements in the functioning of ecosystems, global environmental benefits, and local socio-economic gains resulting from the provision of these services (World Bank, 2002). To a large extent both issues constituted unexplored territories for research and they illustrate the innovative nature of the project (Vaessen and Van Hecken, 2009). However, it was not only the objects of research that were innovative; also the research methodology, which - at least in theory - was based on a randomised experimental design with various participant groups receiving different incentives (payments and/or TA) or no intervention at all (the control group), was unique (Greenstone and Gayer, 2009; Vaessen and Van Hecken, 2009). The experimental design was conceived so as to make it possible to attribute changes to different types of

[31] Dagang and Nair (2003: 149) define silvopastoral systems as 'systems [that] integrate trees into livestock systems for multiple purposes including soil amelioration, shade, fodder, fruit, wood, and habitat for fauna'. According to Pagiola et al. (2008: 304) silvopastoral practices include '(1) planting high densities of trees and shrubs in pastures, thus providing shade and diet supplements while protecting the soil from packing and erosion; (2) cut and carry systems, in which livestock is fed with the foliage of specifically planted trees and shrubs ("fodder banks") in areas previously used for other agricultural practices; and (3) using fast-growing trees and shrubs for fencing and wind screens'.

[32] In other words, the project was thus government-financed, trying to achieve global ecological benefits with global GEF funds.

incentives. It was hoped that, through the use of scientific methods, it might be possible to create a precedent, which would finally separate the impact from a PES intervention from confounders, and could serve to promote further replication of the PES approach throughout the rest of the (developing) world.

In Nicaragua the project was implemented by the research and development institute Nitlapán of the Universidad Centroamericana (UCA) and the Costa Rican-based research centre CATIE[33]. It took place in two micro-watersheds (Bulbul and Paiwas) in the central region of Matiguás-Río Blanco, department of Matagalpa, 140 km northeast of the capital Managua. The region is characterised by a high degree of poverty (Levard et al., 2001), reflected in a low average per capita income of about US$ 340 (Pagiola et al., 2007), a low education level and limited access to basic services such as water and electricity. The site belongs to the so-called 'old agricultural frontier' region; it is situated in the buffer zone of the Cerro Musún nature reserve, and close to the Quirragua nature reserve. The terrain is undulating, with an elevation of 300-500m above sea level. The climate is of the semi-humid tropical type, with average temperature about 25-30°C and average annual rainfall 1300-2500 mm (Pagiola et al., 2007). The rainy season stretches from May to December.

2.2. PROJECT HYPOTHESES AND PARTICIPANTS

The project was based on an experimental approach of targeting groups of farmers with different incentives. In principle, this would offer a solution to the attribution problem[34] in PES impact assessment, as differences between otherwise similar groups could then be attributed to the differences in incentives received from the project (Vaessen and Van Hecken, 2009). The idea of experimental counterfactual analysis is that the situation of a participant group (receiving benefits from and/or affected by an intervention) is compared over time with the situation of an equivalent control group that is not affected by the intervention (ibid). In case of random assignment to either the participant or the control group, the probability that, in sufficiently large samples, both groups are equivalent on all observable and non-observable characteristics except for intervention participation is very high (ibid).

[33] CATIE is the Spanish acronym for 'Tropical Agricultural Research and Higher Education Centre', see http://www.catie.ac.cr/magazin.asp?CodIdioma=ESP.
[34] The attribution problem refers to the question whether changes in certain variables can be attributed to an intervention or whether they should be considered as the result of other factors (Vaessen and Van Hecken, 2009).

Originally, the main hypothesis of the research - that the adoption of silvopastoral practices can be attributed to PES, to TA, or to a combination of both - was to be investigated by subdividing 123 households[35] (mainly small to medium-sized farmers) into three 'treatment' groups[36] (see Table 5). The selection of farmers for the different treatment groups would be done at random so as to assure equivalent groups. Consequently, it would be possible to deduce the effects of different types of incentives directly from a simple comparison of means (of changes over time) between treatment groups (ibid). The largest group (ninety-eight households, almost 80 per cent) belonged to the PES group, which was further divided into two subgroups, depending on whether they received only payments (PES only) or payments and TA (PES+TA).[37] Furthermore, the PES only and PES+TA groups were further divided into two payment scheme subgroups: four-year scheme participants (n=72) were to be paid during the whole project period, while farmers in the two-year scheme (n=26) were only to receive payments during the first two project years. This was done to test and monitor the speed and intensity of adoption behaviour.

In order to distinguish the effects of the treatments, these groups were to be compared to a counterfactual, which was established by assigning twenty-five farmers to a control group. During implementation, however, the use of a control group turned out to be practically impossible, because the implementing project staff considered it politically and ethically unacceptable to exclude certain poor and medium-sized farmers from project benefits in order to serve as a control group (Vaessen and Van Hecken, 2009). Moreover, most of the farmers had already been working with Nitlapán in previous projects, which had resulted in the establishment of longstanding relationships between some of the farmers and the implementing project staff. The project staff, who managed the project primarily as a development project, tried to solve this ethical issue by choosing participants for the control group among more capitalised farmers. As shown in Table 5, the control group members therefore differed significantly from the treatment groups (see annex I for a more detailed discussion of this selection bias). This has the unfortunate consequence that an unbiased comparison on the basis of the experimental data is not possible.

The experimental research set-up was further compromised by 'treatment diffusion' or 'contagion effects'[38], reducing the differences between treatment

[35] Corresponding to 65 per cent of total population in the micro-watershed of Bulbul and 35 per cent in Paiwas.
[36] In fact, the project initially started with 136 participants in the first year (2002), but due to various factors (such as participant decease or property sales) it ended with 123 participants remaining in 2008. In the further analysis we use data from the 123 remaining participants.
[37] TA consisted of monthly workshops, personal farm visits by project staff and interchange of experiences (farmer-to-farmer knowledge extension).
[38] Treatment diffusion refers to the problem that groups of farmers, who are not supposed to be exposed to (or receiving) certain project benefits, are in fact benefiting from a project

groups and invalidating part of the comparison between the groups. Indeed, in practice it proved impossible to use the experiment as a framework for isolating the TA component. Given the proximity between the farmers, the social relationships among farmers and the social relationships between farmers and staff, information about silvopastoral activities and improvements in other land use practices was widely available to all groups. Farmers who were not supposed to receive TA from the project frequently attended project workshops. Farmers from the TA group would also share their newly acquired knowledge on silvopastoral techniques with neighbours or friends (often pertaining to another group in the experiment). Furthermore, several other technical extension organisations were active in the region, often assisting farmers who were simultaneously participating in the RISEMP project. Therefore, what in development projects is usually considered as an important benefit, i.e. the diffusion of project knowledge beyond the participant group, ironically turned out to be a substantial impediment to the validity of the experiment design (Vaessen and Van Hecken, 2009). Finally, the sample sizes of the study population and of the different treatment groups are relatively small. Despite these severe methodological drawbacks, the analysis of the data obtained can still give us important insights regarding the effect of the project incentives and the adopted land uses.

Table 5 shows that the average participating household was composed of six members, and possessed about 34 ha of land and almost thirty-nine heads of cattle. However, the high standard deviations for both area (28.8) and number of cattle (34.4) indicate large differences among households, which become clear when participants are subdivided into three main types of farmers.[39] The poorest group of households, the so-called *campesinos pobres con tierra* (CPT; poor peasants with land) possessed a small amount of land (maximum 20 ha), and generally lacked capital to invest in self-sustaining agricultural production. They had small herds of between two and ten animals. The richest group, the *finqueros ganaderos* (FG; cattle farmers), possessed vast amounts of land, sometimes up to 150 or 250 ha, and had large herds with up to 200 or 300 heads of cattle. The intermediate group of *campesinos ganaderos* (CG; cattle peasants) typically possessed between 20 and 50 ha of land, on which they kept around 20 to 100 animals. The latter two groups of households dedicated themselves almost exclusively to the breeding of dual purpose cattle, with only a small part of their land used for cultivation of basic staples (mainly

---

in one or more ways: by directly receiving the benefits from the project, by indirectly receiving benefits through other participating farmers (e.g. knowledge transfer), or by receiving similar benefits from other organisations (Vaessen and Van Hecken, 2009).

[39] The categorisation into different types of farmers is based on weighted scores that were attributed to every household, depending on their value for different variables selected on the basis of Maldidier and Marchetti (1996) and Levard et al. (2001), and updated by our own field observations. Variables included are farm size, amount of cattle, and types of infrastructure. The categorisation of farmer households into the three main groups obtained by this exercise was ground-truthed during the qualitative research.

corn and beans) for their own household consumption. The poorest group cultivated larger amounts of staple crops, but often also depended on hiring out family labour to the other two groups of farmers or on migration.

Table 5. Project participants by treatment group, 2002 (mean and standard deviation)*

Treatment Group	Group Size	Area (ha)	Household Size	Number of Cattle
PES only	**28**	29,5 (25,1)	6,0 (2,7)	34,0 (35,5)
PES+TA	**70**	31,9 (25,8)	6,3 (2,5)	34,8 (30,9)
Control	**25**	46,7 (37,1)	5,3 (1,9)	53,6 (39,2)
Total	**123**	34,4 (28,8)	6,0 (2,5)	38,5 (34,4)

*Data refer to households who participated during whole project duration (n=123). Standard deviations are indicated between parentheses.
Source: Vaessen and Van Hecken, 2009

2.3. MONITORING AND PAYMENTS FOR ECOSYSTEM SERVICES

Because the measurement and verification of the provision of ES is laborious and would imply huge transaction costs, the project worked with land use proxies likely to provide the desired ES (Pagiola et al., 2004; World Bank, 2002). Furthermore, the project recognised that specific land uses could deliver different combinations or 'bundles' of ES. An 'environmental service index' (ESI) was elaborated, based on the aggregation of the estimated per hectare contribution of twenty-eight different land uses to biodiversity protection and carbon sequestration (see annex II). Farmers' payments were calculated on the basis of the net increase of this ESI - which ranged from value 0 (land use least effective in providing the ES) to 2 (land use most effective in providing the ES)[40] - as compared to the baseline land use data for their farm in 2003.

Payments were made ex post, annually after the observed land use changes. The amount of payment per ESI point was calculated on the basis of the opportunity costs of more attractive land uses (Pagiola et al., 2007). The payments as such did not necessarily cover the full opportunity cost of the ES provisioning, but 'could "tip the balance" of profitability between current and costlier silvopastoral practices, by

[40] For a detailed explanation and overview of this ESI composition, see Pagiola et al. (2004). For a detailed overview and description of the different land use types, see Murgueitio et al. (2003) and World Bank (2002).

increasing the net value of investments in silvopastoral practices and by reducing the initial period in which these practices impose net costs on farmers' (ibid.: 378). Based on calculations of the relative profitability of more attractive common practices, the payments were established at an annual US$ 75 (four-year scheme) and US$ 110 (two-year scheme)[41] per incremental ESI point. In order to eliminate perverse incentives (for example, the risk of farmers cutting down existing trees so as to raise the potential additional payments during project implementation) the baseline ESI points in 2003 were remunerated with a one-time initial payment of US$ 10 per point (Pagiola et al., 2005).

2.4. RESEARCH METHODOLOGY

In our independent[42] research to investigate the motivations for farmers to change (or not to change) land use, we relied on different sources of primary and secondary data. First, we analysed the main surveys conducted during the project period by the CATIE, Nitlapán and World Bank staff. These surveys resulted in two main datasets: a baseline dataset (2002) and corresponding yearly socio-economic follow-up datasets, with detailed information on household characteristics and economic activities over the whole project period[43]; and a land use dataset, with an overview of the land use changes per farm (based on remote sensing imagery[44]) and the corresponding ESI scores and payments during the whole project period. Secondly, we analysed different internal and published documentation on the project. Thirdly, we conducted an extensive field study after project termination. This field study consisted of in-depth responsive interviews (Rubin and Rubin, 2005) with thirty-three former participating and three non-participating farmers in April 2008; and interviews with the Nitlapán project staff in July 2008 (see annex III). The farmers were selected on the basis of maximum-variability and snowball sampling (Glaser and Strauss, 1967), in which all farmers were ranked on the basis of high, low and median values for certain variables in the above-mentioned datasets, such as participant group (PES, PES + TA, Control), received payments, farm size, location and accessibility, gender, herd size, and type of land use changes (see annex IV).

[41] According to the project staff (personal communication) this higher payment for the two-year scheme was established to compensate the farmers of this scheme for their shorter participation time.
[42] By 'independent' we mean that we were not involved in the project design or implementation. We based our research partly on collected 'official' project datasets that we obtained through our long-term institutional links to the Nitlapán institute, and partly on our own qualitative research, which took place after the project was terminated.
[43] Due to several limitations with these socio-economic datasets (e.g. the formulation of the survey questions was changed during the project period; and there were high rates of missing data), we were obliged to mainly rely on the other data sources and our own data recollection methods (qualitative research).
[44] Quickbird imagery with 61 cm resolution. The corresponding land use maps derived from these images were ground-truthed to match each plot to one of the 28 land uses recognised by the project (Pagiola et al., 2007).

The interviews with farmers were conducted in the absence of former project staff and in the name of the University of Antwerp in order to avoid being associated with the project and therefore eliciting socially desired responses. The latter phenomenon is quite common among farmers given the expectations they have vis-à-vis the large number of organisations offering support in the region, as well as more specifically, the long history of cooperation between several farmers and Nitlapán. The first part of every interview was devoted to getting to know the life history and livelihood strategies of every farmer, after which the interview was gradually directed to the topic of projects and institutions that the correspondent had been involved or collaborating with, eventually leading to the discussion of the RISEMP experience (see annex V for a more detailed outline of the interviews). The interviews with the Nitlapán staff were conducted to cross-check some of the main findings of the farmer interviews: by bringing up some experiences or anecdotes from the farmers' interviews, we tried to form a more nuanced context for some of the narratives provided by the farmers. In conclusion, many of the arguments and conclusions in this research rely heavily on triangulation between interviews. This means that they are supported by interviews with different people who independently arrived at the same impression about a certain aspect of the project. Where possible, claims are further supported by (quantitative) project data and documents.

3. ASSESSMENT OF THE RISEMP RESULTS

This section deals with the main results of the RISEMP, focusing on the land use changes and the motivation for these changes, as well as on the overall environmental impact.

3.1. LAND USE CHANGES

One of the main yardsticks the RISEMP used to monitor its impact was the change in land use practices among project participants and the control group. Table 6 reflects the observed changes in land use between 2003 and 2007. While the total area of pasture has remained stable (from 63.8 per cent in 2003 to 62.7 per cent in 2007), its composition has changed significantly. Degraded pastures decreased from 30.9 per cent to 10.1 per cent in five years. They were replaced by improved pastures with trees (up from 9 per cent to 23.8 per cent of the total area) and fodder banks (which more than tripled in area). By 2007, annual crops took up less than half the area they had occupied in 2003, while the quantity of living fences had almost quadrupled. Forests and scrub habitats remained stable, covering about 25 per cent of the total area. The most significant changes occurred during the first two project years. The novelty of the project and the system of payments, which each year repeatedly remunerated the incremental ESI points as compared to the 2003 baseline, stimulated farmers to change their land use as early as possible since this implied higher total payments. Degraded pasture, for example, almost halved between 2003 and 2004 with a decrease of 613 ha, while it decreased by an additional 155 ha during the second year and with 'only' 111 ha during the last two years together. The same pattern, but in the opposite direction, occurred with living fences and improved pasture with trees, which increased over the whole project period, but - again - mainly during the first two years.

Table 6. Land use RISEMP participating households (n=123), 2003-2007

Land Use \ Year	2003		2004		2005		2006		2007		Δ 2003-2007	
	ha	%	ha	%	ha	%	ha	%	ha	%	ha	%
Crops (annual, grains, tubers)	310	7.4	207	4.9	146	3.5	130	3.1	123	2.9	-187	-4.4
Degraded pasture	1306	30.9	693	16.4	537	12.7	468	11.1	425	10.1	-881	-20.8
Natural pasture without trees	53	1.3	129	3.1	129	3.1	94	2.2	74	1.8	20	0.5
Improved pasture without trees	36	0.8	56	1.3	63	1.5	47	1.1	42	1.0	7	0.2
Semi-permanent crops	44	1.1	32	0.8	29	0.7	35	0.8	25	0.6	-19	-0.5
Natural pasture with trees	912	21.6	1179	27.9	1067	25.3	1088	25.9	1081	25.7	169	4.1
Improved pasture with trees	382	9.0	656	15.5	873	20.7	933	22.2	1002	23.8	621	14.8
Fruit crops	21	0.5	23	0.5	25	0.6	26	0.6	25	0.6	4	0.1
Fodder banks	104	2.5	178	4.2	227	5.4	288	6.9	324	7.7	220	5.2
Commercial tree plantations	1	0.0	3	0.1	5	0.1	12	0.3	5	0.1	4	0.1
Shaded coffee	2	0.1	3	0.1	20	0.5	9	0.2	6	0.1	4	0.1
Scrub habitats (*tacotales*)	221	5.2	211	5.0	234	5.5	216	5.1	207	4.9	-14	-0.3
Riparian forest	540	12.8	560	13.3	554	13.1	551	13.1	551	13.1	11	0.3
Intensive silvopastoral	4	0.1	1	0.0	6	0.2	9	0.2	11	0.3	7	0.2
Secondary forest (intervened)	184	4.4	195	4.6	184	4.4	189	4.5	183	4.3	-2	0.0
Secondary forest	43	1.0	45	1.1	63	1.5	61	1.5	65	1.5	22	0.5
Primary forest	41	1.0	37	0.9	40	0.9	33	0.8	37	0.9	-3	-0.1
Infrastructure, housing, roads	15	0.4	13	0.3	18	0.4	14	0.3	19	0.5	4	0.1
Total area	**4221**	**100**	**4221**	**100**	**4221**	**100**	**4203**	**100**	**4206**	**100**	**n.a.**	**n.a.**
Living fences*	127*	n.a.	284*	n.a.	448*	n.a.	448*	n.a.	479*	n.a.	352*	n.a.
Total forests	808	19.1	837	19.8	841	19.9	834	19.9	836	19.9	28	0.7
Total pasture	2693	63.8	2713	64.3	2676	63.4	2639	62.8	2636	62.7	-58	-1.1

* expressed in kilometres instead of hectares

Source: Authors' own elaboration based on project data

3.2. PROJECT INCENTIVES

Hypothetically, the group that would score best on the adoption of silvopastoral practices would be the group receiving both PES and TA, followed by the PES group, and ultimately the control group, which was hypothesised to only marginally adopt the targeted practices, due to the absence of project incentives. Furthermore, it was expected that farmers, triggered by the higher corresponding payments, would mainly invest in land uses with higher ESI scores, such as forests or scrub habitats (*tacotales*).

Figure 4. Changes in land use, per treatment group (*), 2003-2007

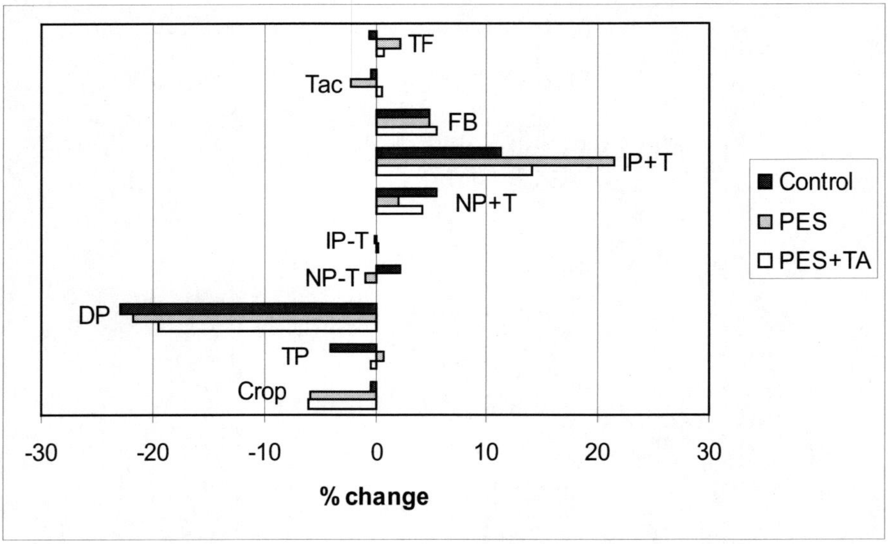

	Crop	TP	DP	NP-T	IP-T	NP+T	IP+T	FB	Tac	TF	LF**
PES+TA	-6.0	-0.4	-19.4	0.0	0.3	4.2	14.1	5.5	0.5	0.8	214
PES	-5.8	0.8	-21.7	-0.9	-0.1	2.0	21.5	4.9	-2.3	2.2	164
Control	-0.4	-4.0	-23.0	2.3	0.1	5.5	11.3	4.9	-0.4	-0.5	1364

* Changes in land use: the additional percentage of the selected land use within the total land size of every treatment group.
** The per cent for LF is calculated as an increase in the length, compared to each group's initial LF length in 2003.
Legend:
Crop = annual crops; TP = total pastures; DP = degraded pastures; NP-T = natural pastures without trees; IP-T = improved pastures without trees; NP+T = natural pastures with trees; IP+T = improved pastures with trees; FB = fodder banks; Tac = tacotales (scrub habitats); TF = total forests; LF = living fences.
Source: Authors' own elaboration based on project data

Figure 4 gives an overview of land use changes across the treatment groups. It indicates that degraded pastures have decreased in all groups, with the highest reduction surprisingly in the control group (-23 per cent). Also, living fences have increased most in the control group (eight times more than in the PES group). Fodder banks show a very similar pattern across the groups, while the highest increase in natural pastures, with and without trees, was also in the control group. The establishment of improved pastures with trees, however, has been highest in the treatment groups (14.1 and 21.5 per cent for the PES+TA and PES groups respectively, with an increase of 'only' 11.3 per cent in the control group). The control group is also the only group in which forest area decreased (-0.5 per cent). The amount of scrub habitats slightly increased in the PES+AT group (0.5 per cent), while it slightly decreased in the control and the PES group.

Although these data confirm that farmers have recognised the benefits of at least some silvopastoral practices and have increasingly adopted these practices, the comparison of land use changes among treatment groups does not provide firm evidence for the RISEMP hypothesis (Pagiola et al., 2005; World Bank, 2002) that observed changes are exclusively attributable to the payment incentive. Pagiola et al. (2007) argue that the similar results of treatment and non-treatment groups are attributable to the poorly chosen control group (see section 2.2), with relatively more capitalised farmers from the FG and CG group. Thus, they conclude that the data on the control group are not useful, and choose to exclude them in their analysis. We acknowledge this problem with the control group, but do not think it justifies ignoring the information on this group altogether. The control group data - no matter how biased - indeed indicate that there were other incentives triggering farmers' adoption of silvopastoral practices. An alternative distinction among participants and control group on the basis of types of farms helps to shed more light on the reasons why certain groups have (not) adopted certain practices, and how this emanates from different opportunity costs and livelihood strategies among the types of farmers.

3.3. MOTIVATIONS AND INCENTIVES TO ADOPT SILVOPASTORAL PRACTICES

Costs for establishing silvopastoral practices are relatively high. In the study region, they range from US$ 170/ha for sowing improved pasture on degraded pastures to US$ 390/ha for converting degraded into improved pasture with high tree density. Establishment of fodder banks ranges from US$ 170 to US$ 270/ha, and establishment of living fences costs about US$ 110 to US$ 160/km (Pagiola et al., 2008). Their on-farm benefits are mainly linked to increased carrying capacity and thus higher milk and meat productivity (Yamamoto et al., 2007)[45]. The fact that all

[45] Yamamoto et al. (2007) have shown that silvopastoral practices in the RISEMP project region have effectively led to higher milk production, mainly through the establishment of pastures with moderate tree density (tree cover approximately 20 per cent).

farmers, with or without payments, have invested heavily in silvopastoral practices bears witness to their intrinsic profitability. This represents a reversal of the traditional extensive production logic in the region, where CPTs maintain low cattle numbers because they lack capital, and CGs and FGs focus on the maximisation of the return on their scarce input factor 'labour', translating this into very extensive cattle breeding and a constant drive to purchase more land (Maldidier and Marchetti, 1996).

Since payments were made ex post, land use changes had to be pre-financed by the farmers, some of whom turned to local microfinance institutions. Since the capacity to access higher project payments hinged on the farmers' ability to pre-finance the investments, this created a tendency towards the exclusion of the poorer CPT farmers, who had more difficulties self-financing or securing loans. This unintended 'bias' against poorer farmers is not only socially undesirable, but also raises doubts about the environmental effectiveness of the project. Nor does it help to slow the advancement of the new agricultural frontier, which is at least partially the consequence of migrating poor farmers selling their land in regions like Matiguás-Río Blanco to richer farmers, who can exploit it more effectively, in order to buy cheaper, unexploited land further down the frontier (see further below in section 3.4)

3.3.1. DIFFERING CONSTRAINTS AMONG DIFFERENT TYPES OF FARMER HOUSEHOLDS

Differences in capital constraints and broader factor opportunity costs go a long way towards explaining the observed difference in investment strategy between the different producer types, largely independent from the payments. Figure 5 re-examines the main land use changes, this time according to the type of household. All farmers have invested in improved pastures and fodder banks, mainly by transforming degraded pastures to these more productive uses. Living fences have also been very popular among all groups[46]. The relative changes in productive uses (mainly improved pastures and fodder banks) have been highest in the more capitalised groups (FG and CG), with the CG group accounting for the most significant intensification (+5.6 per cent in fodder banks and +18.1 per cent in improved pastures with trees), and the lowest decrease in degraded pasture (-16.6 per cent). Increases in areas of scrub habitats have only taken place in the case of the poorest CPT group.

[46] This should be not much of a surprise, since — besides the productive benefits that they generate — living fences are up to nine times cheaper to establish than traditional 'dead' fences (Pagiola et al., 2008), and require far less labour.

Figure 5. Changes in land use, per type of household (*), 2003-2007

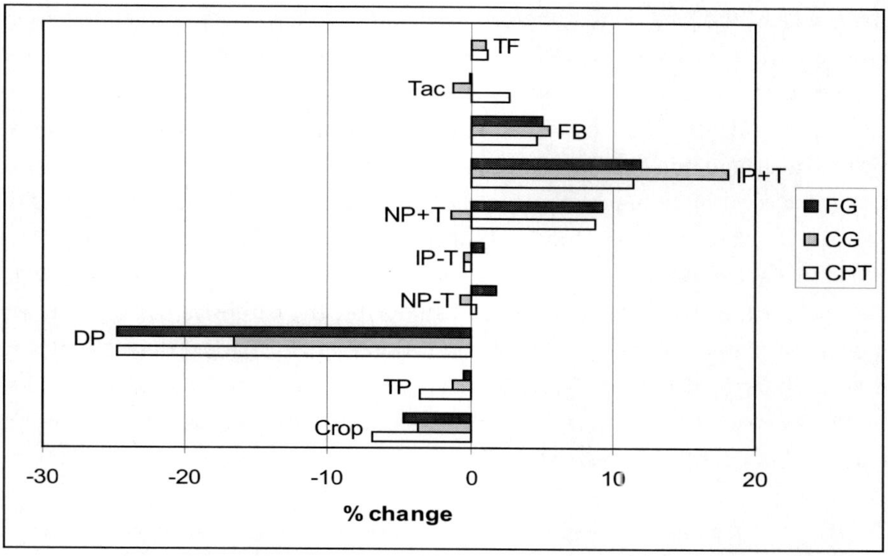

	Crop	TP	DP	NP-T	IP-T	NP+T	IP+T	FB	Tac	TF	LF**
CPT (n = 32)	-6.8	-3.5	-24.8	0.4	-0.4	8.8	11.4	4.6	2.8	1.2	167.6
CG (n = 67)	-3.6	-1.2	-16.6	-0.7	-0.5	-1.4	18.1	5.6	-1.2	1.1	263.0
FG (n = 23)	-4.7	-0.4	-24.8	1.9	1.0	9.2	12.0	5.0	-0.1	0.1	382.5

* Changes in land use: the additional percentage of the selected land use within the total land size of every household type.
** The per cent for LF is calculated as an increase in the length, compared to each group's initial LF length in 2003.
Legend:
CPT = campesino pobre con tierra (poor peasant with land); CG = campesino ganadero (cattle peasant); FG = finquero ganadero (cattle farmer); Crop = annual crops; TP = total pastures; DP = degraded pastures; NP-T = natural pastures without trees; IP-T = improved pastures without trees; NP+T = natural pastures with trees; IP+T = improved pastures with trees; FB = fodder banks; Tac = tacotales (scrub habitats); TF = total forests; LF = living fences.
Source: Authors' own elaboration based on project data

At first sight it seems remarkable how closely the land use changes of the FG group resemble those of the much poorer CPT group, with a similar decrease in the amount of degraded pastures and annual food crops, and increase in fodder banks and in natural and improved pastures with trees in both cases. FGs and CPTs have invested relatively less than CGs in fodder banks and improved pastures, and have relied more on the use of natural pastures. The similar manifestations of land use changes have, however, different origins. Our field research showed that the lower adoption rates of the more productive and intensive land uses (mainly improved pastures and fodder banks) among the CPT group reflect the limitations they often experience due to labour, space and capital constraints[47]. During our interviews, for example, we found that many smaller farmers had tried to invest in fodder banks, but because of the long time lag before the fodder banks could be exploited and the limited alternative pasture available to bridge this time lag, they were often forced to let their cattle enter the newly established fodder banks, which led to their destruction. The same limitations also explain the relatively large increases in natural pastures, which do not require high capital and labour inputs, and thus save precious labour time for crop production or off-farm employment. In the case of the FGs the reliance on natural pastures and lower increases in improved pastures and fodder banks can be explained by the relative land abundance of these farmers, which makes labour the scarce input factor, and stimulates the extensive use of land, with minimal investments in land intensification. However, this land extension strategy has been changing during the last few decades (more on this below), which explains the increases (smaller than among the CGs, but nevertheless positive) in the adoption of more intensive practices.

The increase in areas of scrub habitats in the CPT group should not be much of a surprise; given that this group's main constraint is capital availability and given that parts of the land are underutilised precisely because of these capital constraints, a cheap way to obtain project payments without having to invest much capital or labour has been the simple regeneration of 'low pressure' or underutilised parts of the farmers' land into scrub habitats. Considering that such land is converted regularly into new productive land uses as part of a slash-and-burn system of fertility regeneration, the project payments might have just created a little more space for leaving land fallow for a longer time[48].

3.3.2. BEYOND DIRECT PROJECT INCENTIVES: REVEALED MOTIVATIONS FOR LAND USE CHANGES

In our field interviews most farmers claimed to have changed land use for a number of differing complementary reasons. Payments were a welcome additional incentive but, according to the farmers, did not play a decisive role. Surprisingly, they attributed much more importance to the provision of TA, which deepened their knowledge of silvopastoral practices and strengthened collective motivation to engage in silvopastoral intensification, connected to the ongoing milk boom (see

[47] Nevertheless, fodder banks adoption rates are substantially higher among the poorer farmers, which is probably attributable to this group's lower opportunity cost of labour; the establishment of fodder banks has a relatively high labour/capital ratio of between 1.3 and 4.8. Improved pastures, for example, have a much lower labour/capital ratio of approximately 0.5 (calculations based on project data).

[48] In fact, scrub habitats should not be interpreted as fixed parts of the landscape being in transition to secondary forests, but as cyclical and temporary land uses which serve to recuperate soil fertility in the agricultural slash-and-burn production process (Maldidier and Marchetti, 1996).

below). Various other studies have emphasised the importance of TA in the adoption of silvopastoral practices (see Pattanayak et al., 2003 for an overview). Although most farmers in Matiguás-Río Blanco already knew and used some of the silvopastoral techniques, the TA and the social momentum it generated were said to have stimulated experimentation with new, or expansion of already-known practices and at the same time to have lowered the perceptions of risks. Furthermore, our field interviews confirmed that TA also helped making farms look better-managed, indicating that technology adoption is not only profit-driven, but also linked to social status (see also Chouinard et al., 2008).

At first sight, the quantitative project data (Figure 4) do not seem to provide any evidence that TA played such a decisive role. Comparison between the PES and PES+TA group does not reveal significant differences in adoption rates. However, - and as already explained in section 2.2 - the experiment did not take place in a laboratory but in the real world, where farmers cannot simply be isolated from other interconnected community members. Therefore, participants (not receiving TA) inevitably acquired new knowledge by interacting with other participants (who were receiving TA); they experienced demonstration effects from neighbouring farms and sometimes even attended workshops as substitutes for eligible participants (with TA). Moreover, several other extension organisations were active in the region, some joining the RISEMP momentum and offering TA services similar to those of the RISEMP. Rather than being an indication that TA did not have an effect, this suggests that the adoption of new practices is not solely dependent on individual cognitive capacities and decision making, but is also supported by the emergence and articulation of sufficient social momentum crystallising into coherent collective action that enables collective pathways of change (de Haan and Zoomers, 2005).

Apart from individual and collective project incentives, there have also been strong exogenous incentives which have - contrary to the more traditional extensive production logic in the region[49] - motivated producers to intensify their farming activities. The main incentive derives from the boom in the national dairy market and improved local access of farmers to fresh milk collection centres and (semi-)industrial cheese factories. This has translated into higher demand for milk and a significant increase in regional milk prices. There is also a widespread perception that this rise will continue in the future as a result of recent free trade agreements that will

[49] Traditionally it has never been very interesting for the three types of farmer households to intensify their land use, but each group for different reasons. Generally, CPTs maintain extensive land use practices (with low cattle carrying capacity of pastures), because they lack capital to intensify their land use. CGs and FGs, on the other hand, generally base their production logic on the maximisation of the relative scarce input factor labour, which in practice translates into extensive cattle breeding, with — at least in the absence of attractive dairy markets — little motivation for land use intensification, which is the cheapest way to enhance productivity. (Maldidier and Marchetti, 1996).

reduce barriers to lucrative export markets, including the USA. Until the 1970s most communities in the study region were relatively isolated and lacked access to milk storage facilities, which made the commercialisation of milk unattractive. Increasing interest from international dairy companies through the 1980s and 1990s led to a rapid growth of roads and basic milk storage facilities, which opened up the milk market for many farmers and led to a relative intensification of cattle production. In the late 1990s Salvadoran traders further commercialised the dairy production and offered higher, but seasonally fluctuating milk prices (Levard et al., 2001). The increasing presence of local agricultural extension and development organisations has further promoted and developed milk commercialisation among farmers.

Figure 6. Nominal and real milk prices (in US$/litre) to farmers in Matiguás-Río Blanco, 2004-2006

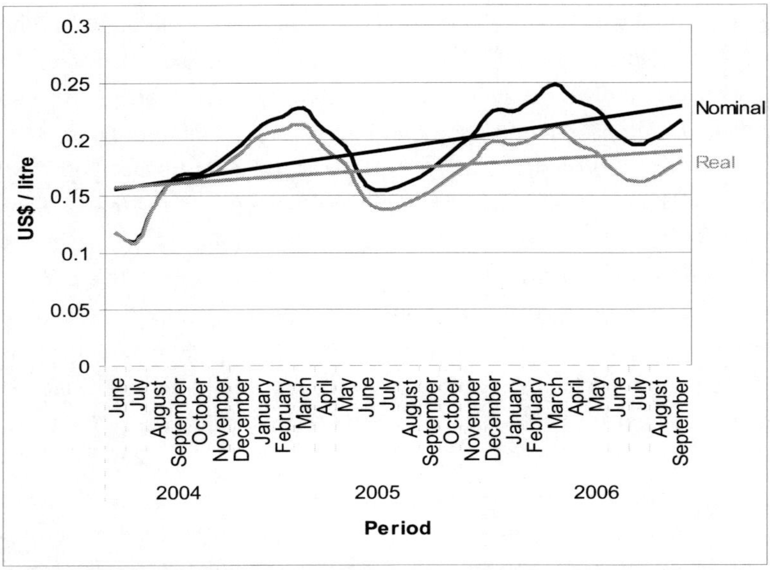

Source: Authors' own elaboration based on project data

Figure 6 shows the evolution of milk prices (in US$/litre), both in nominal and in real terms, in the project region for the period June 2004-September 2006. The cyclical movement represents the seasonal character of milk market prices, while the linear trend line suggests that prices are in an upward evolution. Comparisons between different years reveal an increase of almost 10 per cent in nominal prices in the positive peak price months of March 2005 and March 2006 (dry season), which, however, corresponds with a real price decrease of 1 per cent; and a nominal increase of 38 per cent and 27 per cent (real increase of 25,3 per cent and 16,2 per cent respectively) between the negative peak months of July 2004 and July 2005 and

July 2005 and July 2006 respectively (rainy season)[50]. Compared to the changes in agricultural input prices, these changes in milk prices are substantial; for example, the cost of barbwire, an important input for managing pastures and fodder banks, decreased with 6 per cent in real terms between 2004 and 2006, while herbicides (used for 'cleaning' pastures from undesired vegetation) decreased by almost 13 per cent in real terms. The real cost of hiring day labourers decreased with more than 10 per cent in this same period.

The emergence of and the better access to dairy markets and the corresponding higher milk prices, make intensification of land use through the adoption of silvopastoral practices more attractive for farmers. In order to benefit from these opportunities, dairy farmers need to keep (and feed) their milking cows close to the roads, where milk is collected, dissuading extensive land use in cheaper interior areas and rather favouring land intensification near milk collecting centres and access roads. Milk collection centres - owned by or connected to cheese exporters and national processing plants with a strong interest in maintaining year-round production - pay a significant price premium for a stable supply of milk. Stability of supply means avoiding the usual decline in milk production as a consequence of lower food availability during the dry season. Since the more productive milk cattle breeds are less resistant to heat than the traditional meat cattle breeds, they require the protection of shade from trees. These factors provide private producers with good reasons to invest in natural or improved pastures with/without trees and fodder banks.

Empirical evidence on the local relation between milk production and land use practices was provided by a study of Yamamoto et al. (2007), who analysed the link between milk production and silvopastoral practices in the project region. They concluded that an increase in the meat milk price ratio is likely to decrease tree cover (ibid), or reversely, a decrease in this ratio will probably foster the adoption of certain silvopastoral practices, such as the establishment of living fences that simultaneously provide extra fodder to the cattle (and thus allow cattle grazing on smaller and nearby areas. Our interviews with participants confirmed that farmers share the perception that certain silvopastoral practices have positive effects on cattle production, mainly by increasing milk productivity during dry season and augmenting carrying capacity of pastures. Since various decades farmers in this region have also been affected by scarcity of animal feeding during dry season (Maldidier and Marchetti, 1996). Our interviews showed that farmers attribute these setbacks to changing climate conditions (longer and more severe dry seasons), which have been more salient during the last five to ten years. The combination of these

[50] Milk prices could potentially rise even more in some communities where purchase is currently mainly controlled by middle-men.

factors have increasingly motivated farmers to change animal feeding strategies, which in practice often means resorting to more drought resistant types of pastures and fodder banks. As such, farmers who resort to silvopastoral practices potentially benefit disproportionately more from milk price increases than 'traditional' farmers.

Griffith and Zepeda (1994) and Nicholson et al. (1995), however, emphasise that higher milk prices do not necessarily lead to land use intensification, but could rather 'tend to bring more land into production' (Griffith and Zepeda, 1994: 130), and as such 'do not necessarily reduce the total land in cattle production, although it likely increases total output' (Nicholson et al., 1995: 731). Especially if farmers have access to cheap land in close vicinity, intensification is not a profitable alternative. In a research study of three Latin American countries, White et al. (2001) found that land price is one of the main drivers in farmers' decision of investing in improved forage technologies. They stress that increasing land prices make it harder for farmers to increase their farm size, mainly because of capital constraints. 'Instead, they adopt improved forage alternatives to enlarge their herds for less money' (ibid: 103).

The previous reasoning is also applicable to the RISEMP study site. In Matiguás-Río Blanco real land prices have increased with slightly more than 100 per cent between the end of the 1990s and today, heavily constraining the option of further land expansion within the region. These higher land prices are partly attributable to increasing population pressure, but they mainly reflect the growing (dairy) market opportunities and access, and the gradual disappearance of non-exploited land in close vicinity. They have led to a general perception among farmers that land use intensification is a necessity. In other words, the land constraint, which in the past could be partly evaded by expanding the agricultural frontier, has become increasingly binding (reflected in an increasing land labour price ratio), also for farmers with relative high amounts of land (CGs and FGs). Consequently, one of the most obvious ways to enhance productivity under this constraint is the establishment of higher productive uses per unit of land (White et al., 2001), mainly through the implementation of improved pastures and fodder banks.

In conclusion, although payments have covered a substantial part of the investment costs and have probably played a positive role in motivating and enabling beneficial land use change, the motivation for this change is located in a broader process ensuing from the exogenous incentives created by the milk boom and the related social momentum of knowledge creation and social learning. This provides an indication that farm decisions, whilst clearly affected by market conditions and individual cost–benefit calculations, are also dependent on more diffuse change processes that are collectively deemed beneficial for economic and possibly other reasons. Payments have been welcomed by all farmers, and are likely to have been a real as well as a symbolic factor in creating collective and individual motivation for silvopastoral intensification. Yet, in the absence of credit constraints, many of the investments would probably have taken place anyway, precisely because they 'made sense' economically and socio-culturally. In our interviews, farmers claimed that the project payments did not alter their farm management strategies and that it only promoted the faster adoption of practices which they were already adopting - or at least trying to adopt. The project thus rather legitimised existing but uncertain perceptions of and discourses on new practices and as such generated a collective momentum that 'tipped the balance' in favour of adopting silvopastoral practices. This also explains the high adoption rate among control group participants and the observation that technical assistance was perceived as the most important project component. Project payments might thus have played a less prominent role in behavioural change than expected or claimed. Underlying financial profitability and connected cognitive and social network dynamics might have equal or greater importance as elements of the broader pathways of change.

3.4. SILVOPASTORAL PRACTICES AND ECOSYSTEM SERVICES

Besides the appraisal of PES as a potential policy tool, one of the other main objectives of the RISEMP was the assessment and measurements of improvements in ecosystem functioning (World Bank, 2002). Systematic monitoring at various project farms confirmed the assumed on-site positive effects of silvopastoral practices on carbon sequestration (Ibrahim et al., 2007) and on certain biodiversity indicators, such as bird species richness (Pagiola et al., 2007; Sáenz et al., 2007). Over the whole project period the ESI score increased with slightly more than 48 per cent (from 3,005 in 2003 to 4,467 in 2007), suggesting that the project improved the region's environmental quality. But the overall environmental benefits were claimed to reach much further; intensification of productive land through silvopastoral practices, it was believed, would lead to a decrease in space needed for cattle, which could liberate important and fragile parts of the farmers' land and even stimulate reforestation (World Bank, 2002). This potential positive effect is, however, still widely debated (Dorrough et al., 2007; Kaimowitz and Angelsen, 1998; Swift et al., 2004). Some empirical evidence even suggest that pasture intensification can eventually lead to increased pressure on forested lands, especially if 'greater profitability will create a demand for larger milking and beef cattle herds and pasture to support them' (Vosti et al., 2001: 129).

In the case of Matiguás-Río Blanco the actual overall environmental impact is not very clear. Since the project limited the monitoring of land use changes only to the participating farms, it did not account for possible intra- and inter-regional leakage effects, in which environmentally-damaging activities are shifted elsewhere in space[51]. Our interviews, however, revealed how soaring land prices in the project region have pushed at least some - mainly smaller - farmers to sell their farm and move eastward to the new agricultural frontier where land is still relatively cheap and unexploited. The future plans of farmers further suggest that the agricultural expansion scenario might indeed be the most realistic one. Bigger cattle farmers (mainly FGs and CGs) expounded how their future objectives are mainly centred on two consecutive steps. First, they aim to further intensify their land use and improve their cattle and pasture quality (through silvopastoral practices and genetic improvements), and once they have achieved a new optimal productive equilibrium they will attempt to expand their cattle activities through the acquisition of more productive land. Poorer farmers (mainly from the CPT, but also from the CG group) often mentioned their first priority is the acquisition of (more) cattle, and then the expansion of land size, either in the same region, or by moving to the new agricultural frontier, where land is cheaper. These observations suggest that the overall sustainability of the promoted measures are not unequivocal, to say the least.

[51] A good example is that several participants possessed various plots of land, but participated in the project with only one of them. The non-participating plots (in and outside the project region) were not monitored, which allows for unregistered leakage effects. Participants could obtain a better ESI score — and thus higher payments — for their participating plot, by moving more extractive activities to non-participating plots of land.

4. CAN PAYMENTS ENSURE THE SUPPLY OF ECOSYSTEM SERVICES?

Beyond our immediate empirical reassessment of the 'success of PES' in the RISEMP project, we can now place our findings in a broader theoretical discussion of the potential and the limitations of the market-based PES approach to conservation from an ES supply-side perspective[52].

A first thing to note is that conceptually market-based approaches, almost inevitably, build upon the rational actor paradigm, assuming that people act upon an individual calculus of what maximises their self-interest (Karp and Gaulding, 1995), or at least that we can model human behaviour as if it were solely based upon such a self-interested optimisation exercise. Following this model, it is assumed that people will not undertake environmentally-sound actions unless they contribute to their private utility. More than a decade ago, Cleaver (1998) already warned against such abstractions, when she stated that 'the model commonly offered in literature and policy oversimplifies incentives and motivations, giving primacy to economic/productive considerations and assuming direct causal linkages between such incentives, individual behavior, and collective action' (ibid: 358). Market-based approaches also tend to attribute unrestricted property rights to farmers such that the ES that they provide can be treated and rewarded as positive externalities, rather than at least some of them being considered the result of the normal care of natural resources that could be expected of farmers (see also chapter 2 and 4). The next two subsections will critically reflect on the consequences of these assumptions. They focus on two central themes: 1) the need for a landscape approach and thus cooperation beyond individual decision making; and 2) the effects of market-based institutions on different types of (individual) motivation.

4.1. CONSERVATION AND THE NEED OF COOPERATION BEYOND FARM BOUNDARIES

One of the main conditions for the sustainable protection and provision of ES is a landscape approach to conservation[53] (Goldman et al., 2007; MA, 2005). The Matiguás-Río Blanco project site was chosen because of its potential function as a

[52] Note again that we refer to market-based approaches as a policy tool that is based upon individual decision making mediated by price incentives (see chapter 1). Therefore, the term 'market-based' does not necessarily imply the existence of real-functioning competitive markets where ES are traded through the laws of demand and supply.

[53] The landscape approach to conservation is a holistic approach which in agricultural contexts holds that the provision of ecosystem services from agricultural lands necessitates particular landscape designs or spatial configurations (Goldman et al., 2007: 334). The approach refers to the need of planning, negotiating, and implementing conservation intervention activities across a whole landscape, which usually requires coordination across individual property boundaries.

corridor between two important natural reserves (Pagiola et al., 2004). At first sight the project could thus be considered to take a landscape approach to conservation. However, upon closer analysis the underlying market-based logic of paying farmers for ES entails that the ultimate choice of changing or not changing specific land uses - and thus offering or not offering ES - is entirely left to the grace of individual households. Their decision will be largely based on their economic calculus, which will take into account the opportunity cost of different land uses and the payments that they could potentially attract. This logic is one of the main premises that is believed to make the market mechanism and PES more efficient than other approaches to conservation, precisely because it implies that scarce conservation funds will be allocated to the most efficient and low-cost providers (Engel et al., 2008; Ferraro and Kiss, 2002; Pagiola et al., 2005).

Nevertheless, the reliance on institutions that promote individual decision making has some important implications for conservation. The pieces of land which from the farmer's economic point of view are most interesting to conserve, do not necessarily coincide with ecological priority areas. The payment mechanism might thus enhance the protection of nature on some individual plots of land, but unless it takes additional measures (see below), it basically neglects the importance of landscape configuration. Especially in heavily cleared landscapes, such as Matiguás-Río Blanco, the promotion of corridors and other connecting habitat routes is indispensable for improving habitat quality (Haila, 2002). While coordination is less important for carbon sequestration, which is generally a non site-specific activity (i.e. it does not matter where carbon is captured)[54], it is crucial for biodiversity conservation, which requires a minimal amount of contiguous habitat, in which spatial patterns are one of the main characteristics (Gottfried et al., 1996). It is these 'economies of configuration' (Wear, 1992, as cited in Gottfried et al., 1996) which undermine the effectiveness of market-based mechanisms in solving these collective externality problems. In this context it is worth to fully quote Gottfried et al.'s (1996) summarising reflections on the general failure of institutions that promote individual approaches to conservation:

> 'The location of each landowner's parcel of land plays a critical role in determining the landscape's mix of goods and services. Aggregating landowners' contributions to ecological goods or bads, in order to determine some optimal landscape configuration via a damage or benefit function, loses this critical information. Because landowners jointly affect the landscape's ecological processes, scale problems emerge when taxes, subsidies, or other economic policy instruments attempt to internalise individual

[54] Goldman et al. (2007), however, claim that over the long term configuration of trees for carbon sequestration do play an important role, especially in the tropics where 'trees in small fragments have experienced high mortality from wind exposure, microclimatic stresses (changes in moisture, temperature, or light), and proliferating lianas' (ibid: 337).

landowners' externalities. Instead, owners must be dealt with as a group, for it is at this scale that landscape level processes emerge. Because of these scale problems, individual owners acting alone cannot provide the socially optimal mix of ecologically-provided goods and services. Rather, this requires orchestrating human endeavours across a landscape and across landowner boundaries.' (ibid: 136).

In sum, exclusive reliance on the market-based approach, which leaves land use decisions largely up to individual landowners, without mechanisms that simultaneously stimulate across-farm decision making and cooperation, offers limited perspectives for sustainable environmental conservation. This view is increasingly shared by PES scholars, who have claimed that PES should be embedded within a broader mix of policy instruments (e.g. Börner et al., 2010; Engel et al., 2008). Nevertheless, the still dominant focus on efficiency considerations has motivated a growing number of authors to look for solutions to spatial configuration and coordination problems entirely within a market-based framework. Some potential is seen in so-called agglomeration or coordination bonuses (Goldman et al., 2007; Parkhurst et al., 2002; Parkhurst and Shogren, 2007), which would encourage habitat connectivity by additionally remunerating environmentally-friendly land use changes that border on any other 'conserved' area. Nonetheless, empirical evidence on these systems is still very limited (and almost exclusively limited to experimental research), and indicates that the proposal falls short of practical on-field applicability as it is too complex (Pagiola et al., 2004) and would exacerbate the already critical transaction costs problem. Vatn (2005) emphasises that it would be a 'category mistake' to invoke the market perspective in the context of ES provision, as the issue is really about a collective and not an individual good. In the next section we will draw the line even further by temporarily making abstraction of the coordination requirement and by reflecting on whether payments are the appropriate incentives to induce 'individual' environmental action.

4.2. LINKS BETWEEN MOTIVATION, CONSERVATION AND INSTITUTIONS

In a market-based approach such as applied in the RISEMP, the purpose of PES is logically to alter human behaviour by affecting the (monetary) incentives, thereby creating an extrinsic motivation for the introduction of more environmentally-sound practices. This is achieved by altering the relative prices that determine the profitability of underlying economic activities (Frey and Stutzer, 2006). However, this reliance on extrinsic motivation overlooks the fact that institutions - in this case a market-based institution - cannot be treated as mere neutral transmitters of incentives. They also influence and interact with people's intrinsic motivations, which are related to their sense of enjoyment, satisfaction, (social) responsibility and/or obligation (Bénabou and Tirole, 2003; Paavola and Adger, 2005; Reeson, 2008; Vatn, 2005). Intrinsic motivation cannot be treated as exogenous and fixed. This interaction of external monetary incentives and people's intrinsic perceptions, values and social norms needs to be recognised (Paavola and Adger, 2005; North, 1990; Vatn, 2005). As Reeson explains, 'the way in which a situation is perceived can determine the extent to which intrinsic motivations are applied' (ibid: 18). With respect to the PES approach, the framing of agricultural decision making in an implicitly individualistic, full private property rights set-up, in which private producers need to be rewarded for the ES they provide, obviously tends to affect intrinsic motivations, with respect to both the prevalence of minimum social norms regarding responsible natural resource management, and the individual value of the enjoyment and satisfaction derived from the existence of natural resources.

Some scholars fear that the penetration of market logic for ES provision entails the risk that extrinsic price incentives erode intrinsic motivations, leaving the ultimate outcome for responsible natural resource management indeterminate (Anderson, 2006; Bowles, 2008; Frey and Oberholzer-Gee, 1997; Gómez-Baggethun et al., 2010). In the same vein, Vatn (2005: 215) emphasises that 'people apply different behaviours in different institutional settings' and Reeson and Tisdell (2006: 20) argue that the introduction of market logic may 'trigger people to behave in a self-interested way, rather than in the more cooperative or reciprocal ways in which they behave in other situations'. The danger is that the ensuing 'motivation crowding-out' (Frey, 1997) will destroy existing environmental ethics and associated social practices of co-operation and mutual control, thereby engendering significant 'hidden costs of rewards' (Lepper and Greene, 1978).

From the same pessimistic perspective, Heyman and Ariely (2004) analyse this problem in terms of the erosion of 'social markets'. In such social markets, individual efforts and co-ordination are based upon mutual exchanges embedded in social relationships and prevailing social norms and values. Introducing a market institution changes the locus of responsibility and leaves the choice up to the individual land users who will make their (uncoordinated) individual environmental efforts conditional upon receiving sufficient compensation. For example, the decision of a land owner to cut down trees, which in present-day Nicaraguan law is an illegal act, could become justified by the foregone monetary payments of this 'improved' land use (*mejoras*), since the principle of (foregone) monetary compensation implicitly contributes to legitimise such illegal land use practices (Ravnborg et al., 2007; Young et al., 2003) as it attributes to the farmer a *de facto* entitlement to destroy trees. The associated change of individual perceptions can also imply 'that landholders will come to expect to be paid for actions they are currently doing voluntarily' (Reeson,

2008: 20)[55] or, even worse, that they could start to use the 'environment as ransom' (Young et al., 2003), threatening to excessively mine the available natural resources unless they receive monetary compensation for not doing so.

During field research, we found worrying indications that such an unanticipated effect may be taking place in certain areas of the RISEMP region where the PES idea has been widely publicised. In the neighbouring Quirragua nature reserve, which plays a critical role in the local urban water supply, farmers are at present strategically expressing this threat, allegedly demanding compensatory PES for protecting the remaining forests on their properties (see also chapter 4). Anticipating the possibility of a (municipal) PES system (such as exists in the neighbouring municipality of Río Blanco), they have moved to create a local environmental association, in order to capture any future natural resource rent from PES and other environmental initiatives. In this way, the introduction of market logic could indeed lead to 'token economies' (Frey and Stutzer, 2006) in which people expect to be paid for actions they previously did out of moral obligation and/or social pressure[56]. Another possible effect is that the existing social institutions that co-ordinate and manage practices related to the environment might start to exert less influence. As noted by Wells (1998: 830), 'there is a danger that existing institutional actors may take less responsibility for biodiversity if they see a new institution created for this purpose'.

The phenomena of unanticipated motivation crowding-out and the erosion of 'social markets' would raise serious doubts about the effectiveness and sustainability of PES. Indeed, because of these neglected feedback effects it would no longer be self-evident that the introduction of payments would have a net positive effect on ES provisioning. The creation of PES mechanisms might actually do more harm than good, if the motivation crowding-out effect outweighs the relative price effect and/or if existing social institutions disintegrate under the pressure of the penetration of market logic (Bowles, 2008; Kosoy and Corbera, 2010; Martin et al., 2008). Even if the net effect is positive in the short run, there are still justified concerns about the long-term sustainability and thus the ultimate effectiveness of the programme (Bénabou and Tirole, 2003). A reliance on extrinsic monetary incentives implies that payments would indeed need to be ongoing, rather than short term (Pagiola et al., 2002). If the resulting increase in environmental funding levels cannot be sustained, payments might decline or disappear, leaving destroyed

[55] Psychological and economic experiments have already indicated how incentives can transform over time in *de facto* entitlements, implying diminishing returns for same payments (Bénabou and Tirole, 2003).
[56] This is exactly what Heyman and Ariely (2004) warn against when they assert that 'the social aspects of reward are fragile and a social reward can easily be made into a non-social extrinsic reward by merely mentioning monetary circumstances or perhaps just promoting comparisons to other tasks or other individuals' reward levels' (ibid: 793).

environmental ethics and weakened social institutions. This might lead to a scenario similar to the effects of the substitution of community management of natural resources by state command-and-control, now widely recognised as disastrous, in which the failure of state governance resulted in a shift from more or less effective local governance to *de facto* open access (Ostrom, 2002). It thus seems to be a valid concern to ask if 'not-for-profit conservation motives [can] be reborn once their cultural basis has been diminished?' (Martin et al., 2008: 4).

A key issue is the extent of any pre-existing intrinsic motivations and social norms that contribute to environmentally-sound practices. If these are few, there is not much to destroy in terms of 'social markets' and 'intrinsic motivation'. On the Nicaraguan agricultural frontier, a strong individualistic peasant work ethic prevails, collective action and mutual control are often weak, and the historically dominant logic with respect to the environment was to consider trees as a hindrance for production and cleared parcels as *mejoras* (improvements) (Bastiaensen et al., 2006: 15–16). In a context of gradually changing local perceptions, a positive interaction between extrinsic and intrinsic motivation might also exist (see e.g. Kosoy et al., 2008); in that case, the PES signal that environmental protection is highly valued by outsiders who are willing to pay significantly for it, could support changes in local perceptions, values and norms concerning 'accepted' and 'desirable' agricultural practices. Although the region of Matiguás remains - in both a physical and a cultural sense - far removed from the urban society of the capital and the 'developed' world, ecological messages of endangered species, climate change and increasing pressure on water and forest resources have found their way to local cultural arenas, mainly through schools, television[57] and the discourse of some development organisations. While many producers find it hard to believe that anyone wants to pay to keep trees, exposure to the global discourse of ecological catastrophe gives a better understanding of where this international willingness to pay is coming from. Add a number of local examples of ecological crises, in particular increasing scarcity of water and heightened incidence of draughts and floods in recent years, and it is clear that local norms and values related to the environment might be susceptible to change. In this context, positive 'motivation crowding-in' through PES rather than the alleged 'crowding-out' does not seem impossible. It remains quite unlikely, however, that individualised payments alone could contribute to the strengthening and emergence of more environmentally-friendly norms and 'social markets'. Payments will need to be embedded in broader processes and discourses of change.

[57] With solar panels, television has now reached even the most isolated communities, and cell phone technology is bringing internet and cable television within reach. Even rural Matiguás is thus rushing into the global society.

Our case study material found differences in the 'rate of success' in adopting the silvopastoral practices between different communities of the RISEMP area, suggesting that payments can be expected to have most impact when they are tied into existing or emerging local environmentally-responsible institutions (see also Corbera et al., 2009; Kosoy et al., 2008). In one community (San Ignacio), with a tradition of strong local organisation and relatively high degrees of co-operation and mutual trust, there were pre-RISEMP local institutions for environmental governance[58] (such as a local committee to protect critical areas for water supply). Other participating communities had very low levels of organisation, higher levels of disarticulation and distrust; and very weak or no local institutions for environmental governance. The first community picked up the pro-environmental discourse of the RISEMP much more effectively than the other communities[59]. Individual payments thus need not be detrimental to non-market environmental governance. In the case of the RISEMP, and in line with our previous interpretation of its success due to its articulation with a broader pathway of change, the best local setting for PES to have an impact was the village with the highest institutional capacity, indicating the importance of processes of institutional interplay.

A PES mechanism might thus thrive best in a dynamic context of motivational and institutional reinforcement (Kosoy et al., 2008). From both a pessimistic and an optimistic viewpoint, it seems irresponsible to rely uncritically upon the ES market as the 'magic bullet' for saving the environment. There is a clear need to take account of the whole socio-institutional landscape before 'pushing' the provision of ES in a market framework only. It is important to approach human beings not simply as selfish utility maximisers, but to take due account of the existence of environmental ethics and of how the latter can be further developed and utilised through

[58] The specific community (San Ignacio) was part of a group of communities that were formed in the mid-1980s through a process of church-led agrarian reform at a time when the region was the main 'hot zone' of the war between the Sandinista revolutionary government and the right-wing contra-revolutionary rebels. At the time, the latter had already been transformed from a mere mercenary army, formed of previous National Guard soldiers, into a genuine peasant guerilla force with ample participation of the younger generation of the rural population of (among others) Matiguás. Precisely because of these strong links, the land reform process through the church (as an alternative for usual Sandinista-led land reform which was hated by the contra) gained the acceptance of the contra-revolutionaries and also managed to displace the war to the Northern part of the country. According to Peter Marchetti, one of the promoters of the land reform in Matiguás, in terms of agro-ecological conditions no marked differences existed between the different communities at the time of its implementation (personal communication, November 2008). He attributes today's differences mainly to the exceptional quality of the local leader in San Ignacio, who had also picked up the idea of the usefulness of planting trees on the cattle farm 'from the very beginning'.

[59] This is also reflected in the land use change patterns in the first community as compared to the other communities. At the end of the project, in the first community forests covered an additional extra 4.1 per cent of total land (as compared to 2003), while all other communities knew a change of maximum 0.7 per cent. Improved pastures with trees increased from 11 per cent to 33.8 per cent of total land use in the first community, which means an additional cover of 22.9 per cent; the closest follower knew an increase of 'only' 14.4 per cent.

deliberative institutions that enable co-operative actions and foster what Agrawal (2005) has called 'the making of environmental subjects'. Inspired by Cleaver (2002), we therefore believe that the crafting of an acceptable mix of institutional solutions requires a complexity-sensitive, site-specific, path-dependent and ongoing 'bricolage' towards better local-global institutions.

5. CONCLUSION

This chapter analysed the potential and limitations of PES incentives from a supply side perspective. It did so by systemising and empirically reassessing the 'success of PES' in ensuring farmers' supply of environmental services in the RISEMP project, one of the main experimental pilot PES initiatives worldwide. The project's results indicate how project participants assimilated their agricultural practices to the project's narrative and how they successfully invested in the envisaged land uses. The project's use of a flawed experimental design set-up, however, only marginally touches upon the explanatory importance of broader dynamics that are simultaneously taking place. The effect of other variables on pro-environmental behaviour, such as social dynamics and the interplay with existing formal and informal institutions (e.g. local rules and social norms), are unduly neglected in such an approach. The project set-up therefore implicitly confirms Ervine's (2010) claim that environmental governance is increasingly moulded into a universal blueprint, that in effect 'does away with the historical, spatial and temporal particularities of specific ecological problems' (ibid: 774), and a priori fashions the causes of and solutions to biodiversity loss in a market-based framework. In line with previous empirical research (e.g. Corbera et al., 2007, 2009; Kosoy et al., 2007, 2008), our study has indicated that a narrow market-based approach might not adequately explain the complex dynamics that are taking place. From a broader institutional analysis perspective we showed how a mixture of economic and non-economic factors motivated farmers to adopt the envisaged silvopastoral practices. PES interacted with exogenous economic factors and broader local institutional processes, which together generated renewed and environmentally-sound collective pathways towards intensified silvopastoral milk production. The payments were thus an additional objective and symbolic factor in this broader dynamic.

We also indicated that the market-based PES approach is difficult to be linked with the required 'economics of configuration', necessary to create connected biological corridors or to protect sites critical for water or biodiversity conservation. PES on their own probably do not provide sufficient direct incentives towards cooperation between different actors at the landscape scale. Indeed, we argued that the spread of the market-based logic of monetary rewards may even tend to erode existing environmental ethics and social norms, unless PES are matched to effective local institutions enabling it to promote 'motivation crowding-in'. This leads us to conclude that more sophisticated and ideologically flexible approaches that recognise the advantages and disadvantages of 'market', 'state' and 'community' governance as well as their varied and complex local manifestations in each particular circumstance, and that modestly try to generate ways to build better institutional mechanisms which improve overall outcomes, might thus be more appropriate. In line with McAfee and Shapiro (2010) we conclude that successful conservation via PES or PES-like approaches requires the explicit recognition and greater institutional support of farmer agriculture and community economies. We thus fully support the emerging institutional approach to PES (Corbera et al., 2009; Farley and Costanza, 2010; Muradian et al., 2010; Vatn, 2010), which sheds more light on the importance that institutions play in the design and performance of PES, and explicitly recognises the variety of cultural, political and social contexts in which PES operate.

REFERENCES

Agrawal, A. (2005) *Environmentality: technologies of government and the making of subjects*, Durham, North Carolina and London: Duke University Press.

Anderson, C.L. (2006) "Understanding the supply response of local public goods to environmental service payments", Evans School Working Paper 2006-03, Seattle: University of Washington.

Bastiaensen, J., D'Exelle, B. and Famerée, C. (2006) "Political arenas around access to land: a diagnosis of property rights practices in the Nicaraguan interior", IDPM-UA Discussion paper 2006-08. Antwerp: University of Antwerp-Institute of Development Policy and Management.

Bénabou, R. and Tirole, J. (2003) "Intrinsic and extrinsic motivation", *Review of Economic Studies* 70: 489-520.

Bowles, S. (2008) "Policies designed for self-interested citizens may undermine 'the moral sentiments': evidence from economic experiments", *Science* 320: 1605–1609.

Börner, J., Wunder, S., Wertz-Kanounnikoff, S., Rügnitz Tito, M., Pereira, L. and Nascimento, N. (2010) "Direct conservation payments in the Brazilian Amazon: Scope and equity implications", *Ecological Economics* 69(6): 1272-1282.

Chouinard, H.H., Paterson, T., Wandschneider, P.R. and Ohler, A.M. (2008) "Will farmers trade profits for stewardship? Heterogeneous motivations for farm practice selection", *Land Economics* 84(1): 66-82.

Cleaver, F. (1998) "Incentives and informal institutions: Gender and the management of water", *Agriculture and Human Values* 15: 347-360.

Cleaver, F. (2002) "Reinventing Institutions and the Social Embeddedness of Natural Resource Management", *European Journal of Development Research* 14(2): 11–30.

Corbera, E., Brown, K. and Adger, W.N. (2007) "The equity and legitimacy of markets for ecosystem services", *Development and Change* 38(4): 587-613.

Corbera, E., González Soberanis, C. and Brown, K. (2009) "Institutional dimensions of payments for ecosystem services. An analysis of Mexico's carbon forestry programme", *Ecological Economics* 68: 743–761.

Dagang, A.B.K. and Nair, P.K.R. (2003) "Silvopastoral research and adoption in Central America: Recent findings and recommendations for future directions", *Agroforestry Systems* 59: 149–155.

de Haan, L. and Zoomers, A. (2005) "Exploring the frontier of livelihood research", *Development and Change* 36(1): 27-47.

Dorrough, J., Moll, J. and Crosthwaite, J. (2007) "Can intensification of temperate Australian livestock production systems save land for native biodiversity?", *Agriculture, Ecosystems and Environment* 121: 222-232.

Engel, S., Pagiola, S. and Wunder, S. (2008) "Designing payments for environmental services in theory and practice: an overview of the issues", *Ecological Economics* 65: 663–675.

Ervine, K. (2010) "Participation denied: the Global Environment Facility, its universal blueprint, and the Mexico-Mesoamerican biological corridor in Chiapas", *Third World Quarterly* 31(5): 773-790.

Farley, J. and Costanza, R. (2010) "Payments for ecosystem services: from local to global", *Ecological Economics* 69: 2060-2068.

Ferraro, P.J. and Kiss, A. (2002) "Direct payments for biodiversity conservation", *Science* 298: 1718-1719.

Frey, B.S. (1997) Not Just for the Money: An Economic Theory of Personal Motivation. Cheltenham, U.K.: Edward Elgar.

Frey, B.S. and Oberholzer-Gee, F. (1997) "The cost of price incentives: An empirical analysis of motivation crowding-out", *American Economic Review* 87: 746–755.

Frey, B.S. and Stutzer, A. (2006) "Environmental morale and motivation", Working Paper N°288, Zurich: Institute for Empirical Research in Economics.

Glaser, B.G. (1992) Basics of grounded theory analysis, Mill Valley, CA: Sociology Press.

Glaser, B.G. and Strauss, A.L. (1967) The Discovery of Grounded Theory – Strategies for Qualitative Research, New York: Aldine De Gruyter.

Global Environment Facility (GEF) (2007a) "Biodiversity Focal Area Strategy and Strategic Programming for GEF-4", GEF Policy Paper, Washington, D.C.: GEF.

Global Environment Facility (GEF) (2007b) "Project Details Regional Integrated Silvopastoral Approaches to Ecosystem Management", On-line available at http://www.gefonline.org/projectDetailsSQL.cfm?projID=947 (last consulted: 12 December 2008).

Goldman, R.L., Thompson, B.H. and Daily G.C. (2007) "Institutional incentives for managing the landscape: Inducing cooperation for the production of ecosystem services", *Ecological Economics* 64: 333-343.

Gómez-Baggethun, E., de Groot, R., Lomas, P.L. and Montes, C. (2010) "The history of ecosystem services in economic theory and practice: from early notions to markets and payment schemes", *Ecological Economics* 69(6): 1209–1218.

Gottfried, R., Wear, D. and Lee, R. (1996) "Institutional solutions to market failure on the landscape scale", *Ecological Economics* 18: 133-140.

Greenstone, M. and Gayer, T. (2009) "Quasi-experimental and experimental approaches to environmental economics", *Journal of Environmental Economics and Management* 57: 21-44.

Griffith, K. and Zepeda, L. (1994) "Farm level trade-offs of intensifying tropical milk production", *Ecological Economics* 9: 121-133.

Gutman, P. and Davidson, S. (2007) "The Global Environment Facility and Payments for Ecosystem Services. A review of current initiatives and recommendations for future PES support by GEF and FAO programs", PESAL Papers Series No. 1, Rome: WWF Macroeconomic for Sustainable Development Program Office.

Haila, Y. (2002) "A Conceptual Genealogy of Fragmentation Research: From Island Biogeography to Landscape Ecology", *Ecological Applications* 12(2): 321-334.

Heyman, J. and Ariely, D. (2004) "Effort for payment: a tale of two markets", *Psychological Science* 15(11): 787-793.

Ibrahim, M., Chacón, M., Cuartas, C., Naranjo, J., Ponce, G., Vega, P., Casasola, F. and Rojas, J. (2007) "Almacenamiento de carbono en el suelo y la biomasa arbórea en sistemas de usos de la tierra en paisajes ganaderos de Colombia, Costa Rica y Nicaragua", *Agroforestería en las Américas* 45: 27-36.

Kaimowitz, D. and Angelsen, A. (1998) *Economic models of tropical deforestation: a review*, Bogor, Indonesia: Center for International Forestry Research.

Karp, D.R. and Gaulding, C.L. (1995) "Motivational underpinnings of command-and-control, market-based, and voluntarist environmental policies", *Human Relations* 48(5): 439-465.

Kosoy, N., Martinez-Tuna, M., Muradian, R. and Martinez-Alier, J. (2007) "Payments for environmental services in watersheds: Insights from a comparative study of three cases in Central America", *Ecological Economics* 61: 446-455.

Kosoy, N., Corbera, E. and Brown, K. (2008) "Participation in payments for ecosystem services: Case studies from the Lacandón rainforest, Mexico", *Geoforum* 39: 2073-2083.

Kosoy, N. and Corbera, E. (2010) "Payments for ecosystem services as commodity fetishism", *Ecological Economics* 69(6): 1228–1236.

Lepper, M.R. and Greene, D. (eds.) (1978) The hidden costs of reward: New perspectives on the psychology of human motivation, Hillsdale, New York: Erlbaum.

Levard, L., Lopez, Y.M. and Navarro, I. (2001) Municipio de Matiguás: Potencialidades y limitantes del desarrollo agropecuario, Managua: UCA/FIDA/Nitlapán.

Maldidier, C. and Marchetti, R. (1996) El Campesino-Finquero y el potencial económico del campesinado nicaragüense, Managua: Nitlapán.

Martin, A., Blowers, A. and Boersema, J. (2008) "Paying for environmental services: can we afford to lose a cultural basis for conservation?", *Environmental Sciences* 5(1): 1-5.

McAfee, K. (1999) "Selling nature to save it? Biodiversity and green developmentalism", *Environment and Planning D: Society and Space* 17(2): 133–154.

McAfee, K. and Shapiro, E.N. (2010) "Payment for Environmental Services in Mexico: Neoliberalism, Social Movements, and the State", *Annals of the Association of American Geographers* 100(3): 579-599.

Millennium Ecosystem Assessment (MA) (2005) *Millennium Ecosystem Assessment. Ecosystems and Human Well-being*, Washington, D.C.: Island Press.

Muradian, R., Corbera, E., Pascual, U., Kosoy, N. and May, P. (2010) "Reconciling theory and practice: An alternative conceptual framework for understanding payments for environmental services", *Ecological Economics* 69(6): 1202–1208.

Murgueitio, E., Ibrahim, M., Ramírez, E., Zapata, A., Mejía, C.E. and Casasola, F. (2003) Usos de la tierra en fincas ganaderas: Guía para el pago de servicios ambientales en el Proyecto Enfoques Silvopastorales Integrados para el Manejo de Ecosistemas, Cali, Colombia: CIPAV-CATIE-Nitlapán.

Nicholson, C.F., Blake, R.W. and Lee, D.R. (1995) "Livestock, deforestation, and policy making: intensification of cattle production systems in Central America revisited", *Journal of Dairy Science* 78: 719-734.

North, D.C. (1990) Institutions, Institutional Change and Economic Performance, New York: Cambridge University Press.

Ostrom, E. (2002) "The Puzzle of Counterproductive Property Rights Reforms: A Conceptual Analysis", in A. de Janvry, G. Gordillo, J.P. Platteau and E. Sadoulet (eds), *Access to Land, Rural Poverty and Public Action* (pp. 129–50). Oxford: Oxford University Press.

Paavola, J. and Adger, N.W. (2005) "Institutional ecological economics", *Ecological Economics* 53: 353-368.

Pagiola, S., Agostini, P., Gobbi, J., de Haan, C., Ibrahim, M., Murgueitio, E., Ramírez, E., Rosales, M. and Ruíz, J.P. (2004) "Paying for biodiversity conservation services in agricultural landscapes", Environment Department Paper, vol. 96. Washington. World Bank.

Pagiola, S., Arcenas, A. and Platais, G. (2005) "Can payments for environmental services help reduce poverty? An exploration of the issues and the evidence to date from Latin America", *World Development* 33(2): 237-253.

Pagiola, S., Bishop, J. and Landell-Mills, N. (eds.) (2002) Selling forest environmental services. Market-based mechanisms for conservation and development, London: Earthscan.

Pagiola, S., Ramírez, E., Gobbi, J., de Haan, C., Ibrahim, M., Murgueitio, E. and Ruíz, J. (2007) "Paying for the environmental services of silvopastoral practices in Nicaragua", *Ecological Economics* 64: 374–385.

Pagiola, S., Rios, A.R. and Arcenas, A. (2008) "Can the poor participate in payments for environmental services? Lessons from the Silvopastoral Project in Nicaragua", *Environment and Development Economics* 13(3): 299-325.

Parkhurst, G.M. and Shogren, J.F. (2007) "Spatial incentives to coordinate contiguous habitat", *Ecological Economics* 64: 344-355.

Parkhurst, G.M., Shogren, J.F., Bastian, C., Kivi, P., Donner, J. and Smith, R.B.W. (2002) "Agglomeration bonus: an incentive mechanism to reunite fragmented habitat for biodiversity conservation", *Ecological Economics* 41: 305-328.

Pattanayak, S.K., Mercer, D.E., Sills, E. and Yang, J.-C. (2003) "Taking stock of agroforestry adoption studies", *Agroforestry Systems* 57: 173–186.

Pattanayak, S.K., Wunder, S. and Ferraro, P.J. (2010) "Show me the money: do payments supply environmental services in developing countries?" *Review of Environmental Economics and Policy* 4(2): 254-274.

Ravnborg, H.M., Damsgaard, M.G. and Raben, K. (2007) "Payments for Ecosystem Services. Issues and pro-poor opportunities for development assistance", DIIS Report 2007:6, Copenhagen: Danish Institute for International Studies.

Reeson, A. (2008) "Institutions, motivations and public goods: theory, evidence and implications for environmental policy", CSIRO Working Paper Series 2008/01, Canberra: CSIRO.

Reeson, A. and Tisdell, J. (2006) "When good incentives go bad: an experimental study of institutions, motivations and crowding out", Australian Agricultural and Resource Economics Society (AARES) 50th Annual Conference, Sydney.

Rubin, H.J. and Rubin, I.S. (2005) *Qualitative Interviewing: The Art of Hearing Data*, California: Sage Publications.

Sáenz, J.C., Villatoro, F., Ibrahim, M., Fajardo, D. and Pérez, M. (2007) "Relación entre las comunidades de aves y la vegetación en agropaisajes dominados por la ganadería en Costa Rica, Nicaragua y Colombia", *Agroforestería en las Américas* 45: 37-48.

Swift, M.J., Izac, A.-M.N. and van Noordwijk, M. (2004) "Biodiversity and ecosystem services in agricultural landscapes – Are we asking the right questions?", *Agriculture, Ecosystems and Environment* 104: 113-134.

Vaessen, J. and Van Hecken, G. (2009) "Assessing the potential for experimental evaluation of intervention effects: The case of the Regional Integrated Silvopastoral Approaches to Ecosystem Management Project", GEF Impact Evaluation Report. Washington D.C.: GEF Evaluation Office.

Van Hecken, G. and Bastiaensen, J. (2010) "Payments for Ecosystem Services: A Political View of its Justification, or the Lack of it", *Environmental Science & Policy* 13(8): 785-792.

Vatn, A. (2005) "Rationality, institutions and environmental policy", *Ecological Economics* 55: 203-217.

Vatn, A. (2010) "An institutional analysis of payments for environmental services", *Ecological Economics* 69(6): 1245–1252.

Vosti, S.A., Carpentier, C.L., Witcover, J. and Valentim, J.F. (2001) "Intensified small-scale livestock systems in the Western Brazilian Amazon", in A. Angelsen and D. Kaimowitz (eds.), *Agricultural technologies and tropical deforestation* (pp.113-133), Oxfordshire: CABI Publishing.

Wear, D.N. (1992) "Forest Management, Institutions, and Ecological Sustainability", Paper presented at the Appalachian Society of American Foresters Meeting, Asheville, North Carolina.

Wells, M.P. (1998) "Institutions and incentives for biodiversity conservation", *Biodiversity and Conservation* 7: 815-835.

White, D., Holmann, F., Fujisaka, S., Reategui, K. and Lascano, C. (2001) "Will intensifying pasture management in Latin America protect forests – or is it the other way around?", in A. Angelsen and D. Kaimowitz (eds.), *Agricultural technologies and tropical deforestation* (pp.91-111), Oxfordshire: CABI Publishing.

World Bank. (2002) "Colombia, Costa Rica, and Nicaragua regional integrated silvopastoral approaches to ecosystem management project: project appraisal document", Report No.21869-LAC. Washington, DC: World Bank.

World Bank. (2010) "Payments for Environmental Services: Current projects", On-line available http://web.worldbank.org/WBSITE/EXTERNAL/TOPICS/ENVIRONMENT/EXTEEI/0,,contentMDK:20487983~menuPK:1187844~pagePK:210058~piPK:210062~theSitePK:408050~isCURL:Y,00.html (last consulted: 15 October 2010).

Yamamoto, W., Dewi, I.A. and Ibrahim, M. (2007) "Effects of silvopastoral areas on milk production at dual purpose cattle farms at the semi-humid old agricultural frontier in central Nicaragua", *Agricultural Systems* 94: 368-375.

Young, M., Shi, T. and Crosthwaite, J. (2003) *Duty of care: An instrument for increasing the effectiveness of catchment management*. Department of Sustainability and Environment, State of Victoria, Melbourne.

ANNEXES

ANNEX I. SELECTION OF RISEMP PARTICIPANTS AND CONTROL GROUP SELECTION BIAS

From: Vaessen and Van Hecken, 2009: 14-17.

1) Selection of participants in RISEMP project

In Nicaragua, in 2002, in order to start project activities farmers were selected in a systematic manner and assigned to groups receiving different types of incentives. After the selection of communities (seven communities in two watersheds in the Matiguás-Rio Blanco region) in which the project would intervene, a census was held among all farmers. On the basis of the census the project staff invited farmers to meetings to explain the rules of the game and promote the project. The project objectives were explained to farmers and farmers were selected for participation on the basis of the following criteria (operational manual RISEMP):

- small and medium farmers;
- secure land tenure;
- livestock as principal income activity;
- willingness to sign a contract with the project;
- willingness to collaborate with project monitoring activities;
- willingness to participate in training and receive technical assistance;
- willingness to develop a farm development plan in order to generate environmental services and improve productivity;
- willingness to continue to manage silvopastoral systems after project closure.

In addition, in practice the following criteria for selection were applied:

- proximity to the road;
- farmer should live in the farm;
- farmer should have between 8 and 100 hectares of land.

At the time of project initiation meetings with farmers, the message was that all farmers participating in the project would receive payments for environmental services generated by their changes in land use. Some farmers left as they did not believe that benefits would come forth or they lost interest in the project. Consequently, apart from the formal selection criteria a kind of natural selection process took place in which the most motivated farmers, i.e. those that continued to attend the meetings, would be the first to qualify for project benefits. The interested and selected participants were then assigned to two groups, those that would receive payments and technical assistance (PES + TA) and those that would receive payments only (PES). Preliminary quota for the two groups were established per community. Subsequently, independent of the previous subdivision, the total group of people receiving PES (with or without TA) was again divided into two groups, one receiving only payments during the first two years of the project, and one receiving payments for four years (until the end of the project). The control group was established later on.

2) Control group selection

The control group was selected after the treatment groups and its subdivisions had already been established. The urgency to find a sufficiently large group of willing farmers and the timing of the selection made it impossible for project staff to select farmers randomly (from the same population as farmers selected for the other groups) or even on the basis of certain selection criteria. In the end, the control group comprised farmers who had continued to attend the project meetings (but did not comply with selection criteria for PES), farmers who had ceased to attend the meetings, and others. As a result, comparisons between the treatment groups and the control group would be biased due to severe problems of selection bias on the basis of observables as well as unobservables.

Selection bias on the basis of observables.

Landowners not complying with selection criteria for receiving PES or TA and therefore rejected for receiving PES, in some cases were asked to become part of the control group. This was part of a pragmatic solution to rapidly define groups of sufficient size. The downside of this type of measure was that it introduced a clear selection bias on the basis of observable characteristics. Control group farmers had on average more land, livestock and a relatively smaller proportion of the control group (in comparison with the treatment group) had a history of receiving TA prior to the project. In addition, in the case of land and livestock the standard deviation is much higher in the control group because to a large extent the control group contained farmers with properties that were either too small (less than 8 hectares) or too large (more than 100 hectares) to be considered eligible for receiving PES. Especially the latter type of farmer was quite different from the average participant.

Selection bias on the basis of unobservables.

Some of the farmers who had lost interest in the project at the time of preliminary meetings (before the experimental design was established), were later asked to become part of the control group. While some of the control group farmers were likely to be more reluctant to adopt innovations than the average participant, in practice a subgroup of the control group was triggered by the project to invest in silvopastoral practices (because of treatment diffusion).

Annex II. Environmental services index (ESI) used by the RISEMP

Points per hectare, unless otherwise specified.

Land use	Biodiversity index	Carbon index	ESI
1 Annual crops	0	0	0
2 Degraded pasture	0	0	0
3 Natural pasture without trees	0,1	0,1	0,2
4 Improved pasture without trees	0,1	0,4	0,5
5 Semi-permanent crops (plantain, sun coffee)	0,3	0,2	0,5
6 Natural pasture with low tree density (< 30/ha)	0,3	0,3	0,6
7 Natural pasture with recently-planted trees (>200/ha)	0,3	0,3	0,6
8 New living fence (per km)	0,3	0,3	0,6
9 Improved pasture with recently-planted trees (>200/ha)	0,3	0,4	0,7
10 Monoculture fruit crops	0,3	0,4	0,7
11 Fodder bank	0,3	0,5	0,8
12 Improved pasture with low tree density (< 30/ha)	0,3	0,6	0,9
13 Fodder bank with woody species	0,4	0,5	0,9
14 Natural pasture with high tree density (>30/ha)	0,5	0,5	1
15 Diversified fruit crops	0,6	0,5	1,1
16 Wind break (living fence) (per km)	0,6	0,5	1,1
17 Diversified fodder bank	0,6	0,6	1,2
18 Monoculture timber plantation	0,4	0,8	1,2
19 Shaded coffee	0,6	0,7	1,3
20 Improved pasture with high tree density (>30/ha)	0,6	0,7	1,3
21 Bamboo forest	0,5	0,8	1,3
22 Diversified timber plantation	0,7	0,7	1,4
23 Scrub habitats (*tacotales*)	0,6	0,8	1,4
24 Riparian forest	0,8	0,7	1,5
25 Intensive silvopastoral	0,6	1	1,6
26 Disturbed secondary forest	0,8	0,9	1,7
27 Secondary forest	0,9	1	1,9
28 Primary forest	1	1	2

Note: The ESI is the sum of the biodiversity and carbon indices

Source: Pagiola et al., 2007 and Vaessen and Van Hecken, 2009

ANNEX III. PERSONS INTERVIEWED

FARMERS	
Name	**Treatment group**
Absalón Guerrero	PSA+AT
Agusto Robles	PSA+AT
Albertina Jarquín	PSA+AT
Alberto Saravia	PSA+AT
Angela Alvarado	PSA+AT
Bismarck Barquero	PSA+AT
Carlos Urbina Luna	PSA+AT
Donaldo Barquero	PSA+AT
Eusebio Mendoza Dias	PSA+AT
Fortunato Javier Robles Amador	PSA+AT
Guillermo Garcia Polanco	PSA+AT
José André Jarquín Mendoza	PSA+AT
José Andrés Amador Martinez	PSA
José Roblero Castro	PSA
José Rolando Castillo Ramirez	PSA+AT
Juan José Jarquín Jarquín	PSA
Julia Gadea Amador	PSA+AT
Julio Gutiérrez Obando	CONTROL
Kairo Torres	NON-PARTICIPANT
Orlando Urbina	NON-PARTICIPANT
Pastor Flores Rodríguez	CONTROL
Pedro Reyes Urbina	CONTROL
Pedro Talavera Valle	PSA+AT
Hector René Zeledon Alvarado	CONTROL
Richard José Robles Ortega	PSA
Roberto Urbina	PSA+AT
Rosario Ramírez García	PSA
Santos Genaro Sevilla Suárez	PSA+AT
Severino Vega Martínez	PSA+AT
Simeon Soza Castillo	PSA+AT
Tomas Castro Torres	CONTROL
Tomas Soza Morales	PSA+AT
Trinidad Lanzas	PSA+AT
Victorina Ortega Mondoy	NON-PARTICIPANT
Yamileth Castro	CONTROL
Zoyla Martinez Rubio	CONTROL

PROJECT STAFF	
Name	**Function**
Alfredo Arguëllo	Project staff, Nitlapán
Omar Dávila	Project staff, Nitlapán
Yuri Marín	Researcher, Nitlapán
Guillermo Ponce	Project staff, Nitlapán
Elías Ramirez	Project coordinator, Nitlapán
Bismark Reyes	Project staff, Nitlapán

Annex IV. Participant selection criteria for the qualitative research

The farmer participants were selected on the basis of maximum variability criteria (Glaser and Strauss, 1967). This means that prior to entering the field we made a list of selection criteria which were to guide our initial participant selection. Through this exercise we looked for extreme differences for certain variables among all 123 RISEMP participants. Our initial participant selection was based on the following variables:

- Location (communities, and sectors within communities);
- Payment group (PSA, PSA+AT, Control) and scheme (two- or four-year);
- Received payments during project;
- Farm size;
- Number of cattle;
- Sex of participant;
- Accessibility (close versus far to road);
- Land use and adopted land use changes;
- Membership of organisations.

The participant selection was, however, not entirely fixed from the outset. During field work we maintained an open attitude towards other potential relevant cases. Therefore, additional participants were also selected on the basis of new information obtained during the course of our field work (snowball sampling and theoretical sampling) (e.g. Glaser and Strauss, 1967), and were also selected on the basis of recommendations by former project staff and interviewed farmers. The research design was thus kept flexible in order to accommodate new information, to adapt to the actual experiences that people have had, and to adjust to unexpected situations (Rubin and Rubin, 2005: 35). The amount of interviews was based on the principle of 'theoretical saturation' (Glaser and Strauss, 1997; Glaser, 1992), which means that the sample size depends on whether or not new data is emerging from additional interviews (or other data collecting tools).

ANNEX V. GENERAL INTERVIEW OUTLINE FOR THE QUALITATIVE RESEARCH

In order to guide our interviews with farmers, we used the following general interview outline. Note, however, that the applied outline during field work could differ from the general outline, since the interviews were not fixed from the outset (see annex IV).

General interview outline

Introduction
- Students from University, doing study, no project, no NGO nor governmental organisation
- Research on how farmers live, which problems they experience

Personal data participant/household

Farm data
- Land use (change) – motivation - silvopastoral/agroforestry practices (why?)
- Livestock
- Other farm incomes
- Problems/difficulties and opportunities
- Coping strategies
- Future plans + motivation

Community data
- Presence of institutions/organisations
- Membership organisations
- Community organisations
- Environmental situation

Projects
- Participation projects
- Evaluation of projects

RISEMP (silvopastoral) Project
- Logic
- Participation
- Payments and costs
- Land use changes (during & after project) – (why?)
- Opportunities and limitations project
- Technical Assistance
- Personal opinion/evaluation
- Drivers of change – motivation?
- Future plans (with/without similar projects)
- (Un)successful cases other farmers

CHAPTER 4

A CRITICAL ASSESSMENT OF DEMAND SIDE CHARACTERISTICS IN LOCALLY-FINANCED PES - INSIGHTS FROM A WATERSHED STUDY IN MATIGUÁS, NICARAGUA

Note: This chapter is based upon Van Hecken, G., Bastiaensen, J. and Vásquez, W.F. (2010) "Institutional embeddedness of local willingness to pay for environmental services: Evidence from Matiguás, Nicaragua", IDPM-UA Discussion Paper 2010-04, Antwerp: Institute of Development Policy and Management; and an article submitted to *Ecological Economics* as Van Hecken, G., Bastiaensen J. and Vásquez, W.F. "The viability of local payments for watershed services: Counter-intuitive evidence from Matiguás, Nicaragua".

The chapter has benefited from useful comments and suggestions by Johan Bastiaensen, Tom De Herdt, Guido Erreygers, Kathleen McAfee, Martin Prowse, Griet Steel, William Vásquez, Aviel Verbruggen, Inge Wagemakers and Nanneke Winters. It has also benefited from fruitful discussions with participants at the CERES Summer School Annual Meeting on Global Governance, the Crisis and Development (The Hague, June 2010), and the Institute of Development Policy and Management (IOB) Doctoral Seminar (Antwerp, June 2010). The research was funded by a Ph.D. grant of the Flemish Interuniversity Council (VLIR-UOS). We would also like to thank our local research team in Matiguás for the implementation of the contingent valuation survey. Special thanks go to Dries Cleiren and Jaqueline Zeledón for their unconditional support during the field work. The usual disclaimers apply.

1. INTRODUCTION

The present chapter will inquire into the feasibility of payments schemes from a demand side perspective. More specifically, it investigates the local willingness to pay for watershed services in an upstream-downstream context. In chapter 1 and 2 we already noted how scarcity of public funds make some authors argue that the funding for ES might be further developed by focusing on private demand for conservation (e.g. Pagiola and Platais, 2007; Pattanayak et al., 2010; Wunder et al., 2008). In chapter 2 we also discussed how despite the ongoing political debates at the international level (and most importantly the debate on the implementation of international payments schemes through REDD), at present the quest for sustainable funding is still largely focused on decentralised efforts that capitalise on local demand for certain ecosystem services. The assumed efficiency gains of locally user-financed mechanisms (Engel et al., 2008; Wunder et al., 2008) make watershed contexts an interesting setting for the implementation of PES schemes (Ortega-Pacheco et al., 2009; Pagiola et al., 2007; Porras et al., 2008; Southgate and Wunder, 2009). Pagiola et al. (2007), for example, note that water services offer various advantages: 'water users are easy to identify; receive clear, well-defined benefits; and often already have financing mechanisms' (ibid: 383). In other words, watershed contexts are thus believed to more easily fit the Coasean upstream-downstream externality framework (see Figure 7 for a schematic overview), as they can capitalise on the production of straightforward externalities (water resources) and the generation of relatively low transaction costs by adding ES payments to existing financing structures already established by local water utilities (e.g. Kosoy et al., 2007). Hence, ongoing research is increasingly exploring the potential of local payments for watershed services, and its prospects in securing long-term ecosystem protection (Ferraro; 2009; George et al., 2009; Muñoz-Piña et al., 2008; Ortega-Pacheco et al., 2009; Pagiola et al., 2002; Porras et al., 2008; Southgate and Wunder, 2009; Wunder and Albán, 2008).

So far, however, few studies have explicitly focused on demand-side aspects of locally-financed PES (Postel and Thompson, 2005). Johnson and Baltodano (2004) and Ortega-Pacheco et al. (2009) assessed local rural households' willingness to pay (WTP) for watershed PES in Nicaraguan and Costa Rican communities respectively, but both studies used small sample sizes, found quite diverging WTP results, and none of them explicitly dealt with broader institutional contexts. This chapter attempts to fill this research gap by assessing local WTP for water and related hydrological PES schemes and by identifying and understanding the factors that determine this WTP. The empirical context of our study is the rural town of Matiguás in Nicaragua. In the prospect of the termination of the silvopastoral RISEMP project in Matiguás-Río Blanco (see previous chapter), Pagiola et al. (2007) suggested that potential long-term funding could be secured through the establishment of loca payments for water services, which 'offer the most promising avenue for financing long-term PES programs' (ibid: 383). In this chapter we will critically investigate this proposition. As has already been argued from a supply-side perspective (Clements et al., 2010; Corbera et al., 2007a, 2007b; Corbera et al., 2009; Kosoy et al., 2008; Van Hecken and Bastiaensen, 2010a), our demand-side analysis will show that the feasibility of PES programmes is mediated and constrained by context-related factors within the local socio-institutional context (such as the perceptions of property rights and entitlements), a claim which is increasingly recognised among PES practitioners and scholars, but still under-researched in the PES literature up to now (Muradian et al., 2010; Vatn, 2010).

Figure 7. Externalities and PES on a watershed level

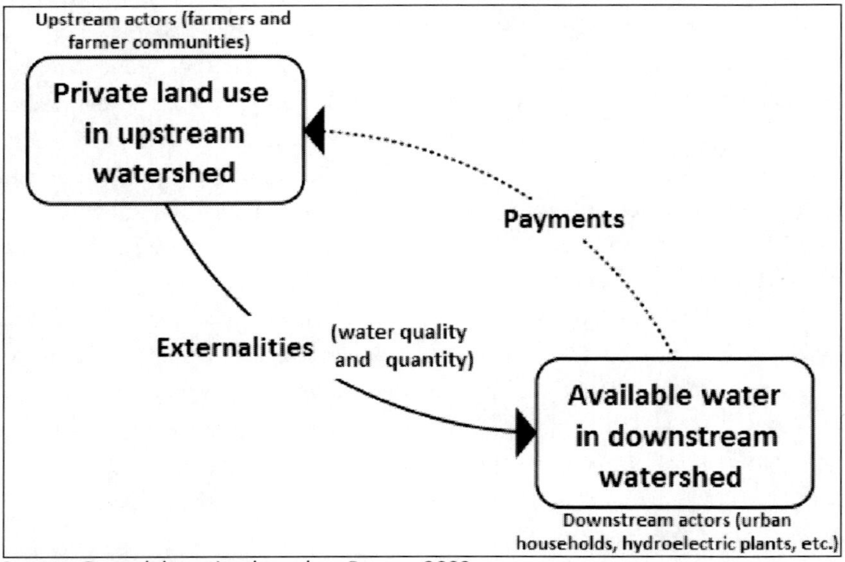

Source: Own elaboration based on Porras, 2003

The next section briefly introduces the study site and explains how the study combined both qualitative and quantitative research approaches to assess the complex reality of environmental governance and the WTP of the local population for improved water delivery and watershed services (Section 2). Based on the qualitative research, section 3 then describes the socio-institutional context and the current approach to environmental governance in Matiguás. Next, section 4 analyses the local WTP for a watershed PES programme in Matiguás with contingent valuation (CV) techniques. The results of this exercise are then critically reassessed and discussed in section 5, mainly by contextualising the result of the quantitative analysis against the local institutional background. The chapter ends with some tentative conclusions.

2. DESCRIPTION OF THE STUDY SITE AND THE APPLIED METHODOLOGIES

2.1. STUDY SITE

Similarly as in the previous chapter, the study site is the rural municipality of Matiguás, located in the central Nicaraguan department of Matagalpa (Figure 8). As mentioned before, the municipality belongs to the so-called old agricultural frontier region (Maldidier and Marchetti, 1996) and contains two protected areas: the Sierra Quirragua (from now on referred to as 'Quirragua') and about 30 per cent of the Cerro Musún. It has an undulating terrain, with elevations in the Quirragua area of up to almost 1,400 metres above sea level. Besides the urban part of Matiguás, which lies at about 250 metres above sea level, the municipality exists of 26 districts and 88 communities, which cover a total area of 1,710 km^2. In 2005 the population of urban Matiguás was estimated at around 9,000, living in about 2,300 houses. The rest of the population, about 32,000 people, lives in the rural areas of Matiguás (INIDE, 2005). Despite the steady economic development during the last decades, the municipality is still part of a region with a high degree of poverty (ibid). Life expectancy is about 65.5 years, and - though some improvements have been made during the last few years - at 41.5 per cent in 2005, the illiteracy rate is still one of the highest in Nicaragua[60] (INIDE, 2005; Levard et al., 2001).

Until one century ago, the area predominantly consisted of forests. However, increasing colonisation of the area in search of pasture for cattle, both by peasants and landlords related to the Somoza government, resulted in rapid deforestation from the 1920s onwards (Maldidier and Marchetti, 1996). According to local estimations, during the last 20 years alone, more than 40 per cent of the forested area in Matiguás has been cut down. Most of its soils naturally possess a low water infiltration capacity and according to the local municipality and local people intensifying agricultural land use has further lowered this capacity, resulting in rivers running dry during the dry season and in uncontrolled run-off and surface water increases during the rainy season[61] (INIFOM, 2004). Inappropriate agricultural practices also pollute water sources with agrochemicals and organic contaminants (PAHO and ENACAL, 2004). These activities have put increasing pressure on the drinking water supply in urban Matiguás, which currently depends on a system that

[60] As shown below (table 7 in section 4.1), our survey research elicited an urban illiteracy rate of 10 per cent. Nevertheless, illiteracy rates are much higher outside the urban centre of Matiguás, which explains the higher regional rate.

[61] As argued further below in this chapter, in the present study the most important factor is what local people *perceive* as a truth, and not so much whether this is really scientifically proven. In fact, — and as already argued in chapter 2 — most PES schemes are based on local perceptions, and not on scientific studies on the link between land use changes and real ES provision, see also Rojas and Aylward, 2003).

captures water from the river Cusiles, which springs in the upstream natural reserve of Quirragua (north of urban Matiguás). Although the Quirragua area is a natural reserve, about 70 per cent of its land is privately owned by farmers who mainly use the land for agricultural activities, such as the cultivation of corn, beans, and coffee, and pastures for cattle. The negative consequences of these upstream activities are locally perceived as an increasing threat to the downstream urban tap water supply, and a clear sign of the urgent need of more effective, negotiated environmental governance.

Figure 8. Matiguás and the protected area of Quirragua

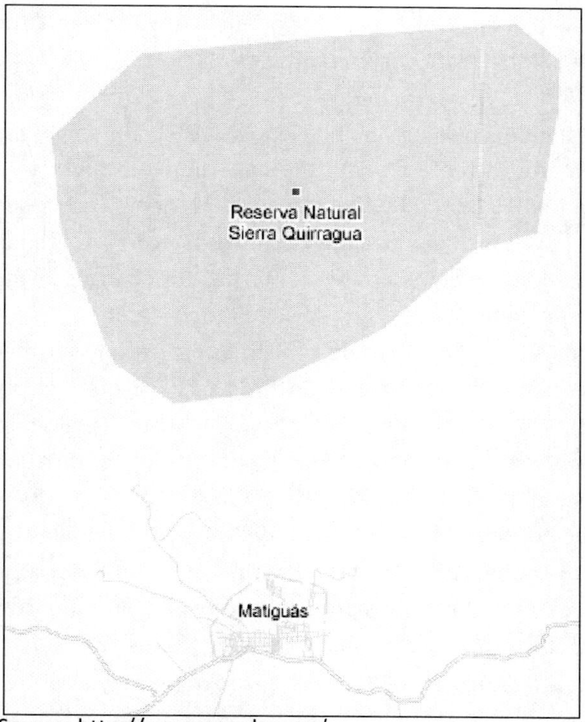

Source: http://maps.google.com/

2.2. RESEARCH METHODOLOGIES

The assessment of local WTP for watershed services and how potential PES programmes fit into local institutional contexts are complex inquiries, which require a combination of several research approaches. In our research we opted for a mixed method approach, combining qualitative and quantitative techniques. The qualitative research, which mainly assessed the institutional setting and the population's perception of the environmental and water problems at stake, was carried out over six months during 2008 and 2009, and mainly consisted of in-depth responsive interviews (Rubin and Rubin, 2005) and observation. More than 25 representatives from different local institutions and organisations were interviewed (see annex I), ranging from consumer group representatives to central institution delegates and from political party secretaries to farmer cooperative presidents. The focus of the interviews was predominantly on the perceptions of environmental problems, their causes, and proposed solutions, as well as on agro-environmental externalities and the potential of PES schemes in dealing with these externalities (see annex II for a more detailed interview outline). Additionally, several inter-institutional meetings dealing with environmental issues in Matiguás were attended. Some of the interviews were taped and verbally transcribed, but most of them were noted down during the interview sessions, as this created a more confidential environment. The data were analysed using the qualitative data analysis software NVivo[62].

In order to further investigate downstream households' WTP for improved water services, we complemented this research with the quantitative analysis of a split-sample CV survey in urban Matiguás. The CV method, in which people are asked hypothetical questions about how much a certain externality is worth to them, assesses the monetary value that respondents are willing to pay for changes in the provision of a (hitherto non-marketed) publicly provided good, such as most environmental services (Carson, 1999). This method is increasingly used in water supply research in developing countries (North and Griffin, 1993; Vásquez et al., 2009; Whittington et al., 1990). We use this method for 'valuing' water services as such while also linking it to specific policy scenarios, thereby generating information about their viability (Farley and Costanza, 2010: 2063). Prior to survey implementation we also conducted three focus group interviews (see again annex II for a more detailed overview of the discussed contents during these interviews), a pilot survey with a random sample of 32 households, and a number of iterations to incorporate feedback and assure respondents' understanding. In-person survey interviews were conducted during August 2009 using a geographically-stratified random sample of 1,015 households[63] (see annex III for a cadastral map of urban Matiguás), covering approximately 44 per cent of total downstream urban households in Matiguás[64]. The surveys were implemented by ten (five female and five male) local university students, who received a five-day training before entering the field.

[62] Nvivo is a software package for qualitative researchers, which helps to manage, shape and make sense of rich text-based information, where deep levels of analysis on small or large volumes of data are required. It provides a workspace with tools that facilitate the coding, classifying, sorting and arranging of information.

[63] Sampling was based on random selection of plots on the latest urban cadastral maps, provided to us by the municipality and the municipal water utility (see also annex III).

[64] Such a large total sample size was required for the analysis of four spit-sampled contingent valuation scenarios (see section 4).

The final version of the survey elicited household responses on the current tap water system, water uses and consumption practices. Several questions were also aimed at eliciting households' perceptions on and attitudes towards local environmental degradation and entitlements, the existence of upstream-downstream externalities and preferred solutions for them. Subsequently, respondents were randomly read one out of four contingent water supply improvement scenarios (which were designed on the basis of the earlier qualitative research, see section 4.2), and were assigned an additional monthly water fee that also randomly varied across the sample. The referendum valuation question (Haab and McConnell, 1998), in which respondents had to answer whether they voted in favour or against the proposed scenario (dichotomous choice), was used to elicit the household's WTP in the presented contingent scenario. Finally, various follow-up questions were asked, which mainly focused on socio-demographic characteristics.

3. THE INSTITUTIONAL CONTEXT OF ENVIRONMENTAL GOVERNANCE IN MATIGUÁS

3.1. ENVIRONMENTAL GOVERNANCE IN MATIGUÁS

Nicaragua has known a long tradition of centralised command-and-control natural resource management, in which the main emphasis has been on the creation of protected areas (Barahona, 2001; Ravnborg, 2010). The main actor responsible for environmental management at the national level is the Ministry of the Environment and Natural Resources (MARENA), which coordinates its tasks with the Ministry of Agriculture, Ranching and Forestry (MAGFOR), and the National Forestry Institute (INAFOR). However, the limited political willingness and capacity of these government agencies to effectively enforce the protected area decrees in the field has turned most conservation efforts into 'paper parks', where deforestation and natural degradation are steadily continuing. During the 1990s the deforestation rate in Nicaragua amounted to about 70,000 to 117,000 hectares/year, corresponding to a forest cover decrease of about 1.7 per cent/year (FAO, 2003, 2010). The apparent failure of halting deforestation through this centralised top-down approach instigated a shift towards decentralisation. Especially after the creation of the 1988 Nicaraguan Municipalities Law and its 1997 reforms, environmental management was increasingly delegated to the municipal level, with municipalities taking up former central competences, though always in coordination with the aforementioned central institutions. Increasing local competences were, however, never accompanied by sufficient municipal budget increases, inhibiting municipalities to effectively take up these competences in practice (Larson, 2002).

Apparently, this decentralisation movement has not succeeded in halting deforestation rates. According to the latest FAO global forest resources assessment (FAO, 2010), the current loss in Nicaraguan forest cover still amounts to about 70,000 ha/year (corresponding to a 2.1 per cent/year). Moreover, the latest national forest inventory (INAFOR, 2009) also warns of an accelerated forest ecosystem degradation observed during the last few years. These observations reflect how national and local governments have so far failed to halt environmental degradation in Nicaragua. Even though it has proven to be very ineffective for various reasons, Nicaragua still seems to stick to its traditional approach of restrictive top-down regulations. The most recent manifestations of this restrictive approach are the 2005 'Law on environmental crimes' (Ley de delitos ambientales) and the 2006 'Law prohibiting the cutting, use, and commercialisation of forestry products' (Ley de veda forestal). Both laws have created more severe punishments (fines and imprisonment) for environmental infractions. They also have complicated the administrative requirements for 'legal' use of trees, resulting in higher timber prices, increased illegal cutting and trafficking (mainly by powerful actors), and only very limited positive environmental results (Marín et al., 2007).

Our qualitative research confirms that Matiguás forms no exception to this general picture. Excessive reliance on poorly-enforced and inadequately-enforceable command-and-control measures has not succeeded in creating and even less in implementing an effective local framework for environmental protection. The presence of national government is very limited; the few local delegates of the environmental ministry, for example, do not dispose of any technical staff while also being responsible for several neighbouring municipalities. To make matters worse, the 'protected' Quirragua reserve does not possess any forest guards or police officers. This lack of state presence makes environmental governance in Matiguás a *de facto* command-without-control approach, which leaves it mostly dependent on local non-state norms and practices.

The cultural perceptions on land and natural resources also influence how environmental governance is locally embedded, and how it interacts with both formal and informal institutions (see also Nygren and Rikoon, 2008). On the one hand, typical of peasant perceptions in areas such as Matiguás is that the entitlement to land is related to the - albeit nowadays imaginary - act of colonisation: i.e. the conquering of the 'savage and unproductive' forest land in order to make it suitable for agricultural and cattle production. In this context, local farmer perceptions view the clearing of forest through hard labour as introducing '*mejoras*' (improvements) which are the foundation of property rights and for which producers logically need to be compensated when their land is sold or expropriated, even when it belongs to a protected area (Bastiaensen et al., 2006: 15-16). At the same time, the agricultural frontier character implies that the region is an 'institutional barrier quite far from established country infrastructure ... in which there is little state presence' (Baumeister and Fernández, 2005: 80), and where extensive social networks, mutual trust, and security are often absent (Ravnborg, 2010).

On the other hand, and as mentioned in the previous chapter, even when Matiguás remains - in both a physical and a cultural sense - far removed from the urban society of the capital and the 'developed' world, ecological messages of endangered species, climate change and increasing pressure on water and forest resources have found their way to local cultural arenas, mainly through schools, radio and television and the discourse of some development organisations, in particular in the urban areas. At the same time the traditional top-down approach to environmental management in Nicaragua has created the general perception among rural and urban communities of environmental conservation as an almost militaristic engagement (see also Ravnborg, 2010). Our observation of inter-institutional meetings and interviews with local urban dwellers demonstrated that narratives on environmental degradation are often linked to the 'malicious' and 'forest-destroying' farmers who should be disciplined by the use of permits and confiscation of chain saws, and by punishing them with fines or even imprisonment as if they were some kind of eco-terrorists. In a certain way the incapacity of the authorised institutions to effectively 'control' farmers has strengthened the narrative among urban dwellers that farmers have a bad 'moral and environmental consciousness' and that their 'economic selfishness' negatively affects the common good. The INAFOR delegate perfectly summarises this common narrative by stating that 'farmers are forests' biggest enemies, they perceive trees as a plague'.

This set-up is further compounded by political frictions that complicate coordination between central and local government institutions. As Nicaragua is characterised by a historical political divide (and previous armed struggle) between 'leftist' Sandinistas and 'rightist' liberals, cooperation and coordination between the liberal local government of Matiguás and the Sandinista ministries prove very difficult and result in very limited cooperation[65]. Furthermore, within each of the factions, vertical-authoritarian governance continues to prevail (Broegaard, 2009). Patron-client relationships, where only a few leading actors (patron-gatekeepers) mediate information and resource flows towards relatively isolated, dependent individuals (clients) and thereby dominate and manipulate local collective action (or inaction), also dominate governance in Matiguás, and even more when we are dealing with more isolated, precariously accessible spaces like the Quirragua mountain area. All these conditions fuel mutual distrust, widespread opportunistic behaviour as well as the prevalence of double standards and deep-rooted pessimism about the possibility to break the negative, non-cooperative and non-rule abiding dynamics typical of vertical patron-client governance (Putnam et al., 1993). Urban dwellers' lack of faith in the potential of state governance mechanisms in restraining farmers from further environmental degradation was aptly articulated by the president of the local consumers defence organisation:

> 'The [local and central] government institutions never have contributed to guaranteeing the rights of the environment... Even in the urban centre, in broad day light, clearly visible to anyone, dairy farmers are cleaning their containers in the river. In the urban centre! And nobody does anything, not even the police, so just try to imagine how the situation is in the [upstream] communities!'

[65] The establishment of so-called local People's Power Councils (CPCs), a -supposedly- apolitical structure of direct democracy that was called into life by the Sandinista government after its victory in 2007, is also seen as a further hindrance to efficient cooperation between local and central governments. Rather than promoting all-inclusive civil participation, it is widely perceived as an additional tool for top-down control of decision making at the local level (see also Cuadra and Ruiz, 2008).

3.2. A SHIFT TOWARDS ALTERNATIVE POLICY MEASURES?

Despite the continued emphasis on failing command-and-control measures, the urgent need of effective environmental policies has also stimulated a few complementary initiatives with the aim of improving environmental conditions in Matiguás. The municipality, for example, recently issued a local regulation exempting land owners from property taxes on forested parts of their land, hoping that farmers would be motivated to leave the forested parts of their property untouched. In practice, however, this measure has had only very limited effects, mainly because property taxes on 'developed' land are already very low, and - due to a lack of control mechanisms - most farmers currently do not even pay property taxes on any land, forested or not. The high administrative barriers to apply for the tax exemption have so far further restricted the practical applicability of this measure.

Local authorities have also focused on reforestation projects, mainly by investing in a so-called vivero forestal (tree farm), in which trees are planted and developed in order to offer farmers the opportunity to buy seeds at low cost and reforest their farms. This initiative has also had very limited results. Indeed, the initiative has so far clearly failed to take into account the underlying drivers of deforestation, and has wrongly assumed that farmers do not reforest merely because they do not possess the resources to do so, neglecting the fact that reforestation or forested land use are mostly not interesting options for them, even if they are offered trees 'for free'. The previous examples - though not classifiable as strict regulatory approaches - again show how local initiatives fail to induce any significant changes as they usually revert to top-down approaches and fail to be part of a broader and coherent environmental policy, in which the perceptions and needs of the - for this matter - most important actors (i.e. the farmers), are also taken into account.

3.3. FAILING ENVIRONMENTAL GOVERNANCE AS A LOCAL MOMENTUM FOR PES?

If the emphasis on top-down regulations has so far failed to trigger effective environmental governance in Matiguás, at the same time, one of the most directly felt impacts of poor upstream environmental governance is the state of water resources in downstream urban Matiguás. The presence of about sixty farmer households and their agricultural practices in the upstream Quirragua area is locally considered to be the main threat to urban water supply by the residents of urban Matiguás. Our survey results showed that on average, households have about 14.2 hours of daily water connection during the dry season and about 3.8 hours of water connection during the rainy season, when heavy rainfall often results in inundations and sedimentation, obliging the water company to shut down the filtration and supply system. Households also perceive water quality problems; about 85 per cent of households think tap water is polluted and almost 50 per cent of households improve tap water before using it, mainly by adding chlorine or boiling it.

At the same time, more than 91 per cent of respondents think Matiguás is struggling with deforestation problems, and about all respondents think that rivers in Matiguás are currently contaminated. The majority of respondents (67 per cent) believe local water resources are badly protected, and about 70 per cent think farmers are not protecting water resources on their farm. Our survey also elicited that 78 per cent and 86 per cent of downstream respondents consider that agricultural activities in the upstream area have negative effects on respectively water quantity and quality, and about 75 per cent think that the negative effects of poor upstream watershed protection mainly affect urban dwellers. Furthermore, 87 per cent and 85 per cent of respondents affirm that reforestation of the upstream watershed would result in an increase of water quantity and quality respectively. Finally, Figure 9 shows that about 66 per cent and 73 per cent of urban households think the best way to respectively improve water quality and quantity in Matiguás is to invest in ecosystem protection, rather than in improvements of the existing water supply infrastructure (pipe system, tanks and filters). For the framing of the latter question — which was based on previous qualitative research — we refer to annex IV.

Figure 9. Preferred investments for solving water supply problems in urban Matiguás

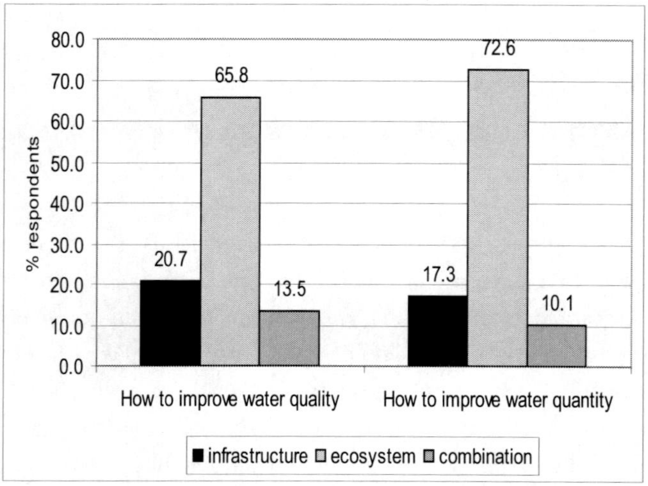

It is exactly in this context of clearly perceived externalities from upstream activities, easily identifiable ES users, and failing regulatory policies that PES advocates advertise the idea of introducing direct incentives to upstream farmers in order to initiate or improve watershed management (Engel et al., 2008; Pagiola and Platais, 2007; Pagiola et al., 2002; Wunder, 2005). The idea of PES is not completely new in Matiguás. In the previous chapter we saw that the concept was first introduced in the region when the GEF-World Bank funded PES pioneering projects in Latin America initiated its activities in several rural communities of Matiguás and Río Blanco. Farmers in the neighbouring Quirragua region, an area that was excluded from the project, have increasingly taken over the project narrative and even organised themselves by starting a local conservation foundation, whose main aim is to attract (international) funds to invest in ecosystem payments to Quirragua farmers. So far, however, the foundation has not succeeded in attracting any funds.

Although local government, NGOs and Quirragua farmer cooperatives are interested in implementing a local watershed PES scheme to solve water-related environmental problems, nothing guarantees, however, a priori that residents are willing to pay or contribute to the conservation bill. Complementary understanding of household preferences and the factors that influence their WTP may provide important inputs into the planning process and the possible role of PES transfer mechanisms.

4. LOCAL WTP FOR IMPROVED WATERSHED SERVICES

In this section we will investigate how much people in Matiguás are willing to pay in order to improve their water supply and how this could be linked with the necessary investments in infrastructure and/or ecosystem services, the latter through a PES system. We will analyse this by using split-sample CV scenarios, which allow us to compare WTP for PES scenarios with infrastructural scenarios. Furthermore, through the statistical analysis we can further investigate which potential factors influence demand-side acceptance or rejection of locally-financed PES programmes. First we will briefly present some basic socio-demographic characteristics of the sample households. Then we will explain the CV scenarios, and the empirical model that underlies the approach. Finally, we will present the main results of three model specifications.

4.1. SOCIO-DEMOGRAPHIC CHARACTERISTICS OF RESPONDENTS

The main socio-demographic data collected during the interviews are summarised in Table 7. It shows that about 75 per cent of respondents are female, which should not be much of a surprise because it is mainly women that stay at home during labour hours, when most of our interviews took place. The average respondent is about 39.5 years old, and has been living about 25 years in the urban part of Matiguás. The average education level is low, about 7 years, which corresponds to finishing the first grade of secondary school. Almost 10 per cent of respondents are illiterate. Household size varies between 1 and 19 members, with an average of almost 5 members. On average, 1.8 household members are currently working, and the average reported aggregate monthly income of a household amounts to about C$ 2,947 (Nicaraguan Cordobas; at the time of fieldwork, August 2009, US$ 1 was equivalent to C$ 20.5), equivalent to approximately US$ 144 (we refer to annex V for more details on the aggregate income variable). About 22.7 per cent of urban households reported to be involved in agricultural or cattle activities.

Table 7. Socio-demographic data respondents urban Matiguás

Continuous and interval variables					
Variable	**Obs.**	**Mean**	**Std. Dev.**	**Min.**	**Max.**
Respondent's age (in years)	1015	39.47	14.06	15	95
Respondent's time living in Matiguás (in years)	1015	25.04	15.11	0.25	74
Respondent's level of education (in years)	1004	7.17	4.52	0	17
Total number of household members	1013	4.78	2.28	1	19
Total number of household members with job	1015	1.77	1.24	0	9
Aggregate household income (in C$/month)	886	2946.95	2788.85	0	>15000

Categorical variables		
Variable	**Obs.**	**Percentage**
Respondent's sex is female	1012	75
Household owns house	1015	89
Respondent knows how to read and write	1015	90
Household involved in agricultural or cattle activities	1007	23

4.2. CONTINGENT VALUATION SCENARIOS

In order to assess WTP for specific water improvement policies, each respondent was randomly confronted with one out of four (two-by-two) contingent valuation scenarios (Table 8), for which the exact phrasing of all scenarios can be found in annex VI. A geographically stratified random sampling strategy was used to select the households to be interviewed from a list of 1,955 households connected to the water system. Half of the respondents were presented a scenario in which the proposed project would improve water supply infrastructure (pipe system, tanks and filters), which would result in the supply of more and better water. The other half of the respondents were presented a scenario in which improvement of the water supply would be realised by transferring a monthly payment to upstream farmers in the Quirragua area, under the strict condition that the latter would not contaminate the river with fertilisers or pesticides, dead animals and animal excrements, and would stop cutting trees close to the river. In both infrastructure and PES scenarios, respondents were told that the project would lead to a situation in which they would have safe-to-drink tap water, without any interruptions. As decentralisation of public services provision and environmental management is high on the agenda in Nicaragua (Larson, 2002), the CV assessment also controlled for an intermediary[66]/administration variable. Half of the respondents in both scenarios were told that the improved water system would continue to be administered by the current departmental water company, while the other half was told that administration would be transferred to the municipality of Matiguás. Furthermore, all respondents were told that in order to finance the proposed project, every household would have to pay an additional monthly fee, which would be added to the current tap water bill. According to our survey results, the average monthly tap water bill amounts to about C$ 115[67]. The proposed additional fee randomly varied across sample households, ranging from C$ 20 to C$ 180, with an interval of C$ 20[68]. Respondents were then asked whether they would vote in favour of or against the proposed project. Of the 1,015 households interviewed in urban Matiguás, 978 answered the CV question (see Table 8). No evidence on systematic non-responses was found.

Table 8. Contingent valuation scenarios used in urban Matiguás surveys

		Type of improvement		
		Infrastructural improvement	ES protection (PES)	**TOTAL**
Type of administration	Current water company	n=240 Average fee=98.0	n=244 Average fee=100.2	n=484 Average fee=99.1
	Municipality	n=249 Average fee=99.1	n=245 Average fee=100.7	n=494 Average fee=99.9
	TOTAL	n=489 Average fee=98.6	n=489 Average fee=100.5	n=978 Average fee=99.5

Note: Average fee presented to respondents is expressed in Nicaraguan C$ (US$ 1 is equivalent to about C$ 20.5 as of August 2009). Total observations are based on households who answered the CV question (n=978).

4.3. MODEL SPECIFICATIONS

Following the standard CV approach it can be assumed that households will be willing to pay for improved water services up to the extent that this improvement compensates for the loss in benefits derived from such payment. One can further

[66] For the importance of intermediary actors in PES mechanisms, see Pham et al., 2010.
[67] Nicaraguan Cordobas; at the time of fieldwork US$ 1 was equivalent to C$ 20.5.
[68] These amounts were established on the basis of the qualitative research and a survey pilot phase.

expect that WTP is a function of specific household's attributes and perceptions. In this study, the WTP function is assumed to follow a log-linear form:

$$LNWTP = X\beta + e \qquad (1)$$

where *LNWTP* represents the natural logarithm of household's WTP for a change in water services. *X* is a vector of covariates including treatment variables (indicating different improvement and administration scenarios), household income, respondent's perceptions, and other relevant household characteristics. β is a vector of coefficients to be estimated, and *e* is the stochastic error term.

The referendum approach used in this study does not allow for direct observation of WTP. However, *LNWTP* can be indirectly identified given that respondents are expected to provide a favourable answer to the referendum voting question only if the household's WTP is greater than or equal to the fee presented in the contingent scenario. This is possible due to the equivalence between the probability of favourable responses and the probability that *LNWTP* is greater than or equal to the natural logarithm of the fee presented to respondents in the referendum question (*LNFEE*). That is:

$$\text{P}(Vote = Yes) = \text{P}(LNWTP > LNFEE) = \text{P}(X\beta + e > LNFEE) = \text{P}(e > LNFEE - X\beta) \qquad (2)$$

On the assumption that the stochastic error term in equation 1 follows a logistic distribution, the error term in equation 1 can be scaled using a parameter *K* that is related to the standard deviation of the error term (i.e. $K = \sigma_e \sqrt{3}/\pi$) (Cameron, 1988). As a result, the following equivalence is obtained:

$$P(Vote{=}Yes) = P(e/K \geq LNFEE/K - X\beta/K) \qquad (3)$$

Thus, when estimating logistic regressions based on the referendum voting responses, we observe that the estimated coefficient of *LNFEE* will be an estimate of *1/K*. Similarly, the estimated coefficients of *X* are estimates of β/K. Therefore, the direct WTP parameters from equation 1 can be calculated by consecutively dividing the estimated coefficients of the independent variables by the estimated coefficient of *LNFEE* and by switching the sign of this resulting parameter.

Table 9 depicts the description and summary statistics of the variables used to estimate equation 1. The dependent regression variable *VOTE* has value one for respondents that voted in favour of the proposed scenario, and zero for those who voted against. *LNFEE* reflects the natural logarithm of the randomly assigned fee in the scenario, and is expected to have a negative coefficient, as a higher fee is assumed to lower the probability of approving the proposed project (incentive compatibility). The covariate vector (i.e. *X*) includes the dummy variable *PES* which indicates the two approaches to improve water services according to the split-sample design. The estimated coefficient is expected to be positive if respondents are willing to pay more for the PES scenario than for investments in infrastructure, and negative if the opposite is true. The dummy variable *CITY* indicates whether the improved water system would continue to be administered by the current departmental water company (*CITY*=0), or would be transferred to the municipality of Matiguás (*CITY*=1). The variable *INCOME* is also included and we expect tap water to be a normal good (i.e. $\beta_{INCOME} > 0$). Since an improved tap water system would increase the substitutability between tap and more expensive purified water, households who currently spend a higher amount of money on buying purified water (*PUREBILL*) are expected to report a higher WTP for both scenarios. Another household characteristic we included is the respondent's years of education (*EDU*). No specific hypothesis is made on the effect of this characteristic on WTP. Respondents who believe that the project is feasible in practice are expected to report a higher WTP (i.e. $\beta_{FEASIBLE} > 0$).

In order to investigate possible relationships between respondents' perceptions of environmental externalities and their WTP, we included two additional variables. It could be expected that *RIVERBAD*, which has value one if the respondent thinks that water resources in Matiguás are currently poorly protected, has a positive coefficient in the PES scenarios since the perception of poor protection would motivate the respondent to vote in favour of a PES project. The same reasoning applies to *URBANEXT*, which reflects the respondent's perception on which stakeholder group is highest affected by poor environmental protection. Respondents thinking that the most affected group are urban people like themselves can be expected to have a higher probability of voting in favour of the PES project.

Table 9. Variables description and summary statistics for all observations

Variable	Description	Mean	Std. Dev.
VOTE	Respondent's vote in the CV scenario (1 = in favour; 0 = against)	0.55	0.50
LNFEE	Natural logarithm of the additional fee charged for water service improvement in the CV scenario	4.42	0.67
PES	Respondent is presented the payments for ecosystem services scenario in the CV scenario (1 = PES scenario; 0 = infrastructure scenario)	0.50	0.50
CITY	Respondent is presented the decentralisation scenario (transfer of water administration to municipality) (1 = municipality administration; 0 = current water company administration)	0.50	0.50
INCOME	Aggregate household income in C$/month	2946.95	2788.85
PUREBILL	Household's weekly expenditure on purified (bottled) water in C$	27.46	60.41
EDU	Education of respondent (in years of schooling)	7.17	4.52
FEASIBLE	Respondent thinks the proposed project could be implemented in Matiguás (1 = yes, 0 = no)	0.82	0.38
URBANEXT	Respondent thinks that mainly urban people of Matiguás will experience bad consequences of no environmental protection in upstream catchment (1 = yes; 0 = otherwise)	0.75	0.43
RIVERBAD	Respondent thinks that water resources in Matiguás are badly protected (1 = badly protected; 0 = otherwise)	0.67	0.47

4.4. ESTIMATION RESULTS

Based on the split-sample approach, the regression results are analysed through the use of three models (see Table 10)[69]. Model 1 uses the pooled sample (all observations) and assesses whether there is a different WTP for infrastructure versus PES scenarios. Models 2 and 3 only use the observations for respondents that were presented the infrastructure (*PES*=0) and PES (*PES*=1) scenario respectively.[70]

[69] For a general overview and summary statistics of the voting behaviour per scenario we refer to annex VII.
[70] Likelihood Ratio tests indicate that there are structural differences between Models 2 and 3 (χ^2=22.30), implying that explanatory variables have different effects on WTP for *PES*=0

They allow us to analyse the potential role that specific variables play in respondents' WTP for a specific policy scenario. Table 10 shows the results for the different models. The first column of every model displays the 'raw' logit results, while the second column displays the WTP parameters, obtained through the transformations explained above.

The estimated coefficients on *LNFEE* are negative and significant at the 1 per cent level throughout all the models and confirm the incentive compatibility assumption (Carson and Groves, 2007). The estimated coefficient of *PES* in the pooled data model is negative and highly significant, clearly indicating respondents' higher WTP in infrastructure scenarios. This result is unexpected, as we also found that the majority of respondents preferred investing in upstream ecosystem protection, rather than in infrastructural improvements (see section 3.3). We will discuss this important finding below. The estimated coefficients on *CITY* are negative in all models, but statistically insignificant. Apparently, households have no significantly different WTP for different administration levels. Similarly, household income seems to have no effect on WTP for improved water services[71]. The coefficient of *PUREBILL* is positive and significant throughout the models, confirming our substitutability hypothesis. The estimated coefficients for *EDU* are positive, but never significant. Households who believe that the project implementation is feasible in Matiguás report a significant higher WTP in all models. This suggests that respondents who believe that the survey will have real policy consequences tend to report higher WTP (Herriges et al., 2010). Finally, we also find that the *URBANEXT* and *RIVERBAD* coefficients are insignificant in model 1 and 2. Nevertheless, and in contrast to our intuitive hypotheses, these coefficients are negative and significant in the PES model. The estimated negative *URBANEXT* coefficient in model 3 is a clear indication that respondents perceiving themselves as most affected by poor upstream protection have a lower WTP for PES projects. Similarly, respondents who think water resources in Matiguás are at present poorly protected have a lower WTP for a PES project that would precisely improve watershed protection[72]. Again, we will discuss these counterintuitive results in the discussion section.

---

and *PES*=1. However, those structural differences become statistically insignificant after including *PES* as an explanatory variable in Model 1 (χ^2=12.64).

[71] This insignificant relation should be interpreted with care. It is a common phenomenon in household surveys that participants underreport or are reluctant to report their (aggregate) income (Turrell, 2000). One possible reason is that the respondent may be unaware of the full range of income-generating activities of all household members. Another reason is that respondents may fear the tax consequences of accurately reporting their incomes. For a further discussion on the relation between the income variable and the voting response, we refer to annex VIII.

[72] Note how the WTP parameters can be interpreted as semi-elasticities of median WTP with respect to the associated variable (Southgate et al., 2009). A one-unit increase in the household's weekly expenditure on purified water in model 1, for example, increases median WTP with 0.9 per cent. In this same model 1, the PES option of improving local watershed conditions decreases median WTP with almost 83 per cent. Similar reasoning applies to all other WTP parameters.

Table 10. Estimated WTP regression models for different specifications

	Model 1 Pooled scenarios (all observations)		Model 2 Infrastructure scenario (PES = 0)		Model 3 PES scenario (PES = 1)	
Variables	Regression coefficient	WTP parameter	Regression coefficient	WTP parameter	Regression coefficient	WTP parameter
LNFEE	-0.611 (0.128)***	---	-0.565 (0.186)***	---	-0.682 (0.181)***	---
PES	-0.504 (0.163)***	-0.824 (0.314)***	---	---	---	---
CITY	-0.151 (0.163)	-0.248 (0.270)	-0.143 (0.240)	-0.253 (0.432)	-0.085 (0.227)	-0.125 (0.333)
INCOME	0.043 (0.036)	0.071 (0.060)	0.063 (0.057)	0.112 (0.106)	0.024 (0.046)	0.036 (0.069)
PUREBILL	0.006 (0.002)***	0.009 (0.003)***	0.008 (0.003)**	0.014 (0.007)**	0.004 (0.002)**	0.006 (0.004)*
EDU	0.011 (0.020)	0.019 (0.034)	0.003 (0.031)	0.006 (0.054)	0.020 (0.028)	0.029 (0.042)
FEASIBLE	2.007 (0.241)***	3.283 (0.767)***	2.362 (0.360)***	4.181 (1.472)***	1.690 (0.330)***	2.477 (0.797)***
URBANEXT	-0.135 (0.190)	-0.220 (0.316)	0.395 (0.278)	0.699 (0.545)	-0.604 (0.263)**	-0.886 (0.461)*
RIVERBAD	-0.255 (0.175)	-0.418 (0.301)	0.044 (0.257)	0.078 (0.452)	-0.559 (0.246)**	-0.820 (0.404)**
CONSTANT	1.561 (0.665)**	2.554 (0.708)***	0.376 (0.952)	0.666 (1.511)	2.199 (0.946)**	3.224 (0.787)***
WTP estimates	126.43		244.95		81.58	
Observations	751		377		374	
Log likelihood	-442.71		-209.47		-226.92	
Pseudo R^2	0.137		0.158		0.124	
AIC	905.43		436.94		471.85	
BIC	951.64		472.33		507.16	

Notes: ***, **, * imply significance at 1 per cent, 5 per cent, and 10 per cent levels respectively; numbers in parentheses are corresponding standard errors.

5. DISCUSSION

The CV exercise demonstrates that respondents express a higher WTP under an infrastructure improvement scenario than under a PES approach. This result is surprising especially since - as reported above - a large majority of urban residents identified the negative externalities of upstream agricultural activities and the lack of environmental governance to control them as the main reasons for their poor water services. They also expressed a preference for upstream ecosystem protection over infrastructure improvements as a solution to their water problems. The results for model 3 confirm these results, as the WTP for water under a PES programme is not higher, but lower among respondents that (i) are most aware of environmental externalities and (ii) perceive these externalities as mainly affecting the urban downstream population, to which respondents themselves belong.

In order to explain these seemingly incoherent choices, we believe it is necessary to qualify some of the assumptions underlying most CV studies. Various authors have emphasised that the CV approach wrongly confuses values and choices with preferences (Bromley and Paavola, 2002; Keat, 1997; Sagoff, 1988). Indeed, in line with a Coasean negotiation approach, one would expect that urban residents' perception that environmental governance is more critical for the urban water provision would result in a higher WTP under the PES scenario. Yet, this is not the case. As indicated by North (1990: 18-19) human motivation is more complex than a simple version of the neoclassical model of individual utility maximisation. It is based upon imperfect, subjective and partially collectively informed cognitive models as well as inherited social routines, which underline the crucial role that institutions play in the choices that individuals make (see also Paavola and Adger, 2005; Vatn, 2005). As indicated in the introductory chapter, institutional economists also explicitly recognise concepts of 'value and motivational pluralism', i.e. actors may hold or be informed by many different values, and arrive at either same or different choices, depending on the situation (Paavola and Adger, 2005). This implies that choices (in this case voting in favour of or against the proposed project) do not necessarily reveal preferences, and that choices are not only informed by cost and benefit considerations (ibid). These general principles give us some way to explain the apparent inconsistencies of individual choices that we observe in our WTP results. More importantly, they also allow us to link them with characteristics of the (not necessarily coherent and articulated) cultural repertoire of the local institutional environment that informs human perceptions and individual decision making (Vatn, 2009). In particular, we believe that framing effects, which occur because the CV scenarios get connected to particular discursive parts of that local repertoire, are of great importance here.

The framing effect is not merely a matter of the wording and interview context of the survey questions (which is rightly of great concern in CV studies, see e.g. Carlsson, 2010; Schuman and Presser, 1981), but more importantly it refers to how the CV scenario is contextualised within the institutional background of local society, particularly when it introduces new rules and forms of transaction in the existing institutional framework (O'Neill, 1997). Therefore, to make sense of our CV findings, we attempt to assess our results against the local institutional background of narratives and practices in Matiguás. Our qualitative research findings offer two possible explanations for the observed results. The first is concerned with fairness considerations about the PES, indicating that prevailing urban ideas about farmers' entitlements reject the switch from a negative to a positive externality framework. The second complementary explanation is related to the lack of mutual trust and widespread opportunism under prevailing patron-client governance which tend to undermine the credibility of the transactions in the PES framework.

5.1. EXTERNALITIES, ENTITLEMENTS AND FAIRNESS

As widely discussed in chapter 1 and 2, the PES approach has gained a lot of attention in policy circles as it breaks away from the perception of economic actors as perpetrators of negative externalities, and instead focuses on the potential positive services these actors could provide to society (Gómez-Baggethun et al., 2010; Pagiola et al., 2002; Wunder, 2005). We also saw that much of the dominant PES literature implicitly assumes that this 'externality switch' can be perceived as something 'natural', or at most as a mere technicality, and therefore little further attention is dedicated to the implications of this assumption (Salzman, 2005; Van Hecken and Bastiaensen, 2010b; Vatn, 2010). In chapter 2 we argued that the categorisation of externalities is, however, not a mere technical issue, but is mainly based on social norms and local conceptions of entitlements[73] (see also Farley and Costanza, 2010; Salzman, 2005; Vatn and Bromley, 1997). In other words, in order to understand and assess the possibilities of new policy instruments and their potential embeddedness in the local socio-institutional context, it is important to explore society's perceptions of entitlements.

In section 3 we already discussed how environmental governance in Matiguás has been mainly limited to top-down regulatory approaches, which build on the assumption that farmers should be 'disciplined' in taking care of the environment. An implicit but very present assumption of this approach is the consideration of farmers as producers of negative externalities. Our research showed that most urban

[73] Please refer to footnote 24, in chapter 2 for the conceptualisation of entitlements.

dwellers perceive farmers' practices as 'harming nature' with negative consequences for society and due to the context of ineffective and unjust rule enforcement, they think that - as one respondent aptly expressed - 'farmers have gone unpunished for their depredation of natural resources for too long'. This message has been further institutionalised through the global ecological discourse on connections between deforestation and climate change, which have progressively entered the local cultural arena. As explained by the radio presenter of a local environmental programme, local media outlets, such as the radio have played a key role in reinforcing these discourses:

> 'In my programme I always dealt with several topics, such as deforestation, agricultural fires, dumping of garbage in rivers, contamination of rivers, etc. People started to call and denounce illegal practices on the radio... I informed the population with the law in hand. Those who didn't know the law finally got to know it and some farmers started to detain illegal activities because they got scared for the legal and social consequences of their actions.'

The sudden introduction of a new mechanism that largely contradicts these dominant perceptions generates a new and hitherto unfamiliar framework of reference. Instead of obliging farmers to protect water resources on their property (according to our survey data a preferred solution by 98 per cent of respondents) and fining farmers for bad environmental custody (preferred by 96.8 per cent of respondents), urban households would now be obliged to compensate farmers for refraining from 'bad' land use practices. This change results in reluctance among respondents to pay farmers for the ES that they could provide, as farmers are precisely expected to take measures against harm. The proposed paradigm shift would implicitly allow farmers to demand compensations for actions they are deemed to undertake as responsible caretakers, and thereby implicitly presumes an unrestricted private property right over land and resources of the individual owners. This claim is, however, not self-evident as property rights will typically be restricted by a number of state and non-state rules of entitlements (Merlet, 2007). The majority of urban households (66 per cent of respondents), indeed believes that farmers have a limited entitlement over privately-owned land, restraining them from exercising whatever activity they want on their property.

This is compatible with the CV results which demonstrate that - though both infrastructure and PES scenarios imply the flow of financial resources out of the respondents' pockets to other actors - households clearly prefer the additional fee going to infrastructure investments, although they previously stated they deem investments in upstream ecosystems as more urgent (section 3.3). In other words, they attach a negative premium to rewarding the destroyers of natural resources for their destruction. The same reasoning applies to the negative coefficient of *RIVERBAD* in the PES scenarios. It reflects that it is precisely downstream households who are most aware of farmers' production of negative externalities who are least eager to reward farmers for the conservation actions that they are deemed to undertake out of moral and social duty. One explanation is that they perceive this as unfair. One urban dweller stated to consider it 'unfair asking us to pay farmers for taking care of their property, as in fact, they are already legally obliged to do this', and several other respondents expressed that they 'don't care paying more for tap water, as long as the money does not go to the [Quirragua] farmers'. This is also reflected by the negative sign of the *URBANEXT* coefficient, indicating that respondents who perceive they are the main stakeholders affected by poor upstream protection are precisely more reluctant to pay upstream farmers.

In short, the idea of paying farmers for avoiding environmental degradation seems incompatible with at least part of the local discursive repertoire which has mainly focused on one-sided obligations for farmers, with only very limited emphasis on broader societal responsibilities. Moreover, the physical distance and the absence of any significant negotiation spaces has led to a situation in which most upstream-downstream interactions from the upstream side are 'monopolised' by only a handful of absentee landowners, living in the urban centre, but possessing large amounts of land in the Quirragua area[74]. These better-off farmers are generally the only ones that are attending meetings in representation of the interests of all Quirragua farmers, and the ones that act as the social gatekeepers for upstream communities and thereby further distort the general perception that downstream people have of upstream farmers. One respondent expressed a disenchantment with 'how the lives of ten thousand people in the urban centre are disturbed by only three farmers up there', and another further specified his indignation by stating that he is 'not prepared to pay a handful of rich farmers who on top of that are themselves living and drinking tap water in urban Matiguás'. Sommerville et al. (2010: 1263) confirm that 'perceptions of unfairness can undermine the effectiveness of incentives that provide apparent net benefits ... at the individual scale [and] can have a substantial impact on the participation of the wider community and thus the efficacy of an intervention'. Game theoretical experiments have also shown that parties often prefer no deal to a deal they think is unfair, even if the deal would leave them better off (Oosterbeek et al., 2004, as cited by Markandya, 2009: 1147). The evidence of our case indeed suggests that in Matiguás ideas and emotions about the

[74] Obviously, the upstream-downstream spatial 'divide' that we refer to in this chapter, does not imply a strict social division, as social networks are complex and stretch much further than a simple spatial division between the urban downstream centre and the rural upstream communities (Ravnborg and Westermann, 2002). However, as a manifestation of the prevalence of vertical patron-client governance structures mentioned before the main 'channels' of social interaction and communication between upstream and downstream actors are to a very large extent limited to a few social gatekeepers.

unfairness of PES, even when offering clear win-win perspectives, is still rejected by part of the urban population.

5.2. TRUST AND CREDIBILITY OF THE PES FRAMEWORK

The lack of any representative and multi-stranded upstream-downstream consultation platform where different stakeholders are able to analyze, discuss and negotiate different interests and perspectives of perceived natural resource problems and agree on action strategies (Ravnborg and Guerrero, 1999: 264) has resulted in very limited cooperation between upstream and downstream actors. Our qualitative research suggested that the mainly negative messages regarding upstream farmers emanate both from the existing restrictive regulatory framework and from the way this framework is locally interpreted and translated into dominant discourses in downstream Matiguás. On the other hand, and from the upstream perspective, farmers feel they are mainly marginalised by broader society, carrying a burden of high expectations, without receiving any support or acknowledgement for the activities they are deemed to exercise or to abstain from. This upstream perspective is summarised as follows by one of the Quirragua farmers:

> 'We farmers are not stupid. They [people in urban Matiguás] are telling us we should take care of the river, but what do we get in return? We're not the ones drinking water in Matiguás, but we are supposed to take care of the rivers, so what are they going to offer us in return? … It is a question of giving and taking, but in our case we're only supposed to give. We're sick of promises and promises, the municipality always promises to invest in roads, they were going to build a bridge, but nothing ever happens. So what are we supposed to do?'

Typical in regions such as Matiguás is indeed that the municipal budget is almost entirely invested in urban areas, often resulting in very few resources flowing to rural communities (Larson, 2002), precisely because they are often under-represented in policy-making. The above citation also demonstrates that farmers do not necessarily expect to be paid for undertaking 'social' actions, but they do expect some kind of reciprocity for the efforts they would undertake.

Upstream farmers and downstream urban dwellers are apparently 'trapped' in a collective action problem with a socially-suboptimal Nash equilibrium as they do not manage to overcome the stalemate of individual non-cooperative strategies despite clear opportunities for win-win scenarios (Ostrom, 1990; Ostrom et al., 1994). In particular, the above-mentioned governance deficiencies of inherited patron-client structures, leading to pervasive mutual distrust and widespread opportunism as well as the tensions concerning the fairness of transactions with richer patron-actors, undermine the credibility of the PES framework. Many urban respondents simply do not believe that it will be possible to implement and effectively enforce the conditionality of the payments. Statements such as 'Why would farmers suddenly start protecting the environment, if in the past twenty years they never have done so?' or 'How can we be sure that our money will really go to environmental improvements, and not to the purchase of additional cows?' clearly reflect the worries of urban dwellers. Furthermore - and as already noted in chapter 1 - the location-bounded nature of hydrological services in an upstream-downstream context implies the need for collective action between the sellers of ES; one non-cooperating upstream farmer could jeopardise the efforts of all other suppliers and therefore the credibility of the whole PES scheme. In this context it is not surprising that urban dwellers rather prefer paying for infrastructural improvement, possibly coupled with renewed and intensified efforts at government control of the upstream area, instead of paying farmers for an insecure or even quite improbable outcome[75].

At the same time, we should bear in mind that conservation success is not only dependent on providing tangible and individual benefits to individual farmers, but is mainly 'contingent on developing positive local attitudes' (Struhsaker et al., 2005, as cited by Sommerville et al., 2010: 1263). It is beyond the aim of this study to formulate an answer to which institutional processes would then best fulfil the task of creating these positive attitudes. However, we would suspect that an important first step in developing these positive local attitudes in Matiguás should be centred on breaking the existent negative vicious circle of distrust, through the promotion of processes that facilitate the creation of multi-stranded platforms for negotiating and coordinating collective action between upstream and downstream (institutional) actors. The importance of these platforms and the institutional factors that facilitate or restrict collective action have been the subject of extensive inquiry during the last two decades, especially after Ostrom's ground-breaking work on governing the commons (Ostrom, 1990). One of the main lessons from this research is that actors' resource management is not only 'determined by external structural forces such as the market or the state... Rather, it is shaped by the interplay between such factors and relationships, and individual [actors'] own experiences and perceptions'

[75] With 'insecure' and 'improbable' we refer to the social conditionality aspects and not to the uncertain scientific relation between upstream land management and its downstream ES provision. It is, however, true that the link between tree vegetation and water quantity provision is anything but unequivocal (Kosoy et al., 2007). An increasing number of studies have indicated that these relationships are site specific and thus depend on local physical conditions (e.g. Bruijnzeel et al., 2005). Nevertheless, what matters in our study is the respondents' perception of what the relationship between upstream land management and downstream water provision is. In section 3.3 we saw that the large majority of respondents believe there is a positive link between upstream management and downstream water quantity and quality provision. This also corresponds to the findings of our qualitative interviews, in which almost all respondents recognised a positive relationship between upstream tree cover and downstream water quantity and quality.

(Ravnborg and Westermann, 2002: 43). Ostrom's work thus underlines the potential of local governance systems based on cooperation and reciprocity. The main initial role of external interventions and organisations should then be focused on facilitating the creation of interaction spaces that enable processes of perceptual changes related to entitlements and (shared) responsibilities, and therefore the legitimacy of practices vested in socially embedded institutions (Cleaver, 2002, Ravnborg and Westermann, 2002)[76]. They confirm Muradian et al's (2010) claim that the emphasis in environmental governance should move from the 'internalisation of externalities' to 'incentives for collective action' through hybrid governance structures.

[76] In the Nicaraguan context, some possibilities might be offered by the so-called 'Community drinking water and sanitation committees' (CAPS by its Spanish acronym), which are formally elected and recognised local platforms for local, participative water management and which recently gained some, albeit not necessarily completely adequate, legal recognition (Kreimann, 2010). More research is needed, however, to evaluate whether, how and under what conditions such formalised forums are the right way to proceed in order to strengthen local governance by building cognitive synergies and multi-stranded, horizontal and vertical accountable governance. In this, we should not forget that most of present-day governance operates through non-formal (horizontal and vertical) mechanisms which will inevitably articulate to the formal procedures in what Cleaver (2002) called a process of institutional bricolage.

6. CONCLUSION

The empirical evidence in this chapter suggests that the mere existence of clearly-defined externalities, which is often seen as one of the main necessary conditions for the creation of PES or PES-like compensation mechanisms (Engel et al., 2008; Pagiola and Platais, 2007), does not out of itself offer sufficient potential to solve current water problems in Matiguás. Indeed, the proposed formal institutional solution of PES is 'contradictory to the principles by which local people prefer to interact and take decisions' (Cleaver, 2005: 358). Our research shows how a Coasean framework to PES falls short of capturing a number of essential issues and processes of institutional interplay which preclude rather than create possibilities for PES implementation. Our CV results and our complementary qualitative research findings indicate that WTP is not just a matter of individual consumption of better and more steadily available water, but that WTP is inextricably connected to (informal) perceptions about the underlying problems and responsibilities, and therefore inseparable from context-related socio-political factors that are embedded in the local institutional framework. More in particular, we have argued that the turn from a mainly negative externality framework to a predominant positive externality framework is not as evident as it may seem. Institutional contexts clearly play a critical role in the viability and design of PES schemes, not only from a supply side perspective (e.g. Corbera et al., 2007b, 2009), but also from a demand side perspective.

In line with our conclusions in chapter 2, we saw that different actors assess externalities and the underlying environmental entitlements in a different way. The idea of paying upstream farmers for refraining from practicing illegal and socially and environmentally unacceptable farming practices is perceived as unfair by the downstream urban population, and partly explains their lower willingness to pay for enforcing a PES scheme. As already indicated by Corbera et al. (2007a, 2007b) questions of fairness and legitimity thus clearly matter. Furthermore, the lack of trust that enforcement of the payment scheme would be sufficient to ensure that the service is actually delivered also undermines the establishment of a PES scheme. Indeed, the absence of mutual trust between different 'parties' involved in a possible transaction undermines the foundation of market-based tools, as the latter are social constructs that precisely depend on a minimum level of trust (Cleaver, 2002; Paavola and Adger, 2005). Moreover, the local boundedness of hydrological services (as discussed in table 4, chapter 1) further undermines the feasibility of these kind of schemes, as the non-cooperation of only one upstream farmer could easily jeopardise the efforts of all other suppliers and therefore the credibility of the whole PES scheme.

From these findings we conclude that studies on the feasibility of (locally-financed) PES mechanisms should not be restricted to mere CV or monetary cost-benefit assessments, but should recognise the limited cognitive capacity of the actors involved and therefore also encompass broader analyses on their interactions of 'demand' (and for that matter also 'supply') with local social practices and associated discourses (so-called procedures for learning, participation, and deliberation in environmental decision making; see e.g. Vatn, 2009 or Paavola and Adger, 2005). We need to be aware that each particular ES market will need to be socially and culturally created and sustained (Kosoy et al., 2007, 2008). Obviously our study only hinted at some of the socio-political interactions involved. Additional studies should help to further clarify this important link and generate insights on how PES systems are locally adapted through processes of 'institutional bricolage' (Cleaver, 2002) from within and in relation to the existing repertoires. These studies should rely on multidisciplinary approaches and also capitalise on concepts already developed in other disciplines. Contributions from political ecologists, for example, might offer very useful insights on how cultural meanings attached to the environment shape the range of conservation efforts, and on how efforts targeted at environmental conservation are intrinsically interwoven with questions of power and political discourses (Nygren and Rikoon, 2008).

REFERENCES

Barahona, T. (2001) "Protected Areas and Natural Resources: With or Without People?", *Revista Envío* 242.

Bastiaensen, J., D'Exelle, B. and Famerée, C. (2006) "Political arenas around access to land: a diagnosis of property rights practices in the Nicaraguan interior", *IDPM-UA Discussion paper 2006-08*. Antwerp, University of Antwerp-Institute of Development Policy and Management.

Baumeister, E. and Fernández, E. (2005) Análisis de la tenencia de la tierra en Nicaragua a partir del censo agropecuario 2001, (Analysis of land tenure in Nicaragua based on the 2001 agricultural census). Managua: Ministry of Agriculture, Livestock, and Forestry; National Institute of Statistics and Censuses and United Nations Food and Agriculture Organization.

Broegaard, R.B. (2009) "Land Access and Titling in Nicaragua", *Development and Change* 40(1): 149–169.

Bromley, D.W. and Paavola, J. (2002) "Economics, ethics and environmental policy", in: Bromley, D.W. and Paavola, J. (eds.) *Economics, ethics and environmental policy: Contested choices*, Malden: Blackwell.

Bruijnzeel, L.A., Bonell, M., Gilmour, D., and Lamb, D. (2005) "Forests, water and people in the humid tropics: an emerging view", in: Bonell, M. and Bruijnzeel, L. (eds.) *Forests, Water and People in the Humid Tropics,* Cambridge and Paris: Cambridge University Press/UNESCO.

Cameron, T.A. (1988) "A new paradigm for valuing non-market goods using referendum data: maximum likelihood estimation by censored logistic regression", *Journal of Environmental Economics and Management* 15: 355-379.

Carlsson, F. (2010) "Design of stated preference surveys: Is there more to learn from behavioural economics?", *Environmental and Resource Economics* 46: 167-177.

Carson, R.T. (1999) "Contingent Valuation: A user's guide", *Discussion Paper 99-26,* University of California, San Diego.

Carson R.T. and Groves, T. (2007) "Incentive and informational properties of preference questions", *Environmental and Resource Economics* 37: 181–210.

Casey, J.F., Kahn, J.R. and Rivas, A. (2006) "Willingness to pay for improved water services in Manaus, Amazonas, Brazil", *Ecological Economics* 58: 365-372.

Cleaver, F. (2002) "Reinventing Institutions and the Social Embeddedness of Natural Resource Management", *European Journal of Development Research* 14(2): 11–30.

Clements, T., John, A., Nielsen, K., Dara, A., Setha, T. And Milner-Gulland, E.J. (2010) "Payments for biodiversity conservation in the context of weak institutions: Comparison of three programs from Cambodia", *Ecological Economics* 69 (6): 1283–1291.

Corbera, E., Brown, K. and Adger, W.N. (2007a) "The equity and legitimacy of markets for ecosystem services", *Development and Change* 38(4): 587–613.

Corbera, E., Kosoy, N. and Tuna, M.M. (2007b) "Equity implications of marketing ecosystem services in protected areas and rural communities: Case studies from Meso-America", *Global Environmental Change* 17: 365-380.

Corbera, E., González Soberanis, C. and Brown, K. (2009) "Institutional dimensions of payments for ecosystem services. An analysis of Mexico's carbon forestry programme", *Ecological Economics* 68: 743–761.

Cuadra R. and Ruiz D. (2008) "CPCs Around the Country Are Waiting For 'Guidance' from Higher Up", *Revista Envío* 320.

Engel, S., Pagiola, S. and Wunder, S. (2008) "Designing payments for environmental services in theory and practice: an overview of the issues", *Ecological Economics* 65: 663–675.

FAO (2003) Situación Forestal en la Región de América Latina y el Caribe 2002 (Forest situation in the region of Latin America and the Caribbean), Santiago, FAO Regional Office for Latin America and the Caribbean.

Food and Agriculture Organisation (FAO) (2010) *Global Forest Resources Assessment 2010 – Main Report*, Rome: FAO.

Farley, J. and Costanza, R. (2010) "Payments for ecosystem services: from local to global", *Ecological Economics* 69: 2060-2068.

Ferraro, P.J. (2009) "Regional Review of Payments for Watershed Services - Sub-Saharan Africa", *Journal of Sustainable Forestry* 28(3-5): 525-550.

Galobardes, B. and Demarest, S. (2003) "Asking sensitive information: an example with income", *Social and Preventive Medicine* 48(1): 70-72.

George, A., Pierret, A., Boonsaner, A., Valentin, C., Orange, D. and Planchon, O. (2009) "Potential and limitations of Payments for Environmental Services (PES) as a means to manage watershed services in mainland Southeast Asia", *International Journal of the Commons* 3(1): 16–40.

Glaser, B.G. (1992) Basics of grounded theory analysis, Mill Valley, CA: Sociology Press.

Glaser, B.G. and Strauss, A.L. (1967) The Discovery of Grounded Theory – Strategies for Qualitative Research, New York: Aldine De Gruyter.

Gómez-Baggethun, E., de Groot, R., Lomas, P.L. and Montes, C. (2010) "The history of ecosystem services in economic theory and practice: from early notions to markets and payment schemes", *Ecological Economics* 69(6): 1209–1218.

Haab, T.C. and McConnell, K.E. (1998) "Referendum Models and Economic Values: Theoretical, Intuitive, and Practical Bounds on Willingness to Pay." *Land Economics* 74(2): 216-229.

Herriges, J., Kling, C., Liu, C. and Tobias, J. (2010) "What are the consequences of consequentiality?", *Journal of Environmental Economics and Management* 59: 67-81.

Instituto Nacional de Información de Desarrollo (INIDE) - National Institute for Development Information) (2005) *VIII Censo de población y IV de vivienda (VIII Population Census and IV Housing Census)*, On-line available at http://www.inec.gob.ni/censos2005/CifrasMun/tablas_cifras.htm (last consulted: 15 May 2010).

Instituto Nicaraguënse de Fomento Municipal (INIFOM) (2004) *Matiguás: Ficha municipal (Municipal data sheet on Matiguás)*, On-line available at http://www.inifom.gob.ni/municipios/documentos/MATAGALPA/matiguas.pdf (last consulted: 8 March 2011).

Insituto Nacional Forestal (INAFOR) (2009) Resultados del Inventario Nacional Forestal: Nicaragua 2007-2008 (Results of the National Forest Inventory: Nicaragua 2007-2008), Managua: INAFOR.

Johnson, N.L. and Baltodano, M.E. (2004) "The economics of community watershed management: Some evidence from Nicaragua", *Ecological Economics* 49(1): 57–71.

Keat, R. (1997) "Values and Preferences in Neo-Classical Environmental Economics", in: Foster, J.B. (ed.) *Valuing Nature?*, London: Routledge.

Kosoy, N., Martinez-Tuna, M., Muradian, R. and Martinez-Alier, J. (2007) "Payments for environmental services in watersheds: Insights from a comparative study of three cases in Central America", *Ecological Economics* 61: 446-455.

Kosoy, N., Corbera, E. and Brown, K. (2008) “Participation in payments for ecosystem services: Case studies from the Lacandón rainforest, Mexico”, *Geoforum* 39: 2073-2083.

Kreimann, R. (2010) “The Rural CAPS: Ensuring Community Access to Water”, *Revista Envío* 347.

Larson, A.M. (2002) “Natural resources and decentralization in Nicaragua: are local government up to the job?”, *World Development* 30(1): 17-31.

Levard, L., Lopez, Y.M. and Navarro, I. (2001) Municipio de Matiguás: Potencialidades y limitantes del desarrollo agropecuario (Municipality of Matiguás: Opportunities and limitations of agricultural development), Managua: UCA/FIDA/Nitlapán.

Maldidier, C. and Marchetti, P. (1996) El Campesino-Finquero y el potencial económico del campesinado nicaragüense (The Finquero Peasant and the Economic Potential of the Peasantry), Managua: Nitlapán.

Marín, Y., Defeltsen, G., Fernández, M., Aguilar, A. and Rivas, R. (2007) “La política y legislación forestal nicaragüense: implicaciones para el fomento y aprovechamiento arbóreo en fincas ganaderas” (“Nicaraguan Forest Policy and Legislation: Implications for the Promotion and Use of Trees in Cattle Farms”), *Encuentro* 77: 29-52.

Markandya, A. (2009) “Can climate change be reversed under capitalism?”, *Development and Change* 40(6): 1139-1152.

Merlet, M. (2007) “Land Policies and Agrarian Reforms”, Proposal Paper, Nogent Sur Marne, France: AGTER.

Muñoz-Piña, C., Guevara, A., Torres, J.M. and Braña, J. (2008) “Paying for the hydrological services of Mexico’s forests: Analysis, negotiations and results”, *Ecological Economics* 65: 725-736.

Muradian, R., Corbera, E., Pascual, U., Kosoy, N. and May, P. (2010) “Reconciling theory and practice: An alternative conceptual framework for understanding payments for environmental services”, *Ecological Economics* 69(6): 1202–1208.

North, D.C. (1990) Institutions, Institutional Change and Economic Performance, New York: Cambridge University Press.

North, J.H. and Griffin, C.C. (1993). “Water source as a housing characteristic: hedonic property valuation and willingness to pay for water”, *Water Resources Research* 29(7): 1923–1929.

Nygren, A. and Rikoon, S. (2008) "Political Ecology Revisited: Integration of Politics and Ecology Does Matter", *Society and Natural Resources* 21: 767-782.

O'Neill, J. (1997) "Value Pluralism, Incommensurability and Institutions", in: Foster, J.B. (ed.) *Valuing Nature?*, London: Routledge.

Oosterbeek, H., Sloof, R. and van de Kuilen, G. (2004) "Differences in Ultimatum Game Experiments: Evidence from a Meta-Analysis", *Experimental Economics* 7: 171–88.

Ortega-Pacheco, D.V., Lupi, F., and Kaplowitz, M.D. (2009) "Payment for Environmental Services: Estimating Demand Within a Tropical Watershed", *Journal of Natural Resources Policy Research* 1(2): 189–202.

Ostrom, E. (1990) Governing the Commons: The Evolution of Institutions for Collective Action, New York: Cambridge University Press.

Ostrom, E., Gardner, R. and Walker, J. (1994) *Rules, Games, and Common Pool Resources,* Michigan: The University of Michigan Press.

Paavola, J. and Adger, N.W. (2005) "Institutional ecological economics", *Ecological Economics* 53: 353-368.

Pagiola, S. and Platais, G. (2007) *Payments for Environmental Services: From Theory to Practice*, Washington D.C.: World Bank.

Pagiola, S., Bishop, J. and Landell-Mills, N. (eds.) (2002) Selling forest environmental services. Market-based mechanisms for conservation and development, London: Earthscan.

Pagiola, S., Ramírez, E., Gobbi, J., de Haan, C., Ibrahim, M., Murgueitio, E. and Ruíz, J. (2007) "Paying for the environmental services of silvopastoral practices in Nicaragua", *Ecological Economics* 64: 374–385.

PAHO and ENACAL (2004) "Análisis Sectorial de Agua Potable y Saneamiento de Nicaragua" ("Sectoral Analysis of Drinking Water and Sewage in Nicaragua"), Nicaragua: Panamerican Health Organization (PAHO) and Empresa Nacional de Acueductos y Alcantarillados (ENACAL).

Pattanayak, S.K., Wunder, S. and Ferraro, P.J. (2010) "Show me the money: do payments supply environmental services in developing countries?" *Review of Environmental Economics and Policy* 4(2) 254-274.

Pham, T.T., Campbell, B.M., Garnett, S., Aslin, H. and Hoang, M.H. (2010) "Importance and impacts of intermediary boundary organizations in facilitating payment for environmental services in Vietnam", *Environmental Conservation* 37: 64-72.

Porras, I.T. (2003) "Valorando los servicios ambientales de protección de cuencas: consideraciones metodológicas" ("Valuing ecosystem services for the protection of watersheds: methodological considerations"), Paper presented at 3rd Latin-American Congress on Watershed Management, Arequipa, Peru, 9-13 June 2003.

Porras, I., Grieg-Gran, M. and Neves, N. (2008) *All that glitters: A review of payments for watershed services*, London: International Institute for Environment and Development (IIED).

Postel, S. L. and Thompson, B. H. (2005) "Watershed protection: Capturing the benefits of nature's water supply services", *Natural Resources Forum* 29: 98–109.

Putnam, R., Leonardi, R. and Nanneti, R. (1993) *Making Democracy Work. Civic Traditions in Modern Italy.* Princeton N.J.: Princeton University Press.

Ravnborg, H.M. (2010) "From declaration to real protection: Biodiversity and local participation in the management of four protected areas in Nicaragua", *Danish Institute for International Studies (DIIS) Report 2010:04*. Copenhagen: DIIS.

Ravnborg, H.M. and Guerrero, M.P. (1999) "Collective action in watershed management – experiences from the Andean hillsides", *Agriculture and Human Values* 16: 257–266.

Ravnborg, H.M. and Westermann, O. (2002) "Understanding interdependencies: stakeholder identification and negotiation for collective natural resource management", *Agricultural Systems* 73: 41–56.

Rojas, M. and Aylward, B. (2003) "What are we learning from experiences with markets for environmental services in Costa Rica? A review and critique of the literature", Markets for Environmental Services N°2, London: International Institute for Environment and Development.

Rubin, H.J. and Rubin, I.S. (2005) *Qualitative Interviewing: The Art of Hearing Data*, California: Sage Publications.

Sagoff, M. (1988) *The Economy of the Earth*, Cambridge: Cambridge University Press.

Salzman, J. (2005) "Creating markets for ecosystem services: notes from the field", *New York University Law Review* 80: 870–961.

Schuman, H. and Presser, S. (1981) Questions and answers in attitude surveys: experiments on question form, wording and context, New York: Academic Press.

Sommerville, M., Jones, J.P.G., Rahajaharison, M. and Milner-Gulland, E.J. (2010) "The role of fairness and benefit distribution in community-based Payment for Environmental Services interventions: A case study from Menabe, Madagascar", *Ecological Economics* 69(6): 1262–1271.

Southgate, D. and Wunder, S. (2009) "Paying for Watershed Services in Latin America: A Review of Current Initiatives", *Journal of Sustainable Forestry* 28(3-5): 497-524.

Southgate, D., Haab, T., Lundine, J. and Rodríguez, F. (2009) "Payments for environmental services and rural livelihood strategies in Ecuador and Guatemala", *Environment and Development Economics* 15: 21–37.

Struhsaker, T.T., Struhsaker, P.J., and Siex, K.S. (2005) "Conserving Africa's rain forests: problems in protected areas and possible solutions", *Biological Conservation* 123(1): 45–54.

Turrell, G. (2000) "Income non-reporting: implications for health inequalities research", *Journal of Epidemiology and Community Health* 54: 207-214.

Van Hecken, G. and Bastiaensen, J. (2010a) "Payments for Ecosystem Services in Nicaragua: Do Market-based Approaches Work?", *Development and Change* 41(3): 421-444.

Van Hecken, G. and Bastiaensen, J. (2010b) "Payments for Ecosystem Services: A Political View of its Justification, or the Lack of it", *Environmental Science & Policy* 13(8): 785-792.

Vásquez, W.F., Mozumder, P., Hernández, J. and Berrens, R.P. (2009) "Willingness to Pay for Safe Drinking Water: Evidence from Parral, Mexico", *Journal of Environmental Management* 90: 3391-3400.

Vatn, A. (2005) "Rationality, institutions and environmental policy", *Ecological Economics* 55: 203-217.

Vatn, A. (2009) "An institutional analysis of methods for environmental appraisal", *Ecological Economics* 68: 2207-2215.

Vatn, A. (2010) "An institutional analysis of payments for environmental services", *Ecological Economics* 69(6): 1245–1252.

Vatn, A. and Bromley, D.W. (1997) "Externalities – A market Model Failure", *Environmental and Resource Economics* 9: 135-151.

Whitehead, J.C. (1995) "Willingness to pay for quality improvements: comparative statistics and interpretation of contingent valuation results", *Land Economics* 71: 207-215.

Whittington, D., Briscoe, J., Mu, X. and Barron, W. (1990) "Estimating the Willingness to Pay for Water Services in Developing Countries: A Case Study of the Use of Contingent Valuation Surveys in Southern Haiti", *Economic Development and Cultural Change* 38(2): 293-311.

Wunder, S. (2005) "Payments for environmental services: some nuts and bolts", *CIFOR Occasional Paper 42,* Jakarta: CIFOR.

Wunder, S. (2008) "Necessary Conditions for Ecosystem Service Payments", Paper presented at the Workshop on Economics and Conservation in the Tropics: a Strategy Dialogue, San Francisco, USA, 31 January–1 February, 2008.

Wunder, S. and Albán, M. (2008) "Decentralized payments for environmental services: the cases of Pimampiro and PROFAFOR in Ecuador", *Ecological Economics* 65(4): 685-698.

Wunder, S., Engel, S. and Pagiola, S. (2008) "Taking stock: A comparative analysis of payments for environmental services programs in developed and developing countries", *Ecological Economics* 65: 834-852.

ANNEXES

ANNEX I. LIST OF INTERVIEWED PARTICIPANTS AND ATTENDED MEETINGS (QUALITATIVE RESEARCH)

(The names of the participants are omitted to maintain confidentiality.)

Interview/meeting date	Institution/organisation/function
Various occasions between 02/03/2009 and 17/08/2009	Responsible for environmental management in the Municipality of Matiguás
Various occasions between 14/03/2009 and 21/08/2010	Quirragua coffee farmer; President Quirragua farmers' cooperative; Co-founder and member of the Quirragua conservation foundation
Various occasions between 16/03/2009 and 17/08/2009	Various urban dwellers Matiguás (n = 23)
24/03/2009; 02/04/2009	Co-responsible water company (AMAT) Matiguás
24/03/2009; 01/04/2009	Responsible community electricity and water projects in the Municipality of Matiguás
24/03/2009	Municipal council member Sandinista Party (FSLN); member of municipal environmental commission
25/03/2009	Executive Secretary Sandinista Party (FSLN) Matiguás
25/03/2009; 17/04/2009	President consumers defence organisation Matiguás
25/03/2009	Municipal Forestation Commission (COMUFOR): Inter-institutional Meeting
25/03/2009	Mayor Matiguás (Liberal Party PLC)
25/03/2009	Public prosecutor environmental crimes
26/03/2009	Local delegate Ministry of Health (MINSA) Matiguás
26/03/2009; 27/03/2009; 21/04/2009	Municipal council member Liberal Party (PLC); ex-vice mayor Matiguás
26/03/2009; 03/04/2009	Quirragua cattle farmer; Co-founder and secretary Quirragua conservation foundation
27/03/2009	Local delegate of Ministry of Agriculture, Ranching and Forestry (MAGFOR) Matiguás
31/03/2009	Responsible water company (AMAT) Matiguás
31/03/2009; 04/04/2009	Radio journalist Matiguás (presenter radio programme 'Protection and conservation of the environment'); Teacher local secondary school
01/04/2009	People's Power Councils Meeting (CPC and GPC): Inter-institutional Meeting
01/04/2009	Local delegate Ministry of Environment and Natural Resources (MARENA)
01/04/2009	Local delegate National Forestry Institute (INAFOR)
01/04/2009	President consumers defence organisation Matiguás
02/04/2009	Commandant fire department Matiguás
02/04/2009	Police chief Matiguás

Annex II. Contents of individual and focus group interviews during qualitative research

The main objective of the qualitative interviews was to reveal the existing perceptions and discourses of the participants on environmental and water-related issues in Matiguás. Through the interviews we also tried to gain knowledge on participants' perceptions on potential interdependencies (or externalities) between upstream agricultural activities and downstream (environmental) consequences, the associated responsibilities of environmental problems, and the (potential) institutional arrangements that deal with these problems. Much the same as in the previous chapter, the research design was kept flexible in order to accommodate new information, to adapt to the actual experiences that people have had (Rubin and Rubin, 2005: 35). The amount of qualitative interviews was based on the principle of 'theoretical saturation' (Glaser and Strauss, 1997; Glaser, 1992). In order to guide our interviews with participants, we used the following general interview outline. Note, however, that the applied outline during field work could differ from the general outline, since the interviews were not fixed from the outset.

General interview outline

Introduction
- Academic study, no project, no NGO nor governmental organisation
- Study about environmental problems in Matiguás
- Assure confidentiality (data only used for academic purposes)

Basic personal data participant(s)/organisation
- Name, age, professional activity, agricultural activities (?)
- Organisation's activity (if applicable); How functions?; When founded? Whom does it work with?

State of the environment in Matiguás (general)
- Environmental problems?
- Why problem?
- Causes
    - *How?* Responsible practices?
    - *Who?* Responsible actors or phenomena?
    - *Where?* Where is the problem situated?
    - *Why?* Why is the problem there (drivers)?
    - *When?* When did problem start?
- Consequences
    - *How?* How affected/what are the consequences?
    - *Who?* Who is affected?
    - *Where?* Where affected?
    - *Why?* Why is there an effect? Why is it a problem?

  - *When?* When affected? When started?
- Solutions
  - *How?* How should problem be solved? How can individual or society help improve environment?
  - *What?* What solutions have already been tried out?
  - *Who?* Who should solve problem?
  - *Why?* Why should problem be solved (by specific actor)?
  - *When?* When should problem be solved?

Water problems

- Same outline, and focus explicitly on the difference between water issues as environmental problem and as infrastructural problem

Upstream-downstream relations and interdependencies

- Which link exists (environmental, social, economic)
- Existing spaces where upstream-downstream problems discussed?
- How collaboration between upstream and downstream?
- Role farmers? As persons (social object) or polluters?
- Why difficult to convince farmers to improve environment?

Instruments to improve environmental/water problems

- What kind of instruments could and should be used?
- In case of organisation: which (environmental) projects? How did/can project contribute to solving the problem? How can collective action between upstream farmers and downstream people be stimulated?
- How are payment mechanisms perceived to help in environmental problems? What are the opportunities of these mechanisms?
- Who should be paid?
- Who should pay?
- Why should pay/be paid?
- Which initiatives exist?

Conclusion

- Recommendations? Other people/organisations we should talk to?

ANNEX III. CADASTRAL MAP OF URBAN MATIGUÁS, USED FOR GEOGRAPHICAL RANDOM SAMPLING

ANNEX IV. SURVEY QUESTIONS ON PREFERENCES FOR INFRASTRUCTURE OR ECOSYSTEM INVESTMENTS

1. In your opinion, what would be the best way to improve the drinking water quality in Matiguás? Investing in improvements of the installations and water equipment of the current water system, or investing in improving the protection of the water resources in the [upstream] area of the river Cusiles and the Quirragua zone?
2. In your opinion, what would be the best way to improve the drinking water quantity in Matiguás? Investing in improvements of the installations and water equipment of the current water system, or investing in improving the protection of the water resources in the [upstream] area of the river Cusiles and the Quirragua zone?

ANNEX V. AGGREGATE HOUSEHOLD INCOME

It is a common phenomenon in household surveys that participants underreport or are reluctant to report their (personal or aggregate household income (Turrell, 2000). One possible reason is that the respondent may be unaware of the full range of income-generating activities of all household members. Another reason is that respondents may fear the tax consequences of accurately reporting their incomes. Galobardes and Demarest (2003) argue that in this context a close-category question increases response rate, and in some cases may even provide more valid information (ibid: 70). On the basis of the feedback during our pilot survey and focus group interviews, we decided to work with close-category income questions, as they were perceived to be less obtrusively than open-ended income questions. The different category intervals were established on the basis of the input from our pilot surveys and qualitative interviews.

The following table displays the results to the aggregate household income question:

Monthly household income (in C$)*	Frequency	Relative frequency (%)
No income	36	3.55
1 – 1,000	152	14.98
1,001 – 2,000	234	23.05
2,001 – 3,000	146	14.38
3,001 – 4,000	118	11.63
4,001 – 5,000	65	6.40
5,001 – 6,000	36	3.55
6,001 – 7,000	23	2.27
7,001 – 8,000	25	2.46
8,001 – 9,000	11	1.08
9,001 – 10,000	15	1.48
10,000 – 15,000	13	1.28
> 15,000	12	1.18
No response	129	12.71

* Nicaraguan Cordobas; at the time of fieldwork, August 2009, US$ 1 was equivalent to C$ 20.5

According to these results, about 52 per cent of households in urban Matiguás have a monthly aggregate household income of about 1 to C$ 3,000. 3.6 per cent of respondents reported not having a household income at all. Less than 2.5 per cent of households earn more than C$ 10,000/month. Still more than 12.7 per cent of households preferred not to answer this question.

ANNEX VI. PHRASING OF CONTINGENT VALUATION SCENARIOS

Keep in mind that the current water service in Matiguás is frequently interrupted and that water is sometimes unsafe to drink. Suppose that the Matiguás residents would have the opportunity to vote in favour of or against a project that would improve the current tap water service.

Scenarios A and B: Infrastructure investments

The project would consist of replacing the current pumps, tanks, pipes, filters, and purification system with more advanced technology to collect and treat water from the river Cusiles. The new system would collect more water, and would treat the water in order to reduce the levels of chemicals and residuals from farmers and farmer communities upstream. Therefore, with the new system, you will have tap water that would be totally safe to drink and with good pressure 24 hours per day, every day of the year, and without any interruptions.

- ***Scenario A*** (administration at departmental level): The new system would be administered by the current Water Utility of Matagalpa.
- ***Scenario B*** (administration at municipal level): Furthermore, as part of the project, the water service administration would be transferred to the municipality by creating a municipal water utility to be administered by the municipality of Matiguás, which would locally manage the water system.

Scenario C and D: Ecosystem investments (PES)

The project would consist of establishing a fund which would pay a monthly amount of money to the farmers and farmer communities in the upstream area of the river Cusiles and Quirragua, in order and under the condition that these farmers would refrain from polluting the river with garbage, washing of clothes, human and animal excrements, fertilisers and pesticides, and would not deforest the river banks. The project would increase the water quantity in the river Cusiles and would reduce the amount of chemicals and pollution that these upstream farmers currently discharge. Therefore, with the new system, you will have tap water that would be totally safe to drink and with good pressure 24 hours per day, every day of the year, and without any interruptions.

- ***Scenario C*** (administration at departmental level): The project and the payments to the farmers would be administered by the current water company as part of the tap water service.
- ***Scenario D*** (administration at municipal level): Furthermore, as part of the project, the water service administration would be transferred to the municipality by creating a municipal water utility to be administered

by the municipality of Matiguás, which would locally manage the water system and the payments to the farmers and the farmer communities.

However, this project would cost money. In order to finance the project, it would be necessary to increase the water bill of all water users in Matiguás. Your water bill would increase by an amount of **C$ FEE** per month, in addition to what you currently pay. Keep in mind that the increment of **C$ FEE** per month that you would pay for the improved water service will not be available to purchase other things such as food, clothes and other items needed in your household. Would you vote in favour of or against the project?

ANNEX VII. GENERAL OVERVIEW OF VOTING BEHAVIOUR IN CV SCENARIOS

Pooled voting behaviour (all observations)

As shown in Table A, of the 1,015 respondents that participated in the survey, 43.4 per cent voted against the proposed project, while 53 per cent voted in favour of the proposed project. 3.7 per cent of participants did not vote.

Table A. General voting behaviour

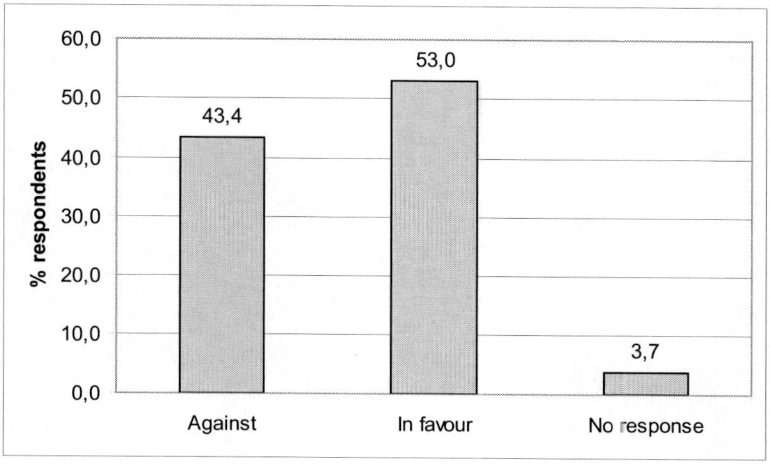

Voting behaviour per scenario

Table B shows the voting behaviour per scenario. It depicts that the odds of voting in favour of the proposed project are higher in the infrastructure scenarios than in the PES scenarios.

Table B. Voting behaviour per scenario

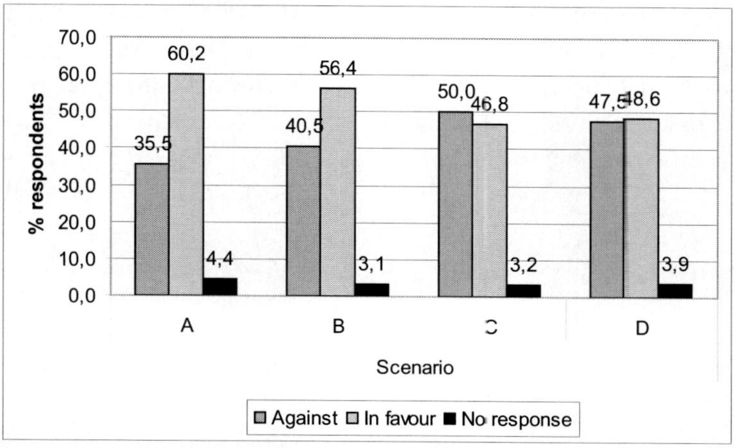

Note: Scenario A = Infrastructure & water company
Scenario B = Infrastructure & municipality
Scenario C = PES & water company
Scenario D = PES & municipality

Voting behaviour per fee for every scenario

Table C depicts the percentage of positive voting behaviour (i.e. votes in favour) per scenario and per randomly-assigned fee (ranging from C$ 20 to C$ 180). It clearly shows the negative correlation between the fee and the odds of voting in favour of the specific scenario (incentive compatibility).

Table C. Votes in favour per fee and per scenario

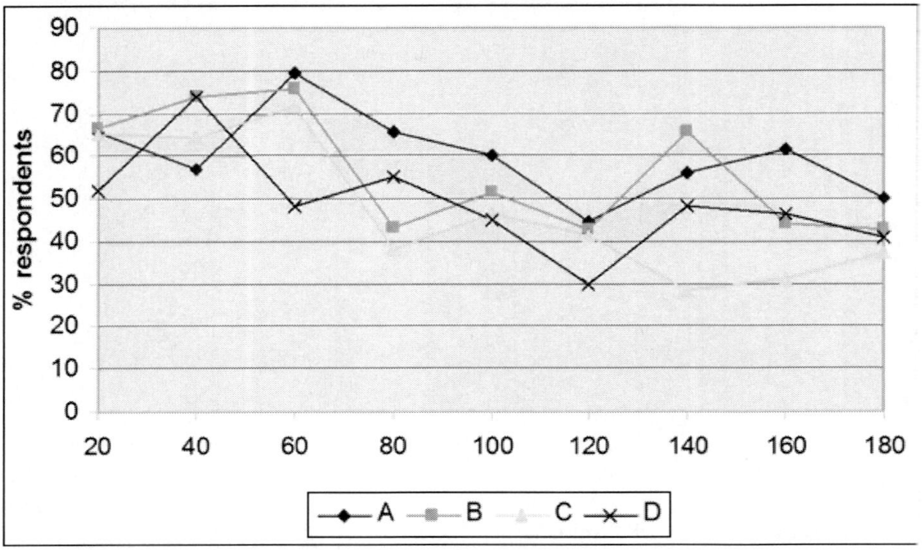

Note: Scenario A = Infrastructure & water company
Scenario B = Infrastructure & municipality
Scenario C = PES & water company
Scenario D = PES & municipality

Voting behaviour per fee for the PES and infrastructure scenarios

Table D depicts the percentage of votes in favour for the infrastructure and PES scenarios, and per randomly-assigned fee (ranging from C$ 20 to C$ 180). Again, it shows the negative correlation between the fee and the odds of voting in favour of the specific scenario. It also shows that the odds of voting in favour for the same fee are generally higher in the infrastructure scenario when compared to the PES scenario.

Table D. Votes in favour per fee for the PES and infrastructure scenarios

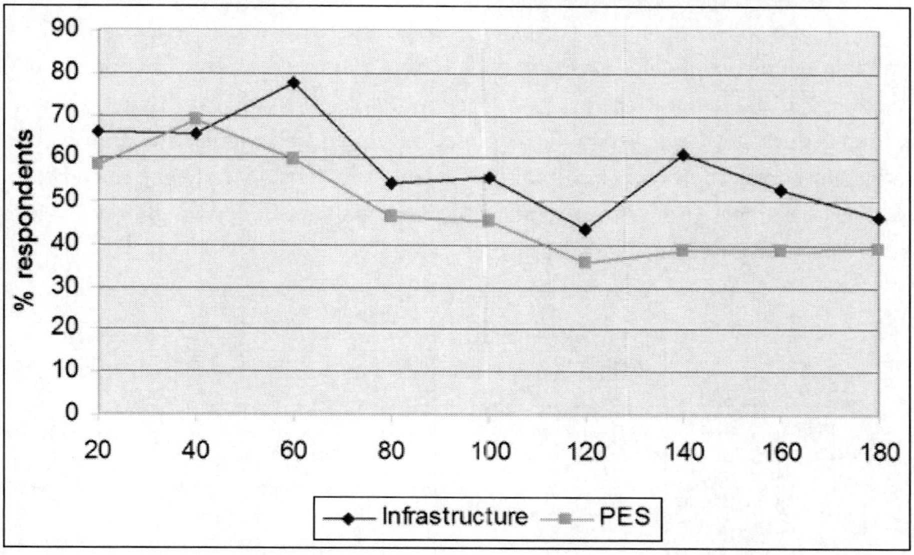

ANNEX VIII. RELATIONSHIPS BETWEEN VOTING BEHAVIOUR AND THE INCOME VARIABLE

In annex IV we already explained how and why we assessed the income variable by means of close-category questions. Contrary to what we hypothesised in section 4.3, the estimation results in section 4.4 seem to indicate that the income variable does not have a significant effect on voting behaviour. This annex briefly provides some additional information on the relationship between income and voting behaviour. The following table displays two-way tables for different voting scenarios on voting behaviour per income category.

		Voting behaviour					
		Pooled scenarios		PES		Infrastructure	
		Against	In favour	Against	In favour	Against	In favour
Monthly household income	No income	16	17	13	9	3	8
	1 – 1,000	67	79	39	37	28	42
	1,001 – 2,000	100	125	53	53	47	72
	2,001 – 3,000	61	83	29	43	32	40
	3,001 – 4,000	52	62	26	27	26	35
	4,001 – 5,000	35	28	16	11	19	17
	5,001 – 6,000	11	24	6	10	5	14
	6,001 – 7,000	10	11	9	5	1	6
	7,001 – 8,000	8	15	3	6	5	9
	8,001 – 9,000	5	6	4	4	1	2
	9,001 – 10,000	3	12	1	7	2	5
	10,000 – 15,000	7	6	6	2	1	4
	> 15,000	3	9	3	3	0	6
	Pearson χ^2	13.10 (p=0.36)		13.91 (p=0.31)		12.77 (p=0.39)	
	Cramer's V	0.1238		0.1809		0.1723	

We observe that in all cases Pearson's $\chi^2(12)$ test statistic indicates that the null-hypothesis of independency cannot be rejected at the 10% level. Furthermore, the value of Cramer's V is less than 0.2 in all cases, which generally indicates a weak relationship between the variables.

Rescaling the income categories to larger intervals, such as 0 – 3,000; 3,001 – 6,000; 6,001 – 9,000; and >9,000 does not change the association test-statistics. As shown in the table below, neither does it substantially change the coefficients and their significance in the logistic regression models.

The fact that the income variable has an insignificant coefficient does not imply that the CV survey was not understood by respondents. The *LNFEE* coefficient, for example, is highly significant (p<0.01), implying that CV scenarios are sensitive to the price variable. The scenarios are also sensitive to the use of substitute goods: bottled water (*PUREBILL*) has a positive and significant coefficient (p<0.01) in all models. Both effects are consistent with economic theory (Whitehead, 1995). Furthermore, the coefficient of the PES dummy variable is also highly significant (p<0.01), which suggests that the split-sample treatment design was effective, and that respondents understood the CV scenarios.

	Model 1 Pooled scenarios (all observations)	**Model 2 Infrastructure scenario (PES = 0)**	**Model 3 PES scenario (PES = 1)**
Variables	Regression coefficient	Regression coefficient	Regression coefficient
LNFEE	-0.613 (0.128)***	-0.566 (0.186)***	-0.684 (0.181)***
PES	-0.506 (0.163)***	---	---
CITY	-0.151 (0.163)	-0.138 (0.240)	-0.087 (0.227)
RESCALED INCOME	0.118 (0.110)	0.193 (0.177)	0.054 (0.144)
PUREBILL	0.006 (0.002)***	0.008 (0.003)**	0.004 (0.002)**
EDU	0.013 (0.020)	0.004 (0.030)	0.021 (0.028)
FEASIBLE	2.005 (0.241)***	2.364 (0.360)***	1.685 (0.330)***
URBANEXT	-0.135 (0.190)	0.394 (0.277)	-0.607 (0.264)**
RIVERBAD	-0.260 (0.175)	0.042 (0.257)	-0.562 (0.247)**
CONSTANT	1.646 (0.660)**	0.483 (0.947)	2.258 (0.937)**
Observations	751	377	374
Log likelihood	-442.87	-209.48	-226.99
Pseudo R^2	0.137	0.158	0.124

Notes: ***, **, * imply significance at 1 per cent, 5 per cent, and 10 per cent levels respectively; numbers in parentheses are corresponding standard errors. The variable rescaled income rescales the original categorisation into four intervals: 0 – 3,000; 3,001 – 6,000; 6,001 – 9,000; and >9,000

Furthermore, earlier CV studies (e.g. Casey et al., 2006) with similar findings argue that income usually is not a binding constraint, given that the actual price for improved water services is relatively small when compared to household income. Respondents may also perceive the price for improved water services to be small, when compared to current indirect costs of low quality services (e.g. lost labour time, higher expenditure on health care, etc.).

CONCLUSION

CONCLUSION

> 'In the excitement of finding apparent synergies between the interests of different disciplines and agendas, it appears all too easy to lose sight of the lessons of history: in particular, that the motivation and incentives behind actions really do matter. The danger is that conservationists have shifted their alliance, away from social scientists who emphasise equity and legitimacy, to carbon economists who emphasise efficiency. And yet, right from the start of the conservation story, it has been apparent that objectives such as equity and efficiency cannot substitute for each other indefinitely; ultimately they are co-dependent.' (Martin et al., 2008: 4).

The citation above partly summarises one of the main arguments that have been developed in the previous chapters. It warns against the uncritical integration of conservation and market thinking, possibly resulting in unpredictable social and environmental outcomes. The citation, however, does not suggest that economists should stay away from the conservation debate; it rather argues in favour of a multidisciplinary approach in which the efficiency criterion should not by definition prevail over others. Society and nature are very complex indeed, and reducing this complexity in order to make it fit into market-based models can only be done at the risk of overlooking the very important fact that nature conservation inherently is (and unavoidably always will be) an eminently political issue. Decisions on the continued existence (or destruction) of nature should not be left to 'efficiency-enhancing' instruments or to the disposition of autonomous agents who can individually and in a rather discretionary way decide whether or not to contribute to the protection of public goods. Such decisions should be based on transparent and open debate that explicitly recognises the many conflicting interests typically characterising environmental problems and that acknowledges that very often these conflicts cannot be solved through the use of economic incentives. And even where this possibility might exist is it important to reflect thoroughly on the long-term consequences of such mechanisms, because - as argued in chapter 3 and mentioned in the citation above - the motivations and incentives behind actions indeed do really matter.

In this thesis we have argued for a more critical assessment of the manner in which PES mechanisms should be framed, analysed and organised in order to achieve multiple environmental and social goals. Contrary to the Coasean view on PES, which currently dominates the literature, we are not convinced that market-based principles, which mainly emphasise efficiency, lead per definition to the most appropriate institutional arrangements to achieve 'win-win' situations. One should not forget that efficiency arguments were also used to legitimise the creation of global market mechanisms that allow buying conservation at low prices in developing countries, while leaving rich countries' extractive consumption and production practices untouched (Karsenty, 2007; Martinez-Alier, 2004). Creating markets entails the risk of disguising deeper structural problems that in the longer term cannot be solved by quick 'ecological fixes', but inexorably call for major institutional and consequent economic changes (Norgaard, 2010). Moreover, as we showed in chapter 2, 'technical' externality frameworks underlying ES market creation and the associated representation of ecosystems as the producers of segregated ecosystem services may even result in mechanisms that effectively make poor communities pay for the provision of global public goods. Framing the problem as a mere technical and institutionally-simple externality issue of matching supply of and demand for virtually-created ES in separated markets is not helpful for avoiding undesired social distortions that could lead to the dispossession of the poor and further free-riding for the rich, especially in the absence of clear and binding commitments at the global level. These dangers obviously need to be discussed in a transparent fashion and should not be hidden behind the technical façade of environmental impact maximisation per unit of funding.

From an empirical point of view, we have also argued that a narrow market-based or Coasean approach to PES may not be the most adequate perspective to explain the typically complex dynamics operating in the field. As we explained, a more meaningful analysis of the potential and limitations of PES mechanisms should be rooted in a broader institutional framework, allowing to take equity and legitimacy issues more explicitly into account, and acknowledging the complexity of the many social rules and norms that govern the interactions between society and nature. The useful insights this alternative approach can offer, were demonstrated in chapters 3 and 4. Chapter 3 analysed the Nicaraguan component of the experimental GEF silvopastoral project. This, through its experimental approach, tried to attribute the adoption of silvopastoral practices and environmentally-sound land use changes to payment and technical assistance variables. While some unfortunate flaws in the experimental design did not allow for drawing unequivocal conclusions on the correlation between the independent and the dependent variables, our qualitative reassessment suggests that a mixture of economic and non-economic motivational underpinnings stimulated farmers to adopt the envisaged silvopastoral practices. Payment mechanisms most likely played an important role, but they were inevitably embedded within broader local institutional processes, which together generated new and collective pathways towards intensified silvopastoral milk production and necessary silvopastoral practices. The research also indicates how the spread of the market-based logic of monetary rewards entails the danger of eroding environmental ethics and social norms, unless PES are matched to effective local institutions enabling it to promote 'motivation crowding-in'. From these findings we conclude that the narrow and oversimplifying research focus of the Coasean approach is likely to overlook several important social, cultural and economic factors which have been shown to play an important role in the (sustainable) adoption of new land use practices. A more flexible approach recognising the complex (intended and unintended) outcome of institutional interplay and processes of institutional 'bricolage' may therefore be a more appropriate framework for further investigation of these issues.

Although the approach used in chapter 4 is different, it led to very similar conclusions. The starting point was the investigation of the demand-side aspects of locally-financed PES in a typical upstream-downstream watershed context in urban-rural Matiguás. Our research showed how local households perceive their tap-water supply to be negatively affected by upstream farmers' inadequate land uses, suggesting that there is a potential for Coasean PES schemes. However, closer analysis showed that willingness to pay for a proposed compensation programme is significantly and negatively affected by prevailing local perceptions on agricultural externalities and entitlements, questioning the fairness of such compensations. We also found that high levels of distrust and opportunism between urban dwellers and upstream farmers undermine the credibility of the proposed PES framework. From these findings, we conclude that it may be difficult to integrate PES logics in a setting where formal and informal rules are embedded in a framework that prominently places the responsibility for environmentally-sound land management almost exclusively with the farmers. In such a setting, the outside crafting of new and 'simple' institutional mechanisms that attempt to correct the failure of regulatory approaches by exploiting the existence and local recognition of externalities in a mainly individual framework, have a high potential for failure, unless they can be appropriately rooted in more adequate social practices. Once more, the narrow research focus associated with the Coasean perspective contains the risk of overlooking these important processes of institutional interplay.

But we want to be very clear: the present study should not be interpreted as an advocacy against economic incentives and payments for environmental services. Quite the opposite, we think that there is a need for economic mechanisms that help to reconcile hard developmental and conservation trade-offs, especially if they can be targeted at poor land users in developing countries. We also share the PES advocates' belief that it is society's duty to provide economic assistance to poor land users for adopting environmentally-sound but privately unattractive land uses. And we are convinced that debates on the appropriateness of conservation instruments should go beyond ideologically-based dichotomies of market promotion versus government intervention, and should instead acknowledge the strengths and weaknesses of different types of institutions. We therefore think that PES can play an important complementary role in conservation policies, as it can supplement the all-too-common impracticably restrictive and partially ineffective motivational approaches, and can have the potential to induce collective action between stakeholders with opposed interests.

However, based on this study's research results, we think that the contribution of the PES approach can be much more valuable if it is integrated in a hybrid and structural rural governance strategy. It should break away from its rigid focus on efficiency and the underlying institutional logic of individual profit-maximisation, and instead further capitalise on its inherently promising notions and recognition of interdependency, shared responsibility, mutual empathy and the building of cooperation on the basis of reciprocity. Financial transactions could eventually take up a supporting role along the way, but should be carefully embedded in the broader institutional context, as they indeed depend on the preliminary development of a solid social foundation and 'the social trust on which institutions depend' (Cleaver, 2002: 27). Vatn (2005) perfectly captures our point by emphasising that 'choosing policy instruments is thus not simply about changing incentives. First of all it is about instituting certain logics, about understanding which institutional frames people apply, and about influencing these frames' (ibid: 215).

REFERENCES

Cleaver, F. (2002) "Reinventing Institutions and the Social Embeddedness of Natural Resource Management", *European Journal of Development Research* 14(2): 11-30.

Karsenty, A. (2007) "Questioning rent for development swaps: new market-based instruments for biodiversity acquisition and the land-use issue in tropical countries", *International Forestry Review* 9(1): 503-513.

Martin, A., Blowers, A. and Boersema, J. (2008) "Paying for environmental services: can we afford to lose a cultural basis for conservation?", *Environmental Sciences* 5(1): 1-5.

Martínez-Alier, J. (2004) The Environmentalism of the Poor: A Study of Ecological Conflicts and Valuation, New Delhi: Oxford University Press.

Norgaard, R. (2010) "Ecosystem services: From eye-opening metaphor to complexity blinder", *Ecological Economics* 69(6): 1219–1227.

Vatn, A. (2005) "Rationality, institutions and environmental policy", *Ecological Economics* 55: 203-217.

SAMENVATTING (SUMMARY IN DUTCH)

Extensieve landbouw en veeteelt worden vaak beschouwd als de voornaamste oorzaken van tropische ontbossing en biodiversiteitverlies. Verschillende sociale, politieke en economische factoren zetten boeren immers aan steeds meer bossen om te zetten in weide- en andere cultuurgronden. Het gebrek aan aantrekkelijke productiealternatieven draagt ertoe bij dat het veranderen van de bestaande extensieve productiepatronen een moeizame aangelegenheid is. Hoewel geen consensus bestaat over de precieze onderliggende drijfveren die deze ontbossingsdynamieken in stand houden, werden reeds verschillende beleidsscenario's uitgeprobeerd om deze tendensen tegen te gaan, echter veelal zonder de verhoopte positieve effecten. Traditionele regulerende systemen, waarbij de overheid bepaalde gebieden uitroept tot beschermd natuurgebied, houden meestal geen rekening met de lokale bevolking en blijken veelal ondoeltreffend, vooral in ontwikkelingslanden, die vaak te kampen hebben met een chronisch gebrek aan infrastructuur-, controle-, financiële, informatie- en afdwingingsmiddelen. Ook meer educatieve en participatieve gemeenschapsbenaderingen bereiken doorgaans niet de gewenste resultaten, omdat ze meestal uitgaan van een te optimistische visie op de mogelijkheid om de belangen van het milieu en het noodzakelijke levensonderhoud van de verschillende partijen met elkaar te verzoenen. Vaak zijn boeren niet gemotiveerd om alternatieve landgebruiken over te nemen: soms wegens een gebrek aan kennis of technische ondersteuning, maar meestal omdat de nodige economische stimuli ontbreken.

Tegelijkertijd wordt in academische en politieke kringen steeds meer aandacht besteed aan de rol van ecosystemen als leveranciers van zogenaamde milieu- of ecosysteemdiensten. Deze nieuwe benadering benadrukt de potentiële economische voordelen die ecosystemen leveren aan de maatschappij, bijvoorbeeld de capaciteit van bossen om lucht te 'zuiveren' via de captatie van koolstofdioxide en andere broeikasgassen uit de atmosfeer. Hoewel het milieudienstenconcept aanvankelijk werd gebruikt als een louter communicatieve metafoor die tot doel had de aandacht van het publiek te vestigen op het belang van milieubehoud, is het concept stilaan een eigen leven beginnen leiden. Vooral binnen economische kringen wordt steeds vaker verwezen naar de mogelijkheid om een monetaire waarde aan deze diensten toe te wijzen, om zo ecosystemen een volwaardige en competitieve plaats binnen een marktgedreven economie te geven, en op die manier het nodige aanbod van milieudiensten te garanderen.

Binnen dit nieuwe milieubehoudparadigma krijgt vooral het concept 'Betalingen Voor Milieudiensten' (BVM) steeds meer aandacht. Deze benadering is gebaseerd op de veronderstelling dat in normale omstandigheden (dat wil zeggen, bij afwezigheid van directe economische stimuli) landgebruikers niet of matig gemotiveerd zijn om een 'milieuvriendelijker' grondgebruik toe te passen. Dit verandert echter als zij betalingen zouden ontvangen van geïnteresseerde milieudienstkopers die op die manier een deel van de opportuniteitskosten van ecologisch 'betere', maar economisch minder winstgevende landgebruiken zouden compenseren. Met andere woorden, de producenten-landgebruikers zorgen voor een beter milieubeheer door middel van positieve ecologische veranderingen in hun grondgebruik (bijvoorbeeld door herbebossing, of toepassing van duurzame landbouwtechnieken), waarvoor zij dan financieel gecompenseerd worden door de gebruikers van bepaalde milieudiensten die hierdoor gevrijwaard of geproduceerd worden.

BVM-systemen kunnen dus beschouwd worden als nieuwe institutionele mechanismen die de leveranciers van publieke goederen (of zogenaamde positieve externaliteiten) trachten te compenseren voor de gepresteerde 'diensten'. In plaats van 'slecht gedrag' te bestraffen, erkent de BVM-benadering de vaak moeilijke contradicties tussen milieubehoud en economische ontwikkeling, en probeert ze tegengestelde belangen te verzoenen via de monetaire vergoeding van 'goed gedrag'. De BVM-benadering steunt daarbij voornamelijk op marktprincipes, waarbij uitgegaan wordt van de assumptie dat individueel gedrag beïnvloed kan worden door middel van prijsincentiva en de creatie van vraag- en aanbodmechanismen. Dit perspectief bouwt voornamelijk op het Coase theorema, dat stelt dat maatschappelijk suboptimale situaties (het onderaanbod van milieudiensten) verbeterd kunnen worden door middel van vrijwillige marktonderhandelingen, op voorwaarde dat de transactiekosten van deze acties voldoende laag zijn en de eigendomsrechten duidelijk worden omschreven. In economische termen kunnen dergelijke onderhandelingen dus leiden tot de 'internalisering' van positieve en negatieve externaliteiten. Dit dominante Coaseaanse perspectief op BVM ligt aan de basis van een grote hoeveelheid aan eerder technisch-economisch onderzoek en publicaties, waarbij voornamelijk aandacht wordt besteed aan marktgebaseerde en efficiëntieverhogende institutionele structuren. Het creëren van directe financiële prikkels via de markt worden hierbij beschouwd als de meest efficiënte manier om schaarse milieufondsen te besteden.

De enorme populariteit van het concept en de explosieve groei van wereldwijde nieuwe initiatieven illustreren hoe BVM geleidelijk is uitgegroeid tot hét dominante milieubeleidparadigma. De precieze effecten van BVM-systemen zijn tot nu toe echter nog niet aangetoond en vormen een bron van intensieve discussies tussen voor- en tegenstanders. Wetenschappelijk bewijs is voorlopig nog erg beperkt en leidt vaak tot de vaststelling dat de lopende BVM-initiatieven slechts geringe additionele positieve milieu- en ontwikkelingseffecten teweegbrengen. Bovendien is de veronderstelde verhoogde efficiëntie in vele gevallen moeilijk aan te tonen. De veelal onkritische promotie van BVM doet dan ook vermoeden dat de populariteit van het concept vooral is gebaseerd op ideologische argumenten, in plaats van op gedegen empirisch bewijs. Verschillende auteurs stellen inderdaad vast dat een groot deel van de bestaande BVM-literatuur geschreven is door fervente marktvoorstanders, die de creatie van markten bijna automatisch als inherent wenselijk beschouwen, vaak zonder de kritische discussie te voeren over mogelijk negatieve sociale en ecologische gevolgen die marktmechanismen kunnen veroorzaken.

Maar wat zijn nu eigenlijk de opportuniteiten die BVM-systemen bieden? Kunnen zij inderdaad een doeltreffender en efficiënter milieubeleid stimuleren? Welke voorwaarden moeten daarvoor vervuld worden? En wat zijn de mogelijke politieke, sociale, ecologische en economische neveneffecten van deze mechanismen? Houden zij naast het efficiëntiecriterium ook voldoende rekening met andere belangrijke criteria, zoals (de wisselwerking tussen) lokale en globale rechtvaardigheid en ecologische duurzaamheid? En wat zijn de effecten van deze mechanismen op het gedrag van landgebruikers? Hanteren boeren werkelijk duurzamere ecologische vormen van landgebruik wanneer ze daarvoor betaald worden? Is het ethisch verantwoord om landgebruikers te betalen voor het waarborgen van publieke goederen? Zijn er naast monetaire betalingen ook andere drijfveren die boeren motiveren om milieuvriendelijke vormen van landgebruik te hanteren? Hoe interageren betalingsmechanismen dan met deze andere drijfveren? En is er werkelijk een betalingsbereidheid bij de begunstigden van die milieudiensten? Welke factoren beïnvloeden deze betalingsbereidheid dan? Op deze en andere gerelateerde vragen geeft deze doctoraatsthesis een aantal antwoorden. Vanuit de analysekaders van institutionele ecologische economie en politieke economie en door middel van verschillende theoretische en empirische hoofdstukken, die elk een gefocuste reflectie bieden op deze complexe materie, schetst dit doctoraat de mogelijkheden, maar vooral ook de beperkingen van het marktgebaseerde BVM analysemodel. De centrale thesis die daarbij ontwikkeld en verdedigd wordt, is dat een te enge marktgeïnspireerde BVM-benadering niet voldoende rekening kan houden met de lokale institutionele context waarin deze mechanismen geïmplementeerd worden, waardoor ze veelal weinig doeltreffend zijn en ongewenste sociale en ecologische neveneffecten kunnen teweegbrengen.

Om de relevantie van deze onderzoeksvragen en van de centrale thesis aan te tonen, is het essentieel om dieper in te gaan op de precieze bestaansreden van BVM en op de impliciete en expliciete veronderstellingen en theoretische assumpties die aan het concept ten grondslag liggen. Hoofdstuk 1 gaat deze uitdaging aan via een uitgebreide en kritische literatuurstudie. Het schetst de ontwikkeling van de BVM-logica binnen de bredere literatuur rond marktgebaseerde milieubeleidsinstrumenten en toont aan hoe de milieu- of ecosysteemdienstenmetafoor gebruikt wordt als legitimerend kader voor BVM. Vervolgens gaat het over tot een algemene bespreking van marktgebaseerde BVM vanuit een milieueconomisch analysekader dat tot op heden de bestaande literatuur overheerst. Dit kader wordt dan vergeleken met twee alternatieve opvattingen die recentelijk in de BVM literatuur zijn opgedoken. De eerste verwerpt BVM als een ongepast neoliberaal commodificatieproces dat via de creatie van nieuwe markten ook nieuwe opportuniteiten voor kapitalistische accumulatie probeert te creëren door ecosysteemdiensten te monetariseren. De tweede opvatting pleit eerder voor conceptuele wijzigingen van de marktgeïnspireerde BVM-aanpak, waarbij meer aandacht besteed wordt aan andere dan pure efficiëntiecriteria, zoals rechtvaardigheid en duurzaamheid, en waarbij meer expliciet rekening wordt gehouden met de bredere lokale institutionele inbedding van deze mechanismen. Via de uitwerking van een vereenvoudigde typologie schetst het hoofdstuk vervolgens de belangrijkste contrasten tussen deze verschillende perspectieven en geeft het aan welke twistpunten momenteel het BVM-debat domineren. Op die manier verduidelijkt het ook hoe de resterende hoofdstukken van het doctoraat verder bijdragen tot dit debat.

Hoofdstuk 2 analyseert een aantal belangrijke theoretische uitgangspunten van marktgebaseerde BVM, met name het externaliteitenkader, dat ten grondslag ligt aan Coaseaanse of marktgebaseerde BVM. Daarbij wordt op twee belangrijke aspecten ingegaan: de verborgen politieke ambiguïteit die achter het gebruik van het externaliteitenkader schuilt, en het risico dat BVM-mechanismen (vooral wanneer ze gefinancierd worden door lokale gemeenschappen) de regressieve financiering van globale publieke goederen door arme gemeenschappen in het Zuiden versterken. De theoretische analyse in dit hoofdstuk toont aan dat deze belangrijke aandachtspunten grotendeels genegeerd worden in de dominante BVM literatuur, die er doorgaans van uitgaat dat externaliteiten en financieringsmethoden louter technische aangelegenheden zijn, en daardoor voorbij gaat aan het feit dat deze kwesties in werkelijkheid zeer nauw samenhangen met maatschappelijke percepties op eigendomsrechten en geassocieerde verantwoordelijkheden. Het externaliteitenanalysekader impliceert dus het risico dat politieke beslissingen versluierd worden achter de technische façade van economische optimaliseringsmodellen, in plaats van deze op een transparante manier te bespreken.

Hoofdstuk 3 en 4 vormen de empirische basis van dit doctoraat. Ze zijn gebaseerd op twee gevalsstudies in Nicaragua. Dit land vormt immers een schoolvoorbeeld van de nefaste gevolgen van een falend milieubeleid. Gedurende de laatste 15 jaar alleen heeft Nicaragua meer dan 20 percent van zijn bosareaal verloren. De snelle opmars van de landbouwgrens, voornamelijk door de aanleg van graasland voor extensieve veeteelt, maakt van Nicaragua een interessante context om de wenselijkheid van BVM-systemen te onderzoeken. De twee empirische hoofdstukken belichten het BVM-verhaal vanuit twee verschillende perspectieven. Hoofdstuk 3 richt zich op de aanbodzijde van BVM-mechanismen (de leveranciers van milieudiensten), terwijl hoofdstuk 4 zich vooral toespitst op de vraagzijde van dergelijke projecten (de kopers van milieudiensten).

Hoofdstuk 3 analyseert een van de grootste experimentele BVM proefprojecten in Centraal- en Latijns-Amerika: een door het Global Environment Facility (GEF)-gefinancierd silvopastoraal project, dat plaatsvond in Colombia, Costa Rica en Nicaragua. Via een uitgebreid veldonderzoek van de Nicaraguaanse component van dit project, bestudeert dit hoofdstuk de verschillende motivatieaspecten die bepalen of boeren al dan niet investeren in milieuvriendelijkere landbouwpraktijken. Het empirisch onderzoek, dat deels gebaseerd is op 'officiële' kwantitatieve projectdata, maar verder ook op bijkomend eigen kwalitatief veldwerk, toont aan dat een mix van economische en niet-economische factoren bepaalt of boeren al dan niet gemotiveerd zijn om bepaalde landbouwpraktijken toe te passen, en dat de feitelijke rol van BVM daarbij verkeerdelijk wordt opgevat als een simpele kwestie van financiële prikkels. Het onderzoek toont aan dat bijkomende factoren, zoals technische assistentie en de veranderende lokale percepties die voortvloeien uit nieuwe opportuniteiten en wijzigende lokale discoursen, een minstens even belangrijke rol hebben gespeeld bij het toepassen van silvopastorale landgebruiken. Het hoofdstuk betoogt verder dat marktgebaseerde BVM-benaderingen niet in staat zijn om deze verschillende dynamieken adequaat te integreren, en daarom weinig mogelijkheden bieden om tot een duurzaam en effectief aanbod van ecosysteemdiensten te komen.

Hoofdstuk 4 onderzoekt de hypothetische betalingsbereidheid van stadsbewoners om bij te dragen tot een mogelijk BVM-systeem dat boeren betaalt voor het adequaat ecologisch beheer van stroomopwaartse gebieden, om op die manier een betere drinkwatervoorziening in het stadsgedeelte te garanderen. Onderzoek in Matiguás, Nicaragua, waarbij gebruik werd gemaakt van zowel kwantitatieve als kwalitatieve onderzoeksmethoden, toont aan dat stadsbewoners zich zeer bewust zijn van de onderlinge afhankelijkheid tussen stroomopwaartse boeren en stroomafwaartse stadsbewoners, en een positieve betalingsbereidheid hebben voor een betere drinkwatervoorziening. Het onderzoek toont ook aan dat bij de stadsbevolking de opvatting heerst dat een milieuvriendelijker landgebruik effectief zou resulteren in een betere drinkwatervoorziening. Dit impliceert in principe de mogelijkheid tot een Coaseaans BVM-mechanisme, waarbij de stadsbewoners boeren zouden compenseren voor een milieuvriendelijker landgebruik. De resultaten van het onderzoek tonen echter aan dat de haalbaarheid van een dergelijk lokaal gefinancierd BVM-systeem ondermijnd wordt door lokale opvattingen over eigendomsrechten en geassocieerde verantwoordelijkheden, die ernstige ethische vraagtekens plaatsen bij mogelijke betalingen aan boeren die vandaag de waterbevoorrading in het gedrang brengen. Bovendien ondermijnt een laag niveau van wederzijds vertrouwen tussen stadsbewoners en boeren de geloofwaardigheid van een mogelijk BVM-mechanisme nog verder. Vanuit een breder institutioneel perspectief biedt het hoofdstuk alternatieve en meer plausibele verklaringen voor de sociaal-politieke interacties die plaatsvinden op het veld, en stelt het dat toekomstig onderzoek naar BVM zich meer moet concentreren op lokale sociale en institutionele normen en structuren.

Het doctoraat concludeert dat BVM-mechanismen meer mogelijkheden bieden tot doeltreffend milieubeheer indien ze worden geïntegreerd in een bredere rurale ontwikkelingsstrategie, die niet enkel focust op marktprincipes en efficiëntiecriteria, maar explicieter aandacht besteedt aan de rol van lokale institutionele structuren en complementaire beleidsinstrumenten. Verder onderzoek naar de mogelijkheden van BVM moet dan ook vertrekken van een bredere en meer multidisciplinaire onderzoeksagenda, waarbij BVM niet als een óf-óf alternatief voor falend overheidsbeleid wordt voorgesteld, maar als een mogelijk complementair onderdeel in een mix van verschillende beleidsinstrumenten. Op deze manier probeert dit doctoraat via additionele empirische en theoretische inzichten kritisch bij te dragen tot de groeiende literatuur rond BVM.

CURRICULUM VITAE

Gert Themba Van Hecken was born on 5 February 1982 in Maputo, Mozambique, where he spent the first three years of his life. After completing his secondary school, he started in 2000 his Master study in 'Commercial Engineering' with a specialisation in 'International Commercial and Diplomatic Relations' at the University of Antwerp, Belgium. For his Master dissertation he conducted field work in the rural town of Matiguás, Nicaragua, focusing on the links between rural poverty and environmental degradation, and on the potential role of financial incentive mechanisms in stimulating sustainable water governance. He obtained his Master degree in 2005 (with honours). The same year, he started an additional Master degree in 'Environmental Sciences' at the Institute of Environmental Sciences (University of Antwerp). He graduated in 2006 (with honours). He successfully applied for a four year Ph.D. grant of the Flemish Interuniversity Council (VLIR-UOS), and in October 2006 started working as a research fellow in the research group 'Poverty and Wellbeing as a Local Institutional Process (PIP)' at the University of Antwerp's Institute of Development Policy and Management (IOB). In close cooperation with the Research and Development Institute Nitlapán of Nicaragua's Central American University he conducted between 2007 and 2010 field research in the central region of Matiguás-Río Blanco. The research mainly focused on governance of natural resources in rural communities and in particular on the ecological, socio-economic and political consequences of new financing mechanisms such as 'Payments for Environmental Services'. From January 2008 to March 2010 Gert lived and worked in the Nicaraguan capital Managua. During these years he occasionally presented his preliminary research work at academic conferences in the United States, the United Kingdom, the Netherlands and Belgium. He also published various articles in international scientific journals such as *Development and Change* and *Environmental Science & Policy*. Currently, Gert lives and works in Nicaragua where he is the country representative of the Belgian development NGO 'Broederlijk Delen'.